Between Landscape Architecture and Land Art

Udo Weilacher

Between Landscape Architecture and Land Art

**With Forewords by John Dixon Hunt
and Stephen Bann**

Birkhäuser
Basel · Berlin · Boston

Translation into English:
Felicity Gloth, Berlin

Design and Production:
Bernd Fischer, Berlin

Typesetting:
LVD GmbH, Berlin

Lithographs:
Bildpunkt GmbH, Berlin

Printing:
Druck Vogt GmbH, Berlin

Binding:
Heinz Stein, Berlin

This book is also available in a German
language edition (ISBN 3-7643-5270-1).

Library of Congress Cataloging-in-Publication
Data

A CIP catalogue record for this book is available
from the Library of Congress, Washington, D.C.,
USA

Deutsche Bibliothek Cataloging-in-Publication
Data

Between landscape architecture and land art /
Udo Weilacher. With forewords by John Dixon
Hunt and Stephen Bann. [Transl. into Engl.:
Felicity Gloth]. – Basel ; Berlin ; Boston :
Birkhäuser, 1996
Dt. Ausg. u.d.T.: Zwischen Landschaftsarchitektur
und Land Art
ISBN 3-7643-5316-3 (Basel...)
ISBN 0-8176-5316-3 (Boston)
NE: Weilacher, Udo; Gloth, Felicity [Übers.]

© 1996 Birkhäuser – Verlag für Architektur,
P.O. Box 133, CH – 4010 Basel, Switzerland

Printed on acid-free paper produced of chlorine-
free pulp. TCF ∞
Printed in Germany
ISBN 3-7643-5316-3
ISBN 0-8176-5316-3

9 8 7 6 5 4 3 2 1

Contents

Foreword by John Dixon Hunt

Land, Art, Land Art & Landscape Architecture

I: We cannot understand the appeal of Land Art to contemporary landscape architecture without first registering how diverse, not to say fractured, that profession currently is. Its activities cover a wide territory: from strategic planning of regional sites to the redesign of backyards and gardens, from ecological recovery of spoiled territory to historical reconstruction of period designs, from public plazas to private *horti conclusi*. Now, it is true that architects also engage in a wide range of activities, as do other professionals like doctors and lawyers. But landscape architecture, spreading itself across a wonderfully wide range of human territories, seems doomed to lose its sense of coherence(s), of shared energies. One cause of this – or is it an effect? – is the failure to attend to any conceptual concerns. The dread of what is called "theory", at least in the United States, is striking (there are, of course, no theories in the scientific sense of that term in landscape architecture; but even the old meaning of theory as contemplation seems to provoke alarm). Another cause of professional unease is the fear of art, an anxiety that human ingenuity may jeopardise the earth's unique equilibria (or those that survive) for stewardship over which modern landscape architects take particular pride; another way this to be formulated is via the old opposition of science versus art.

II: What has privileged Land Art in the essentially barren conceptual field of landscape architecture is its sense of creative purpose – the confidence of its practitioners and critics alike that has a firm basis in ideas. Ideas of how to respond to land, ideas of art and design, together with no fear of conjoining them. In short, Land Art seems to restore to landscape architecture its old and largely lost concern for the intricate melding of site, sight and insight. I see fundamental and welcome development in this respect from, say, such classic Land Artwork as Robert Smithson's *Spiral Jetty* of 1970, which seems to draw attention more to its own gesture than any *mise en valeur* of the surrounding territory, to a work of Patricia Johanson like *Endangered Garden*[1] of 1988, where the history and ecology of a site are in its subject as well as hers.

Land Art may be seen as a visual, actual, three-dimensional analogue to the poem of Wallace Stevens "Anecdote of the Jar", that has achieved a nearly cult status among landscape architects recently. Take some land – preferably unmediated or (literally) unprepossessing – and add an art object, say a "jar" or vernacular urn and hey presto! the physical terrain is utterly changed. If, as Richard Long or Andy Goldsworthy often propose, the "art" consists of reformulating in the simplest ways the given organic or inorganic materials of the site – a line of stones, a ring of leaves, then the ecological disturbance is minimal (Stevens' "jar" was, of course, wholly imaginary and would have done no damage to the Tennessee hillside that it transformed). This minimalism of Land Art must also appeal enormously to a design art like landscape architecture that has seemed to miss out on many of the opportunities of modernism.[2]

III: But Land Art's great appeal to landscape architecture rests upon other foundations, above all its emphasis on process, its invocation of abstraction and its confidence in its own artistry.

Many of the physical interventions of Land Artists – Nancy Holt's spheres in *Dark Star Park*, Michael Heizer's *Effigy Tumuli* – take abstract form; thus they seem to signal a wholly cultural reformation of natural material. But as ecological priorities force themselves upon attention, the patterns and abstractions of the natural world have again become more striking[3], and so Land Art draws us closer to the recognition of the possible coincidence of our own designs with those of nature.

Further, many interventions of Long and especially Goldsworthy also underline the whole temporal process by which landscape architecture distinguishes itself from other arts (except perhaps the dance). It utilizes as essential ingredients materials which grow and eventually decay.

The renewed emphasis upon the art of landscape architecture (recovering its uneasy

[1] Cf. Barbara C. Matilsky: *Fragile Ecologies. Contemporary artists' interpretations and solutions.* New York, 1992: p. 60–65

[2] Cf. "La traversée du minimalisme"/"Minimalism and Beyond" in Gilles A. Tiberghien: *Land Art.* Paris, 1993/1995

[3] Cf. the wonderful photographs in Murphy, Pat/Neill, William: *By nature's design.* San Francisco, 1993

place in the pantheon of *beaux arts*?) has been given impetus by the sculptural focus of much Land Art: Tony Smith's *Wandering Rocks*, for instance, outside the National Gallery in Washington. But sculpture is not the only possible abstraction. Language too, is abstract. The insertion of inscriptions into a site, a strategy honed to great subtlety by Ian Hamilton Finlay or, to take another example, by Montreal-based artist, Gilbert Boyer, may insert "unnatural" elements, and there is a remarkable nervousness about verbal elements in landscape architecture. Yet the function of such verbal interpolations is strategically to return us to considerations of how place intersects with time and temporality, how ideas haunt cultural appropriations of land, and how the re-presentation of land as art is a fundamental ambition of all landscape architecture.

Foreword by Stephen Bann

Crossing Borders

A recent lecture by a colleague specialised in the history of the French Academy reminded me that disputes about boundary lines in the art of landscape are not simply an affair of today and yesterday. The painter Charles LeBrun, concerned to vindicate the supremacy of the newly founded Academy, conceived his work for the palace of Versailles as a series of framed paintings mounted within the elaborate decorative scheme but forming no part of it. A critic from the more ancient and lowly academy of St. Luke could protest in vain that the paintings offered nothing in the way of illusion or naturalism to the spectator. How could a river flow in mid-air? LeBrun however dismissed such objections with contempt. It was precisely the superior mission of the Academy painter to relegate such cheap effects in favour of the intellectual mission of art.

The particular episode in the more recent past which this story called to mind was connected with the apparently admirable '1%'-scheme devised by the French government. This prescribed that a small proportion of the costs of major building projects in the educational sector should be devoted to a work by an artist. As I have heard from Bernard Lassus – himself the creator of a number of very successful projects under this scheme – the outcome was often compromised by the fact that the artist's first question was: where are the *boundaries* of my contribution? Lassus, for example, devised a whole wall in coloured mosaic, whose colours were to blend into a rainbow-like spectrum as the users of the building passed rapidly along it. But the approach taken all too often implied the 'framing' of an object, whether 'painting' or sculpture, and the provision of lines of sight that would appropriately isolate it from the clutter of its surroundings.

The institutionalised divisions between the 'artistic' and professions are no less rigid today than they were in LeBrun's time. And their consequences are no less evident in the domains of practice. Everyone knows that there is a crucial line of demarcation which separates 'art' from 'decoration'. Everyone knows that the architect belongs to a liberal profession which incorporates, at a lower level, a whole range of different crafts from the draughtsman to the bricklayer, without derogating from its superior status. But does everyone know exactly what it means to be a 'landscape architect'? It would have been obvious at Versailles that Le Nôtre, like Mansard the architect and LeBrun the painter, was a valued servant of Louis XIV, entrusted with providing allegories through which the splendour of the Sun King could be mediated. He was not a person who would be found planting bushes. But what does it mean today?

The answer is probably that the profession of landscape architect is one of the most nebulous as far as the general public is concerned, and that perceptions of it are very little different from those of the architectural profession in general. In the British context, there can be little doubt that the most celebrated contemporary landscape architect is Sir Geoffrey Jellicoe. He is an authentic representative of the profession if for no other reason than he spends a great deal of money – witness the artificial hill and lake created at Sutton Place, not to mention the most substantial of all Ben Nicholson's environmental pieces in solid marble. Not only does he, figuratively, move mountains, but he is also credited with ideas. His Jungian notions form a picturesque adjunct to his grandiose schemes.

The landscape artists featured in this book are, without exception, practitioners who challenge this mode of operation. It is not simply a question of working on a small, rather than a large scale. Indeed Bernard Lassus and Dani Karavan, in their different ways, make a claim to transform large areas of territory which would not be far inferior to the Park at Versailles. Nor is it a question of having, or not having ideas. Ian Hamilton Finlay's cult of the French Revolution is as iconographically adventurous in its implications as the programme of any garden designer, past or present. But it is a matter of reconsidering the relationship between professions and practices, and the pre-modern legacy which still disconcertingly inhibits the landscape practitioner. Above all, it is a matter of focusing clearly on the central issue, which is one of invention. Where in the spectrum of widely differing practices involved in landscape is the crucible of new ideas likely to be found?

Bernard Lassus cuts the Gordian knot by stating quite simply: "Art and landscape architecture are the same thing for me." This does not mean, far from it: every artist concerned with landscape is qualified to take the place of the landscape architect. On the contrary, as we have seen, many such artists simply reproduce, on another level, the anxiety about the limits that renders any global solution impossible. What it does mean could be restated no doubt in the following form. There is no reason why the garden should not be the product of an integral aesthetic vision, which draws on the concepts and practices of modernist art while remaining profoundly imbued with the great tradition of landscape and garden design.

For the history of garden design over the past four centuries leaves us in no doubt about the most important fact. Great gardens have been created, as often as not, by poets and painters, and by specialists who integrated their own practice with the prevailing cultural milieu. It has been a history of eclectic and creative innovators, and certainly not of conventionally trained and academic practitioners. The heirs to this tradition at the present day are to be found, one feels, very predominantly along the interdisciplinary 'migrant' whom Udo Weilacher has selected for this valuable series of studies. It does not matter that some of the examples are relatively small in scale, compared with other, monumentally vapid contemporary examples. We know that William Shenstone's grand neighbours from Hagley Hall took a perverse pleasure in guiding their guests round Shenstone's small but perfect garden, The Leasowes, in such a way as to make little sense of it. But Shenstone has the last laugh. The same will surely be true of any contemporary landscape architect who dismisses Ian Hamilton Finlay's Little Sparta as eccentric and small-scale.

Happily the tradition of the landscape garden is very much alive today. The real problem, however, is to maintain the vital link between this tradition and the contemporary practices which will sustain and rejuvenate it. And the unexpected ways of doing so are often the most worthy to note.

Introduction: Art in Nature

A new language in the landscape

"The interest of the natural sciences in non-verbal languages is growing and, consequently, the question as to an understanding of art as language which communicates with a public on a particular issue is gaining ground in interdisciplinary dialogue."[1]

[1] Belting, Hans. *Das Ende der Kunstgeschichte?* München, 1983: p. 36 [new translation] English edition: *The end of the history of art?* Chicago, 1987.

One of the main issues of our age is the disturbed relationship of man to nature and the ensuing world-wide threat to the ecological balance. Our society is still seeking a technological solution to a crisis generated by this same technology. The realisation that the crisis facing the environment is being caused by man, who is not just a "factor" to be predicted by rational means and researched by science, but is also a being perceiving through his senses and often acting intuitively, is only very gradually gaining acceptance. It is slowly being acknowledged that using scientific objectivity to research the causes of the growing destruction of our environment will be of scant avail unless accompanied by efforts to ensure that the established findings can also be understood and experienced subjectively. Ultimately, the question as to whether we can overcome ecological and social crises is primarily a question of human behaviour.

In the past few years, this realisation has led to calls for an adequate design language in public space. The purpose of such a contemporary language would not only be to achieve greater public discussion on a changed conception of nature, but also to contribute to heightening our perceptivity, which increasingly threatens to be stifled by the mass media and mass tourism.

There are growing calls for landscape architecture, which as *Garden Art* was once respected as one of the most important and influential art forms, to take part in the search for a modern form of expression.[2] It is nearly one hundred years since the pre-eminence of aesthetic quality in landscape architecture was abandoned in favour of functional, sociological and ecological considerations. The accompanying loss of expressive force and stimulus to society had serious implications and marked the beginning of a development which resulted in complete inarticulateness. Neither the constant, unreflective repetition of the classical vocabulary of the French Baroque garden or the English Landscape Garden nor the retreat to the purely functional means of expression of landscaping can be accepted as a contemporary form of dialogue between man and nature. The search for a way out of this crisis and the increasing rejection of a purely technologically-driven approach to nature has led to increasing reinstatement of art as a unique tool of non-verbal communication.

[2] Cf. Burckhardt, Lucius. "Gärten sind Bilder." In *Natur im Griff. Bundesgartenschau am Beispiel Frankfurt*, edited by Michael Damian, Thomas Osmond. Frankfurt am Main, 1989: p. 20

Particularly *Land Art*, which attempts "to win back nature as space which allows sensory perception, space in which a relationship between man and the environment becomes at all possible again",[3] is seen as an exemplary approach to the question of developing a new language in the landscape. Indeed, in this context Land Art has become something of a vogue-word and genuine discussion of the concept is rare. Instead, Land Art is now all too often uncritically applied to virtually any kind of design in public space which appears to have artistic qualities, irrespective of the meaning it conveys.

[3] Smuda, Manfred, editor. *Landschaft*. Frankfurt am Main, 1986: p. 8

The following discussion of Land Art and Nature Art – like all overviews, of necessity not exhaustive and to some extent subjective – is intended to make these art movements more accessible and provide a better understanding of them. At the same time, tentative answers are to be given to the question as to the way in which art in the landscape can make a decisive contribution to a contemporary language in the landscape.

Distinguishing nature from Nature

Until the Romantic Movement drew to a close, the concept of Nature, in particular the concept of natural beauty, was influenced by Platonic and Aristotelian philosophies. It was closely linked with the notion of harmony as inspired unity of microcosm and macrocosm, of which man was an integral part. The subsequent mechanisation of the conception of the world led to a scientific understanding of nature, which no longer availed itself of qualitative conceptions, preferring quantitative ones which gave rise to different notions of aesthetics. However, our thinking is still influenced by the romantic notion of ideal, untouched natural beauty. While the scientific approach to understanding nature provides the background for harnessing nature as a source of raw materials, man is driven by his romantic conception of nature to seek untouched natural beauty – and by the very fact of his intervention places this longed-for paradise at risk.

In the course of history, Nature has become an integrative concept of ever-increasing thematic diversity. However, the inherent conflicting poles have still today not been resolved, but continue to coexist. Within the framework of our pluralistic society, and against the complex historical background, every individual has developed his own personal conception of Nature. This conception is not static, but changes depending on the form of influence exercised by society (for example the image of nature conveyed by advertising) and conforms to cultural norms. Hence, the true meaning of the contemporary concept of Nature probably only exists as the sum of all individual conceptions, and, in consequence, a precise definition of Nature has been rendered impossible – if indeed such a definition was at any time possible.

Nevertheless, the concept of Nature fulfils an important ideological function and can express both progressive and regressive tendencies in society. To use Rousseau's call for a Return to Nature to justify escape to supposedly unspoilt natural surroundings is clearly regressive. This takes on alarming dimensions when the organic, the indigenous and the pure are proclaimed to be ideals by virtue of their outstanding naturalness, and when, by the same logic, extermination of the "unnatural", the strange and the "inferior" is called for.

A progressive definition of Nature could perhaps be described as one based on a moral philosophy which accepts heterogeneity, values diversity, permits sensuousness, respects differences and is able to come to terms with discontinuity. Such a conception would tacitly accept that, being a living organism, man is part of nature, but as a rational being he is autonomous and, hence, must accept full responsibility for his actions.

As the concept of Nature still has strong moral connotations and becomes the basis of actual planning,[4] thus having concrete effects on the way we live, a critical reflexion on both our individual and the generally accepted attitude to nature is indispensable. The global environmental problems we face are essentially attributable to our disturbed relationship to "outside nature" and to our own "inner nature".

Modern man's mistrust of human nature – above all of the "inner wilderness" of his desires – is the consequence of his development into an enlightened rational being in the seventeenth and eighteenth centuries.[5] Since the beginning of this development, which reached its first climax during the Enlightenment, overcoming the sometimes uncontrollable nature of man was one of the fundamental aims of the process of civilisation. That this process did not remain without implications for "outside nature", for the environment is hardly surprising, and today its effects are undeniable. The entire process of industrial and technological progress and its serious implications for the environment is based on man's endeavours to free himself from the restricting forces of all-powerful nature and to harness its resources. At the same time, it was this act of liberation, the subjugation of nature which made the prosperity of the industrialised nations and the general aesthetic enjoyment of nature possible.[6] For example, the enthusiasm of the exponents of Land Art in America in the sixties for natural disasters can only be understood by those whose very existence is not threatened by earthquakes, volcanic eruptions, floods and other such catastrophes.

Rejection of technology per se is scarcely a matter for any serious consideration in today's society. The question we need to ask is how we are to find a meaningful approach to nature and technology in the future. Particularly the disciplines responsible for shaping the environment will, in view of the fact that they share direct responsibility for propagating certain conceptions of Nature, be called upon to take a critical look at their attitude to nature and their conventional approach to landscape planning.

[4] Cf. Burckhardt, Lucius. *Die Kinder fressen ihre Revolution*. Köln, 1985: p. 213

[5] Cf. Böhme, Hartmut. "Die Natur sprechen lassen." In *Kulturstiftung Stormarn (1989): Projekt Schürberg. Die Natur sprechen lassen*. Hamburg, 1989

[6] Ritter, Joachim. *Landschaft, Zur Funktion des Ästhetischen in der modernen Gesellschaft*. Münster, 1978

Land Art and Nature Art

"Land Art is the name given to an art movement which emerged in America in the late sixties in which landscape and the work of art are inextricably linked.

Sculptures are not placed in the landscape, rather the landscape is the very means of their creation. Interventions by the artist, which use earth, stone, water and other natural materials mark, shape and build, change and restructure landscape space; they do so with a sensitivity and care arising from an awareness of ecological responsibility and as the means of expression of a plastic-weary society. Most works are located well away from civilisation, for example in canyons or deserts, and form a record of human presence only when seen from the air. Video recordings are the only means of conserving the transience of such landscape objects."[7]

A precise conceptual distinction between Land Art and other art movements related to landscape ultimately defies definition, and the above definition contained in the exhibition catalogue "Concept Art, Minimal Art, Arte Povera, Land Art", published by Kunsthalle Bielefeld, would probably be hard to surpass. The way art critics have used the term Land Art since its inception in the late sixties has turned it into something of a catch-all concept. Nowadays, virtually every piece of design in the landscape is called Land Art, even if the work in question only uses landscape as a setting in the traditional sense. Whereas the term Land Art has become usual in Europe, the terms *Earthworks* and *Earth Art* are more common in America, albeit not necessarily more precise. "Indeed the term Land Art can probably be taken as summarising a certain theme, but not as an indication of a particular style."[8]

The German term *Natur-Kunst* (*Nature Art*) was coined to describe ecologically orientated art which, working principally with natural materials, emerged in connection with the growing ecological awareness that existed in Europe in the early seventies. Again, the term does not refer either to a coherent movement or to a specific style. The most prominent exponents of Nature Art in Europe include the British artists David Nash and Andy Goldsworthy and Nils-Udo of Germany. Such artists are also known as *Environmental Artists* in England, a term which gives particular emphasis to ecological aspects and, hence, also cannot be understood as a precise definition of this art movement. Seen from the perspective of art history, Land Art can neither be called the "inventor" of art in the landscape nor was it the only avant-garde "art movement" in the late sixties. The societally turbulent years between 1965 and 1970 gave rise to a large number of art programmes which saw themselves as being a reaction to Pop Art, which had lost its impact by the late sixties. Besides Land Art, the other predominant movements of the sixties were Minimal Art and Concept Art.

In order to better understand the complex background to Minimal Art, Concept Art and Land Art, it is necessary to go further back into the history of art. The art historian Karin Thomas points out that the "interpretative study of the complex groupings and conceptions of art of the last few years […] only [appears] fruitful in the context of a critical analysis of the questions raised by Cubism, Expressionism, Dada, Surrealism and Realism, which, rejecting classical and naturalistic-illusionistic art, created the theoretical and painting technique bases of modern art."[9] The artist of the twentieth century no longer sees himself as the inspired creator of reality lying behind the visible world and perceived through the senses. Instead, he analyses reality and his own existence and experimentally explores new mediums, new perspectives and new forms of communication between man and the environment.

The artistic emphasis of *Minimal Art*, which emerged in the sixties and numbered Sol Lewitt, Robert Morris, Carl Andre and Donald Judd among its leading exponents, is on a formal return to primary structures. In a complete rejection of the gaudy imagery of Pop Art, Minimal Art returns to fundamental forms, orders and structures. These have a strong relationship to space and are to be understood as "barriers to sight" rather than sculptures. "Its absolute objectivity was a response to the emotiveness of Abstract Expressionism. Dispensing with any form of representational art, it succeeds in the tradition of European Constructivism, using the basic forms of Cubism."[10]

Like Minimal Art, *Land Art*, which, it is accepted, was "born" in 1967, is to be understood as a protest against the artificiality, plastic aesthetics and ruthless commercial-

[7] Kunsthalle Bielefeld, editor. *Concept Art, Minimal Art, Arte Povera, Land Art. Sammlung Marzona*. Bielefeld, 1990: p. 264

[8] Wedewer, Rolf. "Landart – Vorstoß in andere Dimensionen." In *Dimensionen des Plastischen – Bildhauertechniken (21.03 – 20.04.81)*, Neuer Berliner Kunstverein e.V. Staatliche Kunsthalle Berlin, 1981: p. 154

[9] Thomas, Karin. *Bis heute. Stilgeschichte der Kunst im 20. Jahrhundert*. Köln, 1994: p. 25

[10] Braun, Heinz. *Forum der Kunst. Eine Einführung in die Kunstgeschichte*. München, 1974: p. 443

Carl Andre. *Secant*. 1977. 100 pieces of Douglas fir (30.4 x 30.4 x 91.4 cm). Total length: 91.4 m. Roslyn, New York.

Michael Heizer. *Rift*. 1968. (15.8 m x 45.7 x 30.4 cm) from: *Nine Nevada Depressions*, Jean Dry Lake. Nevada (destroyed)

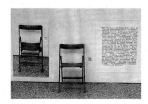

Joseph Kosuth. *One and Three Chairs*. 1965. Museum of Modern Art, New York.

▷ Nils-Udo. *Water-Nest*. 1995. Box, England.

isation of art. Exponents of Land Art reject the museum as the setting of artistic activity and develop monumental landscape projects which are beyond the reach of the commercial art market. "In contrast to the purely objective approach of Minimal Art, Land Art has an intrinsically romantic component in so far as it is the intention of the artist to give nature a specifically human marking as a manifestation of man's spirit and creative power."[11]

As a consequence of the increasing rejection of the conventional object-relatedness of art, *Concept Art* emerged in the late sixties. This movement no longer sees the materialisation of a project or the realisation of an idea as being absolutely essential. In contrast to the traditional concept of material in painting or sculpture, it is the idea itself which becomes the material of art. Artists such as Joseph Kosuth, Hans Haacke, Jan Dibbets and Douglas Huebler number among the leading exponents of Concept Art. Kosuth's project "One and Three Chairs" is a clear example of the way that Concept Art works with various levels of abstraction. Kosuth (born in 1938) combined a chair (reality), a photograph of the chair (sign) and a dictionary definition of "chair" (designation) to create a work which clearly illustrates the limited information value of object, representation and language. This leads to the question as to what information value art possesses.

What is known as *Natur-Kunst* (*Nature Art*) developed in Germany in the early seventies. One of the most important centres of this art in Germany is the Galerie Falazik in Neuenkirchen in the Lüneburg Heath. This was the venue of "Aktion Heidebild" in 1972, the first large-scale project of its kind to try out works which did justice to nature using artistic means and accentuated nature by art.[12] The fact that so far this art form was only able to gain relatively little recognition outside Europe is probably due to the comparatively short life-span of Nature Art works, which are, in comparison with Land Art monuments, in most cases unspectacular and characterised by a picturesque tendency.

Reference should be made of two further contemporary art trends which deserve special mention in view of their relationship to current developments in art in the landscape and landscape architecture: Individuelle Mythologie (Individual Mythology) and Spurensicherung (Securing of Evidence).

The concept of *Individual Mythology* dates back to 1972 and documenta V. Individual Mythology summarises a movement which "counters Minimal Art's desire for objectivity by a firm declaration of belief in subjectivity. The art productions of this subjective, creative message do not have any common denominator, rather their completely open form and the unique identity of the artist defy any typification."[13] Joseph Beuys, Paul Thek, Christian Boltanski, Etienne Martin and James Lee Byars first demonstrated their relationship to the myth at documenta V. Richard Long, Nancy Graves and Jannis Kounellis are also regarded as exponents of Individual Mythology. "The imagery of Individual Mythology is the search for a lost Arcadian ideal, which is to be revealed by immersion in subconscious dreams and mythological notions as well as by meditation."[14] Land Art reflects part of this philosophy and avails itself of typical elements of Individual Mythology.

There are similar links to *Securing of Evidence*, which emerged during the same period and numbers Paul-Armand Gette, Anne and Patrick Poirier, Nikolaus Lang, Rainer Wittenborn and Charles Simonds among its leading exponents. Karin Thomas defines Tracing the Past as "a special movement within Individual Mythology, which uses traces and symbols of past cultures and lives to create highly associative symbols of suggestive emotiveness. Inventories, photographs and scientific research in the fields of archaeology and ethnology serve as the materials of Securing of Evidence, which are given new life of their own by the artist's individual commentary."[15]

In her 1983 essay entitled "Environmental Artists: Sources and Directions" the American journalist, Carol Hall, provides an interesting outline of the development of Land Artists and illuminates the components which make up landscape art.[16] The past five decades led to a pluralistic coexistence which manifested itself in terms of style and theory in Postmodernism. This is the context in which Land Art, Nature Art and contemporary landscape architecture are to be seen.

[11] Thomas, Karin. *Bis heute. Stilgeschichte der Kunst im 20. Jahrhundert*. Köln, 1994: p. 333

[12] Cf. Thiel, Heinz. "Natur-Kunst." In Kunstforum International, *vol. 48 (2–3/82): p. 24–25*

[13] Thomas, Karin. *Bis heute. Stilgeschichte der Kunst im 20. Jahrhundert*. Köln, 1994: p. 347

[14] *Ibid.*

[15] Ibid.: p. 22/cf. Metken, Günter. *Spurensicherung*. Köln, 1977

[16] Cf. Carol Hall. "Environmental Artists: Sources and Directions." (1983) In Sonfist, Alan. *Art in the Land*. New York, 1984: p. 8ff.

Nikolaus Lang. *Kiste für die Geschwister Götte* (*Chest for the Götte Siblings*). 1973/74. Bayersoien.

Michael Heizer. *Double Negative*. Interior View.

▷ Michael Heizer. *Double Negative*. Aerial view. 1969–1970. 240.000-ton displacement in rhyolite and sandstone. At the edge of Mormon Mesa, near Overton, Nevada. Collection the Museum of Contemporary Art, Los Angeles, California.

Nature as the material of art

For the sake of simplicity the "typical" materials of Land Art and Nature Art are commonly referred to as "natural materials". However, in the artistic context "material" is not only to be understood as "malleable means". It is equally the means of conveying inherent meanings and its own history and mythology. Material becomes the medium which influences the figurative and symbolic message of the work.

Earth

"The dirt (or earth) is there not only to be seen, but to be thought about! [...] God has given us the earth and we have ignored it."[17]

It is nearly thirty years since the Land Art exponent Walter de Maria (born in 1935) proclaimed his particular interest in materials which art had previously dismissed as worthless. He discovered the unique quality and specific aesthetic appeal of earth as a medium. He illustrated these qualities when in 1968, in the context of *Munich Earth Room*, he filled a room measuring 72 square metres/775 square feet at the Galerie Heiner Friedrich in Munich with 50 cubic metres/65 cubic yards of soil: muffled sound, perceptibly higher humidity and an earthy smell pervaded an airy gallery room, where the visitor had expected to view art objects at a distance.

Of more lasting significance for the development of Land Art were, however, the large-scale earthworks which were created outside museums and include, for example, works such as de Maria's *Las Vegas Piece* (1969) and Michael Heizer's *Double Negative* (1969/70). "*Double Negative* is the name given to two huge incisions in a plateau near Overton/Nevada, approximately 80 miles north-east of Las Vegas. At the edge of a mesa, along the escarpment which borders the wide valley of the Virginia River, Heizer [born in 1944] used dynamite and a bulldozer to make two cuts. They are axially aligned and are separated by a ravine which has eaten back part of the mesa on the edge of the large river valley. The two cuts on opposite sides of the ravine form a straight line stretching from east to west over a total length of approximately 460 metres/1,500'. The eastern section is 75 metres/246' long, the western section 45 metres/148'."[18] Each cut is 15 metres/50' wide and up to 12 metres/40' deep. Both are accessible from the ravine.

The work is, despite its gigantic dimensions, subject to the inexorable process of weathering and decay. This predictable process of erosion would indeed seem to confirm the transience of Land Art projects. But although the forces of weathering will completely cover the cut in the course of time, the scar which marks the violation of the earth's surface will remain visible as earth of a different colour and will never fully disappear. Heizer underlines the value of soil as an enduring "memory of earth", a quality which has long been appreciated by archaeologists.

Nevertheless, in contrast to many other cultures, our relationship to earth tends to remain contradictory. "Earth, this special matter is bound up with mythology and mysticism, particularly in our culture it has negative connotations, is associated with dirt, filth – the base. The word matter is derived from the lexical family "mater" – mother, a fundamental substance, which contains life and death and rebirth."[19]

The violent manner of artistic intervention in what had been virtually untouched land has repeatedly received strong criticism. How can this approach be reconciled with the special esteem which is supposed to be due to this medium? The art expert Thomas Kellein speaks of a "defilement" of the "landscape along the lines of bourgeois sexual morals with the help of a bulldozer. [...] However, it is only the violent destruction of the earth's surface which marks the fact and the way we move on earth: always in one dimension, always in one direction, rather than with a goal [...] Just as *Double Negative* emphasizes the size of a natural ravine between two artificial incisions like the distance between two planets, de Maria's furrows [Las Vegas Piece] in the Tula Desert evoke the first or last tracks of a human being who wanted to make a mark on an untrodden planet."[20]

A kind of counter-trend to the earthworks movement in America developed in Europe at the end of the sixties. The British artist Richard Long (born in 1945), still today one of the most prominent exponents of landscape art in Europe, attracted particular

[17] Cited from press release *Walter de Maria: The Land Show*, Galerie Heiner Friedrich, München, September 1968

[18] Hoormann, Anne. „Außerhalb des Ateliers: Land Art und Concept Art." In *Moderne Kunst 2. Das Funkkolleg zum Verständnis der Gegenwartskunst*, edited by Monika Wagner. Reinbek bei Hamburg, 1991: p. 593

[19] Falazik, Ruth. In *Frauen Museum: Umwelt – Naturkunst*. Bonn, 1985: p. 5

[20] Kellein, Thomas. "Land Art – Ein Vorbericht zur Deutung der Erde." In *Europa/Amerika*, published by Museum Ludwig, Köln. Köln, 1986: p. 400

attention with his cautious landscape interventions in 1968. "Instead of the new-frontier attitude of the Americans Heizer and de Maria, here was a gardener approaching landscape which was already cultural; his unobtrusive markings formulated the early antithesis of all spectacular interventions in the earth."[21] Richard Long essentially understands walking through virtually deserted regions as a meditative undertaking, seeing this to be very closely linked with a personal experience of nature.

[21] Ibid.: p. 368

The spatial effect and technical execution of the seemingly archaic works created during the course of his walking expeditions are particularly reminiscent of the Nazca Lines in Peru, probably made around 500 B.C. using very simple means. Long's artistic interventions are almost invisible markings in the landscape, sometimes no more than primitive geometrical formations consisting of footprints or places which have been marked by stamping the earth hard. Sometimes his interventions take the form of arrangements in stone and wood, drawings in sand or water, which only remain in the landscape for a brief period, their clear geometrical forms entering into a dialogue with nature. "You could say that my work is also a balance between the patterns of nature and the formalism of human, abstract ideas like lines and circles. It is where my human characteristics meet the natural forces and patterns of the world, and that is really the kind of subject of my work."[22]

[22] Long, Richard cited by The South Bank Centre, editor. *Richard Long. Walking in Circles*. London, 1991: p. 250

The approach to earth as a material takes on a particularly interesting aspect when an American pioneer of Land Art such as Walter de Maria comes into contact with European terrain. The project entitled *The Vertical Earth Kilometre*, which was realised as part of documenta VI in 1977, proved to be an interesting experiment with sociological implications. It provoked heated public debate on account of the expenditure it entailed. In contrast to the works in the deserts of North America, the surface area covered by the project is minimal. Walter de Maria had a hole with an average diameter of just under 30 centimetres/12" drilled in the middle of Friedrichsplatz in Kassel to a depth of 1,000 metres/3,300'. It was an undertaking which – and here it rivals the American works discussed above – involved an immense amount of technical equipment and expertise.

The artist deliberately chose an urban context in which to stage his project. Its dimensions transcend the immediate experience of the individual and, nevertheless, exist anywhere in the world. The stone slab measuring 2 x 2 metres/6½' x 6½', by now much worn down, encases the upper end of the bronze rod (5 cm/2" in diameter, 1,000 metres/3,300' in length, weighing 18 tonnes) beneath the ground. The slab is the only visible sign of the spectacular action and still today causes visitors to the site to reflect on a dimension which remains invisible. Earth as a mythical primordial element is enhanced, revived, seen consciously. "I imagine that public reaction was marked by such uneasiness because people experienced a challenge to the way they conventionally thought and felt. Perhaps because a work such as this startles people into having to reflect on the purpose of our life, our existence."[23]

[23] Friedrich, Heiner cited by Seidenfaden I.: "Da wacht man ganz schnell auf." in: Abendzeitung München, no. 26 (29.05.1977)

Stone

For thousands of years stone was, alongside wood and bone, the most important material worked by man. For this reason, it has always played a central role in art. "The rough, unhewn stones which are to be found in prehistoric cultures as objects of religious veneration, as gravestones, spiritual and ancestral figures or places of ritual worship may be seen as a first form of sculpture. Sometimes the very act of choosing it, deliberately putting it in its appointed place was sufficient to make the stone sacred and imbue it with symbolism."[24] Many artists in Europe and America use unworked stone in this way, evoking its diverse traditional symbolism: stability, endurance, reliability, immortality, permanence, the eternal. Moreover, every stone, in particular the unhewn erratic, tells a piece of landscape history through its location, its type of rock and form, strengthening the relationship of the work to the place. This can be seen as the reason why Nature Art and Land Art prefer, in contrast to conventional sculpture, to use unworked stone.

[24] Billeter, Erika. In *Mythos und Ritual in der Kunst der siebziger Jahre*, published by Kunsthaus Zürich. Zürich, 1981: p. 21

The techniques of linear arrangement, of stacking and particularly of building walls play a more significant role for European environmental artists than they do in America. In

Walter de Maria. *Las Vegas Piece*. 1969. Realised with the assistance of Michael Heizer near *Double Negative*. Desert Valley, Nevada.

Walter de Maria, *The Vertical Earth Kilometre* (cover on Friedrichsplatz), commissioned by the Dia Art Foundation at documenta VI in Kassel 1977.

contrast to traditional sculpture, nature art in particular sees natural, unworked stone as a special medium with many references to past cultural history and, mainly in Europe, also to the present. The technique of building drystone walls is, to a certain extent, a cultivated form of stacking. When the wall is built the individual stone does not lose its own special form, but becomes part of a new order, the clear expression of a creative purpose or of man's agricultural activity (for example the use of drystone walls in the history of cultural landscape). The result is an attractive encounter between a traditional craft and a contemporary art form. "Stacking wood which has been cut, making piles of grass which has been mown, collecting boulders on the edges of fields is always an expression of work and economic activity. The form is determined by the functional necessity of the activity – it is not the product of a conscious design process based on aesthetic principles. Yet, in formal terms the results of a way of working which is based on economic and functional considerations and one based on aesthetic principles are very similar."[25] Particularly the work of Richard Long is a clear illustration of the subtle effect achieved when the artist contrasts the original natural complexity with his own order by consciously arranging the material.

Using the example of his 1988/1989 work *The Wall*, the British artist Andy Goldsworthy (born in 1956) puts the close relationship between art and daily life into a very everyday perspective. He said at the time, "I have been given a small piece of woodland in Dumfriesshire by the Buccleuch Estates. I call this place Stonewood. Part of the lease required me to build a dividing wall. I have made a give-and-take wall between the farmer and myself. Two sheep folds are incorporated into the wall: one opening on the farmer's side for sheep, one opening on my side for sculpture. The sheep will in effect be on my land and the sculpture on the farmer's."[26] Goldsworthy's work not only builds a bridge to a craft tradition but also to the people who give him technical and creative assistance. Thus, Joe Smith, the drystone waller who helped Goldsworthy to build the wall is mentioned by name in the artist's publications as a matter of course.

Wood

Particularly its uses as fuel and as a building material have made wood a material which man has always seen as fundamental to his existence, as a vital symbol of natural growth. Wood as a sculptural material is still today essentially worked in three different ways: "First, the fashioning of a block of wood by carving – probably the oldest and best-known technique –, second, the use of wood as a constructional means in the form of beams and planks, third, the integration of wood in its natural form as tree, trunk, branch."[27] Again, it is the material in its natural state (or worked only minimally) which is particularly preferred in European Environmental Art. North American landscape art tends to use wood to a greater extent as a constructional means. Sawn, planed, nailed and, occasionally, also painted, the natural material loses much of its characteristic form, its distinctive nature.

While wood is most dynamic as living material, only few artists work with living plant material other than grass or lawn as a green surface texture. The living plant often develops an unpredictable momentum of its own and actively alters its environment. Man has traditionally used gardening whenever it was a question of controlling this natural process of change. But in 1968 Robert Smithson asked, "Could one say that art degenerates as it approaches gardening"?[28] Art criticism has, consequently, been unable to come to terms with creative gardening and sees a direct link between works such as David Nash's *Ash Dome* (1977) of living ashes and traditional garden art. Does this gardening tradition of "grooming" provide an explanation for the infrequent use of living plants in Nature Art and Land Art? Or does art choose to steer clear of mediums which develop a momentum of their own?

The use of living plants also tends to be an exception in the work of David Nash (born in 1945). As a rule, he works with dead wood in its natural form and sees this material as a metaphor of life. "I want a simple approach to living and doing. I want a life and work that reflects the balance and continuity of nature. Identifying with the time and energy of the tree and with its mortality, I find myself drawn deeper into

[25] Thiel, Heinz loc. cit.: p. 26

[26] Goldsworthy, Andy. *Andy Goldsworthy*. London, 1990

[27] Rüth, Uwe/Galerie Heimeshoff, Essen, editors. *Material und Raum*. Essen, 1991: p. 26

[28] Smithson, Robert cited in Holt, Nancy, editor. *The Writings of Robert Smithson*. New York, 1979: p. 85–86

Art in Nature

the joys and blows of nature. Worn down and regenerated; broken off and reunited; a dormant faith revived in the new growth on old wood."[29]

Many environmental artists see transience, a fundamental, yet often repressed part of our life and the decay phase in the cycle of nature as playing an essential role. When working with nature, the artist is forced to enter into a dialogue with the independent existence of his subject matter or, at least, to come to terms with it. Natural changes become an immanent element of the sculptural work, they are the expression of an important, new dimension of the open work: "All this explains how contemporary art can be seen as an epistemological metaphor," writes Umberto Eco. "The discontinuity of phenomena has called into question the possibility of a unified, definitive image of our universe; art suggests a way for us to see the world in which we live, and, by seeing it, accept it and integrate it into our sensibility. The open work assumes the task of giving us an image of discontinuity. It does not narrate it: it *is* it. It takes on a mediating role between the abstract categories of science and the living matter of our sensibility; it almost becomes a sort of transcendental scheme that allows us to comprehend new aspects of the world."[30]

Snow and ice

As part of the project entitled *Time Pocket*, the Land Art pioneer, Dennis Oppenheim (born in 1938), used a snow-mobile to make a line in the snow which marks the international time border between Canada and the United States. Andy Goldsworthy fashions fragile sculptures of snow and ice, which melt only a short time later. Such actions focus on the individual, sometimes whimsical encounter with landscape, nature and the phenomenon of time. When no photographs of the object were taken, something which the pioneers of Land Art categorically rejected in the early years, the work only lived on in the memory of the individual. The dividing-line to Minimal Art and Concept Art is a fluid one. "The end product, if it does exist at all, [...] is no longer the objective, but, within the artistic work, its meaning becomes secondary, becomes a relic degraded in favour of visualisation of the process, the movement, the change itself, frequently with references to phenomena which are beyond the visible world, such as time."[31]

Richard Harris. *Cliff Structure*. 1988. Grizedale Forest Sculpture, Cumbria, England.

[29] Nash, David cited by Beardsley, John. *Earthworks and beyond*. New York, 1989: p. 47

[30] Eco, Umberto. *Opera aperta*. Milano, 1962, 1967. English edition: *The Open Work*. London, 1989: p. 90

[31] Jochimsen, Margarethe. "Zeit zwischen Entgrenzung und Begrenzung der bildenden Kunst heute." In *Die Vierte Dimension in der Kunst*, edited by Michael Baudson. Weinheim, 1985: p. 224–225

Archetypal forms

One of the particular features of Land Art is a language of forms characterised by simple, often severe geometries. This language of forms is principally based on symbols which are essentially archetypal. Their origins lie in the earliest history of mankind, their meaning is rooted in the collective mind and can be read via the unconscious. The point, the line, the circle, the spiral, the labyrinth and the pyramid are among the forms which are most frequently used with a symbolic meaning.

The line

The line is one of the most fundamental one-dimensional signs. In contrast to the point, it appears directed, in motion and in a process of development. The meaning of the line as an everyday design element has had a wide variety of connotations in the course of history; the line has often assumed an imaginary character, for example as the fictitious linking of the stars. Land Artists essentially use the line to make the invisible visible. In his project *Time Pocket* marking the international time border between Canada and the United States Dennis Oppenheim made the abstract result of a mathematical operation on the temporal structuring of the world briefly visible as a line in the snow.

Richard Long understands the landscape as a complex structure of superimposed geological and historical layers. His linear marks in the landscape are tracks which for a short time indicate an independent layer. With *Walking a Line in Peru* (1972) Long turned his attention to a country in which the visible lines, elements of the old Indian Nazca Lines, tell an ancient story which is yet to reveal its secrets. Walter de Maria is also aware of the meditative effect of archaic geometry set in a landscape context. In a personal report, the Swiss exhibition organiser, Carlo Huber, describes his first encounter with de Maria's *Las Vegas Piece* as "a walk to the ends of the earth."[32] In the remote desert wastes the linear track of a bulldozer conveys a feeling of orientation which seems to encompass the whole world.

Andy Goldsworthy. *Icicle*. 1987. Scaur Water, Scotland.

The circle

The circle is a universal symbol, conveying a similar meaning in nearly all of the world's cultures. "Whether the symbol of the circle appears in primitive sun worship or in modern religion, in myths or dreams, in the mandalas drawn by Tibetan monks, in the ground-plans of modern towns, or in the spherical concepts of early astronomers, it always points to the single most vital aspect of life, its ultimative wholeness."[33] The circle can signify concentration on the centre as well as radiation from the centre to the surroundings.

Stonehenge in southern England, the largest megalithic site in Europe, has still today not fully divulged its secrets and – perhaps for this very reason – is a reference frequently quoted by Land Art. Robert Morris' *Observatory* in the Netherlands (1977) is an example of a work which makes references to Stonehenge not only formally but also in terms of meaning. The position at which the sun rises at the winter and summer solstices and at the time of the vernal and autumnal equinoxes determines the position of the axes. Thus, the axes which extend from the centre of the circular mound to the horizon anchor the project firmly in the natural time system. As the fourth dimension of art, time takes on central significance in the form of the circle.

The pyramid

The pyramid is a basic phenomenon of perception.[34] Put in perspective, even a parallelepiped is seen as a form resembling the pyramid. As cubical forms the pyramid and the cone symbolise the duality of stability and dynamism. The triangle, the plane section of the pyramid, represents stability, particularly when it rests on one of its three faces. At the same time, the pyramid, which tapers towards its vertex, is a dynamic element.

The pyramid is traditionally seen as symbolising fire, flame, the power of the sun, highest intellectual endeavour, centre of the world, axis mundi. Heinz Thiel, a knowledgeable authority on Nature Art, understands pyramids and cones as forms of

Richard Long. *A Circle in Ireland*. 1975. Ireland.

[32] Huber, Carlo. "Spaziergang ans Ende der Welt. Zu den Werken von Heizer und de Maria in Nevada." In *Kunstjahrbuch 1*. Hannover, 1970: p. 129

[33] Jaffe, A. in Jung, C. G. *Man and his Symbols*. New York, 1964.

[34] Cf. Grütter, Jörg Kurt. *Ästhetik der Architektur. Grundlagen der Architektur-Wahrnehmung*. Mainz, 1987: p. 141

Art in Nature

Robert Morris. *Observatory*. 1977 (during building phase) an 1993. Flevoland, Netherlands.

everyday life. "From the aesthetic point of view, the eye sees mounds as harmonious, and this in itself is reassuring enough for the cone and pyramid not to require any further explanation or inquiry as to their meaning. [...] Conical forms occur frequently in the area of anonymous design, as stacks of wood, sheaves of corn or piles of dry grass."[35]

No discussion of the effect of the archetypal pyramid form would be complete without mention of the pyramids in Egypt, the monumental tombs of the pharaohs which date back approximately four and a half thousand years to the Old and Middle Kingdoms. Although the purpose of the Pyramids of Gizeh is known, as is the manner in which they were built, their meaning is still not fully understood. Many Land Artists were fascinated by the mysterious qualities and formal power of these monuments. In particular, the works of Michael Heizer are frequently compared with ancient monuments. For over two decades Michael Heizer has been working on *Complex One/ Complex Two*, a gigantic ensemble of geometrically configured earth-and-concrete structures in Garden Valley, a high plateau in the Nevada desert. The first part of the ensemble, *Complex One*, an earth-and-concrete structure with a trapezoidal cross-section, is over 40 metres/130' in length and seven metres/23' high and was built by Heizer between 1972 and 1974. "Its imposing isolation in the remoteness and desertedness of the landscape, the alignment of its frame to the course of the sun are not speculative, but direct references to Copán or Teotihuacán."[36] Michael Heizer's father, Robert F. Heizer, was an eminent anthropologist and archaeologist who taught at Berkeley. In his youth Michael Heizer became acquainted with the meaning of the structures of the pre-Columbian advanced civilisations on excavations in Central and South America, an experience which has had a lasting influence on his creative work. The trapezoidal form of the mastabas of ancient Egypt is clearly reflected in *Complex One* in Nevada.

[35] Thiel, Heinz loc. cit.: p. 41

[36] Wedewer, Rolf loc. cit.: p. 156

[37] De Maria, Walter cited by Jochimsen, M. loc. cit.: p. 224

[38] Dewey, John. *Art as Experience.* New York, 1934: p. 206

[39] Pohlen, Annelie/Warin, Isolde. "Vom Denken in Bildern." In Kunsthaus Zürich loc. cit., 1981: p. 34–35

[40] Böhme, Hartmut. "Die Natur sprechen lassen." In *Kulturstiftung Stormarn* loc cit.: p. 96–97

[41] Panofsky, Erwin. *Perspective as symbolic form.* Massachusetts, 1991: p. 29/30

The fourth dimension of Land Art

"The artist who works with earth, works with time."[37] This statement made by Walter de Maria at the beginning of the seventies not only illustrates the connection between material and time generally, but also emphasizes the particular meaning of time in art in the landscape. "Space and time – or rather space-time – are found in the matter of every art product", wrote the philosopher John Dewey. "In the arts, they are neither the empty containers nor the formal relations that schools of philosophy have sometimes presented them to be. They are substantial, they are properties of every kind of material employed in artistic expression and aesthetic realisation."[38] The conscious decision to use transient materials and the incorporation of the aspect of decay are indications of an individual conception of time.

By opening up the desert as an extended area of action, and with the growing rejection of an art which had become faceless and rootless from alienation, time had become an important factor for the pioneers of Land Art. "The further the belief in progress […] crumbled, the more society reached the limits of its material development […], the more plainly time became the focus of reflexions as an element which moves and confines", wrote Annelie Pohlen. "The purpose of intellectual endeavour in the search for experience of the self was not conquest of the physical space, but of time as the non-material dimension of space. The interventions in the landscape by Land Art are, despite their monumental proportions, invocations of time."[39]

To render this invisible dimension visible and to heighten the awareness of time, art in the landscape not only deliberately incorporates transient aspects, but also makes use of certain symbolic forms. These either manifest themselves in the outer form of the work, as in the case of the circular *Observatory* by Robert Morris (born 1931), or underlie it as conceptual lines of movement, as in the case of Richard Long's walk along concentric circles *Four Hours and Four Circles* in 1972, an action which had the subjective experience of time as its focus. Land Art uses both the ruinous and references to structures dating back to early history to put time in a historical context. References to the annual course of the sun are intended to convey an experience of astronomic time.

Like Land Art, European Nature Art not only tolerates the limited life-span of the works, but actually intends such transience. Transience as a temporal process, as a means of experiencing nature directly is the essential dimension of Nature Art. In contrast to traditional sculpture, many works in nature only survive for a few months, days, hours or for no more than a matter of seconds. It follows that documentation of works such as those of Andy Goldsworthy places emphasis on this process of disappearance.

The implications of experimenting with the fourth dimension for our media society, which is geared towards acquisition and accumulation, are summarised by Hartmut Böhme in an article on "Letting nature speak": "Our perceptive abilities are conditioned to identify the information content of images within a matter of seconds. The sensuousness to which we are attuned has, as it were, been decentralised by the frightening speed of our modern means of transport and the unrelenting onslaught of images in both cities and the media, has become restless, nervous, greedy, aggressive. Perception of nature requires a different relationship to time […]. Perception of nature reveals entirely different time forms, rhythms, time figures in which natural processes are organised. Human time, societal and historical time, and the times occurring in nature only overlap in very few zones and are, otherwise, poles apart."[40]

Michael Heizer. *City.* 1972 (east half; in progress). *Complex One.* 1972–1974 (in background). *Complex Two.* 1981 (left foreground, in progress). Central Eastern Nevada.

The other experience of space

"But if perspective is not a factor of value, it is surely a factor of style. Indeed, it may even be characterised as […] one of those 'symbolic forms' in which' spiritual meaning is attached to a concrete, material sign and intrinsically given to this sign. This is why it is essential to ask of artistic periods and regions not only whether they have perspective but which perspective they have."[41] An attempt to answer this question of perspective, which was raised by the art historian Erwin Panofsky with regard to Land Art is made particularly difficult by the fact that many of the transient works now only exist as photographic documentation. The very fact that pioneers of Land Art permitted their works to be photographed frequently led to the reproach of inconsistency: after all, one of the strictest maxims of Land Art was its rejection of the established art market, which it did not want to provide with anything marketable whatsoever.

Richard Serra (born in 1939) sees photography, in particular aerial photography, as clear evidence of Land Art's continued dependence on painting, despite its rejection of the traditional concept of art. "What most people know of Smithson's *Spiral Jetty*, for example, is an image shot from a helicopter. When you actually see the work, it has none of that purely graphical character, [...] if you reduce sculpture to the flat plane of the photograph, you're passing on only a residue of your concerns. You're denying the temporal experience of the work. You're not only reducing the sculpture to a different scale for the purposes of consumption, but you're denying the real content of the work."[42]

Robert Smithson. *Spiral Jetty*. 1970. (1,500' long, 15' wide). Great Salt Lake, Utah.

In consequence, Erwin Panofsky makes single-point perspective, the inventor of which is considered to be the sculptor and architect Filippo Brunelleschi (1377–1446), dependent upon two essential assumptions: "... first, that we see with a single and immobile eye, and second, that the planar cross section of the visible pyramid can pass for an adequate reproduction of our optical image. In fact these two premises are rather bold abstractions from reality. [...] Nowhere in the space of immediate perception can this postulate be fulfilled."[43] Such a critical approach only gradually gained acceptance, and the normative validity of single-point perspective endured for several hundred years. As the natural sciences altered their conception of the world, particularly due to the influence of Einstein's theory of relativity, a profound change of emphasis in favour of aperspectivity took place. The standpoint of the beholder was no longer to be dictated.

The fundamental difference between contemporary sculpture, the foundations of which were not developed until the sixties, and "traditional" sculpture is principally to be understood as a new self-conception and an almost "symbiotic" relationship to the recipient. "This sculpture asks to be used, entered, mounted, touched. In contrast to earlier works of art, it not only wants to be experienced in an aesthetic or intellectual dialogue, but – literally – wants to be lived. [...] Thus, psychology too has recognised that the whole body is an organ of spatial experience: and it is precisely this that sculpture not only uses as a form of action, but takes as its very subject and transmits into the various sensorial dimensions of the body [...] The body is both used and experienced through this use. It is both instrument and sensorium."[44]

Robert Smithson. *Spiral Jetty*. 1970. Great Salt Lake, Utah.

Only a work of art defying unequivocal interpretation and allowing itself to be experienced in individually different ways from both the formal point of view and in terms of its content enables the beholder to discover new dimensions of perception. Umberto Eco uses the concept of "open work" to describe such structures.[45] The open work no longer dictates a specific manner of perception, but opens up a field of interpretative possibilities which allow the individual to make his standpoint a matter of conscious choice. This definition could be understood to imply that every free-standing sculpture was technically to be categorised as an open work. Eco accepts this fundamental objection, but he states: "On the other hand, apart from works that were designed to be seen only from the front (like the statues that adorn the columns of some Gothic cathedrals), most sculptures, though they can be viewed from different angles, are intended to produce a global impression, the cumulative result of various perspectives. [The open work on the other hand] makes one imagine a variety of possible perspectives; and though each perspective is satisfactory in itself, it inevitably frustrates the viewer who would like to apprehend a totality."[46]

Robert Smithson. *Spiral Jetty*. 1970. Great Salt Lake, Utah.

Not all Land Art and Environmental Art works allow this spatial experience within their own structure. Often it is the symbiosis with the landscape space which creates an open, interpretable composition. The spatial conception of Land Art and Nature Art is usually not determined by pre-ordained viewpoints and unequivocal perspectives. Aperspectivity is a rejection of the dictatorship of the fixed eye. Moreover, it is also understood as an invitation to a total spatial experience, as an invitation to the recipient to experience individual, conscious freedom in the sense of the theory of the open work. Thus, photography is essentially a technique necessary to document transient works.

[42] Serra, Richard in an interview of July 1980, cited in The Hudson River Museum, editor. *Richard Serra: Interviews 1970–1980*. New York, 1980: p. 170

[43] Panofsky, E. loc. cit.: p. 29/30

[44] Schneckenburger, Manfred. "Plastik als Handlungsform." In *Kunstforum International*, vol. 34 (4/79), p. 20–31

[45] Cf. Eco, U. loc. cit.

[46] Ibid.: p. 85–86

In the natural environment

[47] Beardsley, J. loc. cit.: p. 7.

"Rather than representing it in paint on canvas [...], a handful of artists chose to enter the landscape itself, to use its materials and work with its salient features. They were not depicting the landscape, but engaging it," writes John Beardsley in his book "Earthworks and beyond". "Their art was not simply *of* the landscape, but *in* it as well."[47] For work in and with nature the relationship to the respective environment is of fundamental significance. Whereas the pioneers of Land Art retreated from the cities to the supposedly untouched natural environment, landscape artists working in Central Europe were, from the very beginning, forced to enter into a dialogue with densely populated, richly structured cultural landscape. The fragmentation of the landscape, the character of the culturally formed surroundings and the incorporation of landscape design in the everyday processes of society, with their specific problems when dealing with art in the public space, have produced works on a distinctly smaller scale and have restricted the freedom of movement.

Desert

[48] Heizer, Michael cited by Wedewer, Rolf loc. cit.: p. 152

The American pioneers of Land Art saw the extensive desert areas of Nevada, Utah, Arizona and New Mexico as unspoilt, meditative natural environments. In contrast to the complexity of the cities, conditions of life here are limited to a few simple parameters. Michael Heizer said that what he was seeking in the desert was "that kind of unraped, peaceful, religious space [...] artists have always tried to put in their work."[48] Perception of the boundless space and the unique quality of the experience of nature were the principal concerns. Desert areas are still today the preferred venues of artists in this tradition, who, such as Charles Ross in New Mexico (*Star Axis*) or Hannsjörg Voth in Morocco (*Himmelstreppe*, *Goldene Spirale*), want to escape the constraints of densely populated cultural landscape.

[49] Norberg-Schulz, Christian. *Genius loci – paesaggio, ambiente, architettura.* Milano, 1979. English edition: *Genius loci: Towards a phenomenology of architecture.* London, 1980

The architecture theoretician Christian Norberg-Schulz speaks of the desert as a cosmic landscape, in which the individual does not encounter the multifarious forces of the earth, but experiences its most absolute cosmic qualities.[49] These cosmic qualities manifest themselves in an openly stereotyped ideal of the desert: endless expanses, arid ground, cloudless sky, scorching sun, remoteness, silence, desolation and the like. Artists experience this kind of landscape as neutral ground which, with the exception of isolated oases, provides the individual with no spatial orientation and, hence, with no existential security. Their resulting interventions are intended to emphasize spatial orientation. This is achieved by using a great diversity of means. "In fact, many works by Andre, De Maria, Long and others can be described more aptly by concepts such as way, axis, place, inside-outside than by conventional terms such as material, mass, negative volume, rhythm, composition."[50]

[50] Schneckenburger, Manfred loc. cit: p. 23

However, orientation in space is not the only reason for the built manifestations by exponents of Land Art. Rather the severity and monumental nature of many works are a clear indication of the will to create on the part of the individual. Their markings on neutral ground are, therefore, mostly in contrast to and a confrontation with the environment. Sometimes this dominant character only reveals itself in an element of surprise. Walter de Maria's *Las Vegas Piece* in the Tula Desert of Nevada may be seen as a structuring line, of which the visitor only becomes aware when already standing on the tracks left by the bulldozer.[51] In contrast, *Himmelstreppe* by Hannsjörg Voth, in the shape of a gigantic stairway, consciously stands out from its surroundings in formal terms, even when seen from a distance, as does Michael Heizer's *Complex One*. As unique examples and markings such monuments transform the nameless site into a place, a topos. Christian Norberg-Schulz calls this process the existential purpose of building.[52]

[51] Cf. personal report by Huber, Carlo loc. cit.: p. 129ff.

[52] Cf. Norberg-Schulz, C. loc. cit.

In his walks in the Sahara in 1988, in Anatolia in 1989 and in the desert areas of Texas in 1990 Richard Long also sought quiet, intimate spaces and deserted neutral ground, not, however, for the purpose of installing monumental symbols but rather to express a very personal experience of nature. He does so with simple, universally understandable placements in the landscape. His marks blend in, becoming recognisable in varied landscape only on closer inspection, showing a sensitive awareness of the inner

Richard Long. *Touareg Circle.*
1988. Sahara.

Richard Long. *Dusty Boot Line*.
1988. Sahara.

Art in Nature

character of a place. Long admits that "nature has more effect on me than I on it".[53] This statement underlines the essential ways in which Land Art's relationship to nature differs from that of Nature Art.

[53] Long, Richard cited in *Richard Long* loc. cit. 1991: p. 12–16

Forest

Central Europe was originally almost entirely covered by forest. Early history of its civilisation is characterised by the battle against "dark forests" from which usable arable and grazing land were wrested. Only after large expanses of forest had been cut down to enable man to cultivate the land did Romanticism discover the "solitude of the forest" as a preferred nature motif. The seemingly endless diversity of the forest's appearance, its self-contained, almost labyrinthine impenetrability and mysterious twilight atmosphere not only inspired fairytales and legends in the past. The partly eerie, partly romantic image of the forest still lives on in our imagination, despite the fact that it has long since become an area used for economic purposes.

The *Grizedale Forest Sculpture* project, realised in Grizedale Forest in the southern part of the English Lake District in the mid-seventies, is one of the few large-scale projects to date which has been developed in a forest area. In particular, nature artists from all over the world have used the ambience of the forest, which covers an area of 35 square kilometres/13,5 square miles, to realise their projects. There are by now over 100 sculptures, some of them only temporary works, others of greater permanence, on sites chosen by the artists. Their uniting feature is a very personal, sensitive interpretation of their particular romantic woodland site.

Andy Goldsworthy. *Seven Spires*. 1984. Grizedale Forest Sculpture, Cumbria, England.

Andy Goldsworthy realised *Seven Spires* (1984) in dense pine woods. He arranged slender pine trunks to form 25-metre/82' high spires, which blend in with their surroundings of dense woods so well that they can first easily be overlooked. Only when the visitor is already standing in the midst of the group of *Seven Spires*, does he suspect that he may have intruded on a secret gathering. "In making the spires I wanted to concentrate the feelings I get from within a pine wood of an almost desperate growth and energy driving upwards. The spire also seemed appropriate with its references to churches and, in particular, the Cathedral with its architectural use of lines leading the eye skyward."[54] The romantic element of this interpretation is undeniable and evokes Michael Heizer's remark on "that kind of unraped, peaceful, religious space" in the desert. In contrast, Goldsworthy's *Sidewinder*, which dates from 1985, depends upon a formal contrast. The artist used twisted trunks which he found in the surrounding area to build a snake approximately 55 metres/180' long. The monster seems to wind its way unchecked through the trees and over boulders, perceptibly disturbing the stasis and silence of the pine forest. "The form is shaped through a similar response to environment," writes Goldsworthy. "The snake has evolved through a need to move close to the ground, sometimes below and sometimes above, an expression of the space it occupies."[55] With its gradual decay – the wood is already covered with moss and is slowly starting to rot – *Sidewinder* is increasingly becoming part of its surroundings and will disappear completely in the foreseeable future.

[54] Goldsworthy, Andy cited by Grant, Bill/Harris, Paul, editors. *The Grizedale Experience. Sculpture, Arts & Theatre in a Lakeland Forest*. Edinburgh, 1991: p. 62

[55] Goldsworthy, A. loc. cit. 1990

Andy Goldsworthy. *Sidewinder*. 1984–1985. Grizedale Forest Sculpture, Cumbria, England.

As was also the case in Richard Long's expeditions, the act of walking as the key to an intense experience of natural environment plays a decisive role in (re)discovering the forest, and is something which cannot be conveyed in photographs. The relaxing rhythm of walking, the free-play of the imagination and the direct perception of nature in the forest bring about significant changes in awareness and the way things are experienced. Here, in places where artistic intervention and landscape do not confront each other, but coexist in an almost symbiotic way, an encounter with nature is an experience full of surprises. The awareness of the beholder of phenomena in his natural surroundings and his ability to experience these are greatly heightened. Varying traces of commercial forestry activities, tracks which have been closed off, clearings and felled trees add to the diversity of experience: the landscape itself evolves into an ever-changing sculpture, through which it is possible to walk.

Discussing the *Schürberg Project* in the Westerwald in Germany, a project which basically resembles the Grizedale Forest Project, Gundolf Winter and Christoph Schreier wrote: "The structures which develop are dialogic, suitable not only to avoid the arbit-

[56] Winter, Gundolf/Schreier, Christoph. "Skulptur im Dialog. Wortelkamps, TAL bei Hasselbach/Werkhausen im Westerwald." In *Skulptur im Tal*, published by Kunstverein Hasselbach. Hasselbach, 1989: p. 53

[57] Cf. Hannsjörg Voth's project *Feldzeichen*: p. 56

[58] Exhibition "Material aus der Landschaft – Kunst in die Landschaft". – Falazik, Ruth. "Entstehung und Entwicklung des Projektes 'Kunst – Landschaft' in Neuenkirchen." In *Das Bildhauersymposium*, edited by Wolfgang Hartmann/Werner Pokorny. Stuttgart, 1988: p. 63

[59] Weichardt, Jürgen. "Material aus der Landschaft. Kunst in die Landschaft." In *Galerie Falazik*, Neuenkirchen, 1977, n.p.

rariness of the sculpture park but also tendencies towards a unified *gesamtkunstwerk* in the sense of the French or English Garden. [...] Here, no all-embracing idea imposes its will on the dialogue between the works and nature or prescribes their inclusion and position [...]."[56]

Agricultural landscape

The intrusion of "pure" art into landscape which has been intensively used for agricultural purposes inevitably leads to tension.[57] In consequence, only very few artists work directly in areas once used for agriculture. By moving her Gallery for Contemporary Art from the city of Bochum to the village of Neuenkirchen in the German Lüneburg Heath in 1966, Ruth Falazik took a conscious decision to meet this challenge. The move marked the commencement of a project which has been successful in exploring the interaction of contemporary art and land utilisation.

The village of Neuenkirchen is surrounded by farmland, woods and protected areas of heath. Most of the works were created on unused areas made available by the villagers. The scope of the exhibitions and symposiums on "art-landscape" which Ruth Falazik, now head of the Springhornhof art society, has organised is reflected by the large numbers of well-known artists taking part. The traditional sculptures, which were realised in the village in the project's early years, have gradually given way to a growing focus on the process of the reciprocal relationship between art and landscape at the annual symposiums. In the context of the 1977 exhibition on "Material from the Landscape – Art in the Landscape", Ruth Falazik noted: "The dialogue with the specific materials of this natural environment also meant a total integration of the work in the countryside. This marked the beginning of what has held true ever since, namely that art is to be understood as an integral part of the landscape."[58]

Beobachtete Veränderung (*Observed Change*), created in 1977 by the artist HAWOLI (born in 1935), was, like many other projects, realised at a place where woodland and fields met. The work is situated at the side of a path. It resembles a pile of long timber and, at first sight, appears to be one of the inconspicuous forms typically found in rural areas. However, at the corner of the forest something quite unexpected happens: the pile follows the contours of the forest. The trunks form a right angle in a way which would not normally be possible. In a process requiring time and skill, the artist bent the trunks until they were parallel to the edge of the forest. He thus wittily draws attention to complicated manifestations of the seemingly simple reality of everyday life, transforming the commonplace into something special and blurring the boundaries between forest reality and art product. In consequence, some of the village farmers, who had previously viewed the landscape entirely as a means of securing their livelihood, were able to see it in a different way. "Here it was possible to gain an insight into the structure of artistic work [...] The fact that, in purely visual terms as well as concerning the effort involved, his work was not very different from everyday work in the country earned the artist general respect."[59]

The interventions by the artist Stanley James Herd in the vast prairies of Kansas have far more in common with the "new frontier" approach of American Land Art than with the sensitive interventions of European Nature Art. Inspired by the Nazca Lines and the awesome view of the prairies from the air, Herd, who comes from a family of farmers, has ploughed and planted giant pictures, mainly portraits and still lifes, in the endless expanses of the prairies. Herd uses the tractor and the plough as his brush and the field as his blank canvas. His still lifes are in the tradition of famous paintings, while his giant portraits of Indians document his admiration for the indigenous inhabitants of North America. The transient field images are entirely intended to be seen from the air and make use of perspective constructions which have their origins in panel painting.

The illusion of perspective in the two-dimensional pictures is undoubtedly very effective for those who find the occasion to see them from a bird's-eye view. In Germany, for example, where the appeal of this landscape design has also been discovered, advertising motifs covering an area of six hectares have recently been planted below the final approach paths to Munich airport. These areas, called "Artfields", cannot fail to

HAWOLI. *Beobachtete Veränderung* (*Observed Change*). 1977. Neuenkirchen, Germany.

Art in Nature

make an impression on the airline's passengers as they see them from a height of approximately 500 metres/1,600'. However, when seen from the ground, the motifs are neither comprehensible nor, indeed, are such decorative interventions intended to heighten the perceptive sensibility. Hence, they cannot be classified as Land Art in the conventional sense. "Crop Art"[60] is reminiscent rather of the – substantially smaller – colourful flower beds at horticultural shows, intended as a brightly-coloured logo or municipal coat of arms.

[60] Cf. Herd, S.J. *Crop Art*. New York, 1994

Stanley J. Herd. *Saginaw Grant*. 1988. Kansas.

Industrial landscapes, disrupted landscapes

Whereas Nature Artists prefer to work in more or less "intact" cultural landscapes, the devastated landscapes of our industrial society such as quarries, coal-mines, ore-mines and so forth have numbered among the preferred sites for avant-garde landscape art not only since the emergence of Land Art.[61]

[61] Cf. Harvey Fite's design for a disused quarry *Opus 40*, 1938, near Woodstock, New York

The continuing fascination which these environments hold for art has a number of reasons. "Disrupted" landscapes bear ultimate witness to the power of man over nature, revealing the technological possibilities of civilisation, their ruins referring, in a way that could almost be described as Romantic, to the transience of man's creations. Whereas there are, generally speaking, hardly any areas left which could be used for experiments in the environment, there are virtually no taboos in many disrupted landscapes. They are places for trying out something new. It is particularly in devastated landscapes that nature most impressively demonstrates its vital regenerative abilities (for example special sites for plants and habitats for rare species of wildlife), and at times these are deliberately included in the context of the artistic intervention. In many cases, landscape art's strong interest in working in such disrupted landscapes coincides with the interest of local authorities and industrial companies in removing the damage to the landscape as effectively as possible and in a way which is aesthetically satisfactory.

Robert Smithson (1938–1973) was one of the first Land Artists to recognise the challenge which lies in an artistic dialogue with the devastated landscape. From the outset, he was interested in the aesthetic and fundamental experiences of human and natural destruction, and he even pleaded for experience of the "catastrophic" as an ultimate experience of nature.[62] In 1970 Smithson discovered the site for a project – which was to become an icon of Land Art – on the north-east shore of the Great Salt Lake in Utah, close to the point at which the eastern and the western sections of the transcontinental rail network meet. "The north shore of the Great Salt Lake, which had been exploited for both economic and military purposes [...] owed its appeal not only to mud, salt crystals, boulders and water but also to the dead birds, plastic containers and rusting machinery. *Spiral Jetty* reflects this configuration. A bulldozer and trucks drove mud, salt and stones into the lake to form an anti-clockwise spiral. Smithson saw this as an allegory of the demise of the machine age and the eve of a natural disaster. [...] He knew that the anti-clockwise spiral symbolised destruction and entropy, the end of civilisation by global warming."[63]

[62] Cf. Smithson, Robert. "Entrophy Made Visible. Interview with Alison Sky." In *The Writings of Robert Smithson*, edited by Nancy Holt. New York, 1979: p. 196

[63] Kellein, Thomas loc. cit.: p. 397–398

It was necessary to move 6,650 tonnes of material in order to create a spiral-shaped jetty which was 450 metres/1,500' long and approximately 4.5 metres/15' wide. "Walking along the spiral lifts one out into the water into a breathless experience of horizontality. [...] It is a moist and earthy causeway with salt caking on the rocks and on the visitor. The landscape is [...] evoking past time with placid insistence."[64] Anyone walking along the spiral – Smithson called it "lifeline" – from the shore to its innermost point had to retrace his steps to return to the shore and was, as in early initiation rites, able to experience a kind of rebirth.[65]

[64] Alloway, Lawrence. "Robert Smithson's Development." (1972) In Sonfist, A. loc. cit.: p. 139

[65] Cf. Lippard, Lucy R. "Art Outdoors, in and out of the Public Domain." In *Studio International*, 1977: p. 87

Spiral Jetty, which by now has been submerged due to the rise in the level of the lake, derives much of its sustained effect not only from its spectacular setting and the fascinating spatial experience of the archetypal spiral form. For Smithson, the "Piranesi of Land Art", the linking of three levels was of major significance: the microscopic level with the salt crystals and their spiral-shaped microstructure, the macroscopic level and the mythological level: during work on *Spiral Jetty* Smithson learnt of the legend according to which the Great Salt Lake was linked to the Pacific Ocean by a whirlpool and subterranean channels.

[66] Smithson, Robert cited in Holt, Nancy loc. cit.: p. 220

"Across the country there are many mining areas, disused quarries and polluted lakes and rivers. One practical solution for the utilisation of such devastated places would be land and water re-cycling in terms of Earth Art." (Robert Smithson)[66] In 1979, the King County Arts Commission used Smithson's proposal as the basis of the project "Earthworks: Land Reclamation as Sculpture", which it organised in and around Seattle/Washington. Eight artists, Robert Morris, Herbert Bayer, Ian Baxter, Lawrence Hanson, Richard Fleischner, Mary Miss, Dennis Oppenheim and Beverly Pepper, were invited to create designs for four gravel pits, a deserted area close to an airport, a refuse tip, a disused military airfield and a heavily eroded canyon. In contrast to Smithson, most of the artists virtually completely remodelled the devastated landscapes, paying hardly any attention to their genius loci. The design by Robert Morris converted a gravel pit into a green amphitheatre. With the project *Mill Creek Canyon Earthworks* (1979–1982), Herbert Bayer (1900–1985) restored an eroded streambed by constructing a site which functioned both as a storm-water retention basin and a public park and recreation area for the city of Kent, a suburb of Seattle. But whereas the local authorities welcomed the artistic, low-cost landscape repair, many professional landscape designers were angered by the interference of the artists. The "green cosmetic treatment" which landscape architecture had often been accused of providing had here become a celebrated, supposedly ecological art happening. Robert Morris took up the question of the moral problems the approach entailed: "Will it be a little easier in the future to rip up the landscape for one last shovelful of a non-renewable energy source if an artist can be found (cheap, mind you) to transform the devastation into an inspiring and modern work of art?"[67]

[67] Morris, Robert. "Robert Morris Keynote Address." In *Earthworks: Land Reclamation as Sculpture*, Seattle Art Museum. Seattle, 1979: p. 16

[68] tumulus [Latin] = prehistoric burial mound

One of the most ambitious projects of the eighties was Michael Heizer's *Effigy Tumuli Sculptures*,[68] built between 1983 and 1988 near Ottawa/Illinois. The five sculptured mounds in the abstracted forms of frog, catfish, turtle, snake and water strider are located on an 80-hectare site which was used for opencast mining in the thirties and was heavily contaminated with industrial waste. As part of the extensive reclamation work, approximately one million dollars was made available for artistic works. The individual earthen sculptures are up to 700 metres/2,300' long and around 5 metres/16' high. While the manner of construction of the abstract, geometric figures is reminiscent of Heizer's *Complex One*, they are no longer as abstract in formal terms as the artist's early works. Their models are clearly to be found in the culture of the Indians who once inhabited the Midwest, particularly in the burial mounds which they often built in the shape of an animal. In contrast to Morris, Heizer categorically rejects cosmetic "reclamation art" and attaches importance to it being clear that his work is pure art. Like Smithson, he makes use of different levels of meaning in order to react to the devastated landscape. He opposes the artificially restored cultural landscape with clear forms of abstracted nature. He counters devastation of macroscopic proportions with greatly enlarged depictions of microscopic organisms, which will be the first to recolonise the site.

While disused quarries and gravel pits have also been popular venues for symposiums on sculpture in Europe for many years, reclamation projects in which landscape art of the American type plays an essential role were extremely rare in Europe until only recently. In many European countries, industry is required by law to clean up the pollution it causes, but has preferred to leave this task up to its own specialists. International economic changes over the past few years have also led to numerous closures of mines and industrial companies in Europe. These closures have left substantial environmental problems, particularly when the devastated areas are as extensive as the huge sites in the former German Democratic Republic where brown coal was once mined. Prior to German unification, the operators were not required to set aside any funds for reclamation. Consequently, landscape art has recently played a more important role in developing new perspectives with regard to a changed awareness and a modern approach to "devastated" landscape.

The European Biennial for Land Art, Object Art and Multimedia, which was first held in a disused opencast mining area near Cottbus/Germany in 1991, is one of the few initiatives in Germany seeking a new interpretation of "devastated" landscape with

Michael Heizer. *Effigy Tumuli* (*Water Strider*). 1983–1985. Buffalo Rock State Park, Ottowa, Illinois.

Art in Nature

the help of landscape art. Elsewhere, such as in the Bitterfeld East German region, new approaches are being sought using the vision of an "Industrial Garden Realm" analogous to the Wörlitz Garden Realm of Prince Leopold Frederick Franz von Anhalt-Dessau of 1770.[69] In the context of the 1991, 1993 and 1995 Biennials at Cottbus, international artists realised a wide variety of both temporary and permanent works over a number of weeks, in some cases in collaboration with the miners.

In contrast to the works of the American pioneers of Land Art, many of the works realised in this context still have a strong object bias. They use the bizarre mine landscape in a traditional way, treating it as a wild and romantic artistic background. It was only possible to achieve an exciting dialogue between the work and the overburden landscape when the artist entered into direct confrontation with the vast disused mines, which extend over an area of approximately 3,000 hectares. With the project of a gigantic stairway, *Treppe nach oben* (1993), the French artists Gilles Bruni (born in 1959) and Marc Babarit (born in 1958) ventured to the precipice of the mine and, using the fascine method for erosion control, laboriously constructed by hand steps which descend almost 100 metres/330'. Step by step, they fashioned their own access to the mine. The steps link a small grove of trees at the foot of the embankment with a mound of brown coal on the shoulder of the slope. The laborious work of a miner, man's progress towards an energy-consuming future, the process by which vegetation is transformed into a fossil fuel … many layers of meaning are superimposed in this transient work. Very simply in formal terms, it changes the conventional way of reading a bizarre "cultural landscape", which was formerly created by using enormous technical means.

As part of the Emscher Park International Building Exhibition in the Ruhr district of Germany, attempts are being made in collaboration with artists to find a new interpretation for the former industrial region, which is characterised by slag-heaps, industrial plants, blast furnaces, railway tracks and so forth. Works of art are intended to be points of identification in order to convey the fascinating conflict between industrial landscape and natural landscape.[70] However, judging by the outcome of numerous art competitions and symposiums on the question of designing "slag-heap landscape", fears seem justified that here, too, the industrial landscape will either be used as an attractive background or will be landscaped virtually beyond recognition in the sense of "Land Reclamation as Sculpture".

Nevertheless, art and especially landscape art will be indispensable as a language in the search for a new interpretation of landscape. Provided that landscape artists achieve a critical view of their own traditional conception of landscape art's role and purpose and get involved in the typical changes which take place in nature with the passing of time, they will be capable of contributing to the changed understanding of cultural landscape. The designs and concepts presented in the second section of this book illustrate the enormous potential of an open approach to industrial landscape.[71]

Urban landscape

Before Land Artists demonstratively turned their back on the urban context, in order to work in virtually uninhabited desert regions, they realised a small number of projects in urban space to underline their determination to break with the conventional understanding of art. Together with Walter de Maria, whose *Munich Earth Room* challenged the expectations of gallery visitors as far back as 1968, Michael Heizer, in particular, has adopted a clearly confrontational approach: anyone who visited the Galerie Heiner Friedrich in Munich in 1969 in order to see the scheduled exhibition did not find the object he had anticipated displayed in a gallery room, but was, instead, confronted with Heizer's "negative" outside sculpture *Munich Depression* on a building site in the city district of Perlach. Heizer provoked visitors by means of an accessible, circular, conical hole in the ground with a diameter of approximately 30 metres/100' and a depth of 4.50 metres/15', which was filled in shortly afterwards. A few years later De Maria's *Vertical Earth Kilometre*, which he realised in the context of documenta VI in Kassel, made a similar impact on consumers of art in view of the fact that it was invisible and, thus, contrary to the conventional conception of art.

Bruni & Barbarit. *Treppe nach oben* (*Steps leading up*). 1993. Disused opencast browncoal mine. Greifenhain, Pritzen, Germany.

Bruni & Barbarit. *Treppe nach oben* (*Steps leading up*). 1993. Disused open-pit browncoal mine. Greifenhain, Pritzen, Germany.

[69] Cf. Toyka, Rolf. *Bitterfeld: Braunkohle-Brachen. Probleme – Chancen – Visionen.* München, 1993

[70] Cf. Kunstverein Gelsenkirchen, editor. *Dokumentation Kunstmeile Gelsenkirchen.* Gelsenkirchen, 1992

[71] Cf. the works of Herman Prigann and Peter Latz: in this book p. 173 and p. 121

72 Heizer, Michael cited by Wedewer, Rolf loc. cit.: p. 152

Just as Richard Serra's steel sculptures, which are Minimalist in formal terms but realised on a large scale, are frequently interpreted as criticism of architecture and the city, it was clearly the intention of Michael Heizer to develop "alternatives to the absolute city system".[72] He often formulated this criticism – as the example of his monumental *Complex One/Complex Two/City* in Nevada clearly illustrates – with architectural means, procedures, scales and, occasionally, even architectural materials, as well as with a corresponding language of forms. However, Heizer – like all other pioneers of Land Art – avoided direct confrontation with the urban system and sought contact with primary nature. It is only today, concludes John Beardsley under the headline "Beyond Earthworks: The New Urban Landscape", that the legacy of the Land Art movement is manifesting itself in the urban context.[73]

73 Beardsley, John loc. cit.: p. 127

A number of artists whose work is often mentioned in the context of Land Art have sought, in contrast to pioneers such as Michael Heizer and Walter de Maria, direct contact with urban surroundings in their environment-related art. However, their intentions were not the same as those of Land Artists.

Christo (born in 1935) is one of the best-known project artists whose works are popularly associated with Land Art. His landscape-related projects such as *Wrapped Coast* (1969), *Valley Curtain* (1972), *Running Fence* (1976), *Surrounded Islands* (1983) and *The Umbrellas* (1991) have made a significant contribution to the popularity of art in the landscape. However, in terms of the history of art, he is probably to be seen as an exponent of New Realism, and the elaborate art events he stages are actually happenings or environments. Christo seeks the urban context, as in the recent case of *Wrapped Reichstag* in Berlin in 1995, not primarily for spatial and formal reasons, but for social reasons in order to include people in his media-orientated public art. His urban projects do not create new objects, rather he makes use of existing forms, which he temporarily alienates and removes from their context by wrapping them. Christo's purpose is to make the unseen visible. The fascination of his projects has little to do with the real intentions and approaches of Land Art, but originates rather from the general feeling of the "changeability of the world"[74] which his work evokes.

74 Kellein, Thomas loc. cit.: p. 397

Since the mid-sixties the works of Alan Sonfist (born in 1946) have been concerned with achieving greater public awareness of ecological issues. He does not see the purpose of an artist to be the creation of marketable objects, but defines the traditional, socially rooted role of the artist as being to enter into a dialogue with society in order to make the experience of aesthetics accessible to the community.[75] While still in his teens, he worked out a plan, which he called *Time Landscapes*, to return some areas in major cities to their natural condition prior to settlement by planting trees native to the particular area. It was not until 1978, following years of research and negotiations with New York City's public authorities, that the first trees were planted by Sonfist with the collaboration of local residents and Manhattan schools on the 14 x 61 metres/ 45 x 200' site of *Time Landscape*.

75 Cf. Sonfist, Alan loc. cit.: p. 209

The reaction of the city's inhabitants to the special little park, a living work of art, was most positive also on account of their involvement in its creation. Using only very simple means, Sonfist succeeded in making the city dweller aware of the natural basis of his existence. In retrospect, there may not seem to be much difference between the impact of such a project and conventional, ecological designs for urban parks and green areas. However, in the mid-sixties Sonfist's project was little short of revolutionary and may be regarded as a precursor of present Environment Art in an urban context. Whether Sonfist's recent proposals, which date from 1991, to realise a series of *Time Landscapes* to the north of La Défense in Paris as a walled nature and culture reserve are still adequate in today's context seems, however, questionable.

Wheatfield, Battery Park City – A Confrontation, a project by the Hungarian artist, Agnes Denes (born in 1938) in Manhattan, dating from 1982, may be considered to be a successful contemporary project in keeping with the ecological and social approach of Alan Sonfist. The artist had the refuse and rubble on an area of waste land near the World Trade Center removed and covered the site with a few centimetres of topsoil. She then sowed wheat on half of the site, which measured approximately 1.6 hectares. The wheatfield in the heart of the city was watered and tended for a period of

Post Ars. *Die Partitur (The Score)*. 1993. Disused open-pit browncoal mine. Greifenhain, Pritzen, Germany.

Art in Nature

Alan Sonfist. *Time Landscape*. 1965–1980. New York City.

Agnes Denes. *Wheatfield, Battery Park City – A Confrontation*. 1982. New York City.

four months; it went through its natural cycle until August, when a combine harvester brought in the harvest beneath the towering skyscrapers of Manhattan. For a brief time, the artist transformed an inner city site, usually a much sought-after object of speculation, back into valuable, fertile land which is still able to yield essential food-stuffs. While the straw which was produced was used as fodder for the horses of New York's mounted police, some of the wheat was donated to the "International Art Show for the End of World Hunger", an exhibition held at the Minnesota Museum of Art.

Whereas ecologically orientated Environmental Art, as illustrated by the project of Agnes Denes, continues to enter into a dialogue with the city in a typical way, it is far more difficult to identify the legacy of Land Art in the urban context. The American examples of "New urban landscape" beyond earthworks described by John Beardsley[76] either broadly follow the traditional concept of sculpture in the public space or the conventional principles of open space design using architectural means. Perhaps it lies in the nature of the urban context that it requires an emphasis on objects and permanence and is less suited to Land Art's willingness to experiment and openness, to its conscious use of the factor of time. Nevertheless, Land Art has, as shown in the second section of this book, set new standards for designing space which have influenced many contemporary approaches in landscape architecture and landscape art.

[76] Cf. Beardsley, John loc. cit. p. 127 ff.

Social dimensions of Land Art:
distance, myth, Romanticism

Distance: escape or new beginning?

As the sixties drew to a close, the United States, the birthplace of Land Art, was a country shaken by crises at home and abroad, beset by bloody race riots, massive anti-war protests, student revolts and so forth. The energy crisis and major environmental disasters at the beginning of the seventies seriously challenged the American belief in the inexhaustibility of natural resources, while the first pictures of the Earth relayed from space brought home the finiteness of the Earth for the first time. The spirit of the affluent society was celebrated by Pop Art, its gaudy visual language elevating objects of everyday modern life to works of art. There were reasons enough to consider fleeing society.

Against this volatile background, an unprecedented exodus took place in the American art scene in spring 1968, the impact of which was also felt in Europe. In an expression of vehement rejection of the traditional understanding of art and the prevailing system of social values, young avant-garde artists moved out of the city to the supposedly peaceful and untouched desert areas of Nevada, which had, in fact, already served as nuclear testing sites for years. Land Art no longer wanted to provide the property-owning classes with any objects of speculation. However, the need to secure their material existence ultimately forced the artists to come to an arrangement with leading galleries. In fact, it was the exhibitions at these galleries which gave the new movement its name: "Earthworks".[77]

[77] *Earthworks*, exhibition at the Virginia Dawn Gallery in New York in October 1968

Not least on account of the allegedly inconsistent attitude of the American avant-garde has the exodus to the desert attracted different kinds of critical interpretation. Some speak of flight from reality in the face of a lack of control over nature and extremely restricted individual freedom of movement in a rationalised and perfected world. Others interpret the flight from society as an act of liberation necessary to define a new stance: "The distance which such works are able to maintain is their answer to the age of technical reproducibility of the work of art,[78] which could equally well be described as the age of its omnipresence: art, present everywhere and everybody's whore. The fact that today's artists prefer to distance themselves from this kind of faceless product churned out for masses, is undoubtedly connected with this latest trend in the development of art [...]; so one may say that the technical reproducibility of the work of art did not only result in the decline of the aura, but, in a further step, with a certain historical delay, in its re-emergence from an insuperable distance: from an airplane, in the desert, in the sea."[79]

[78] Cf. Benjamin, Walter. "Das Kunstwerk im Zeitalter seiner technischen Reproduzierbarkeit." In *Zeitschrift für Sozialforschung* 5 (1936)

[79] Salzinger, Helmut. "Fragen zur Aktualität des Mythischen." In *Kunsthaus Zürich* loc. cit.: p. 76

Land Art countered the constraints of the positivistic and functional world with archaic symbolism and the revival of myths. This was not without its dangers. "The phenomenon of not-understanding, not-wanting-to-understand the complex ways in which our life and our world interact is no longer reflected upon critically, but in the very act of flight we make ourselves a part of this attitude."[80] Irrational conceptions of the world are liable to give rise to irrational practices with fatal consequences. However, this risk was always less pronounced for the artists in Europe working within the Land Art movement. They were, as the work of Hannsjörg Voth demonstrates, compelled, almost as a matter of necessity, to enter into a far more conscious dialogue with the complex historical and sociological influences on the structure of the cultural landscape. It remains to be said that the flight of Land Art, making it necessary for the viewer to embark upon a journey of inner and outer discovery in order to experience the work, was, despite all inconsistencies and dangers, a preparatory step towards a return to a social dialogue, which opened up new horizons and should be developed further in the future.

[80] Cf. Wedewer, Rolf in Städtisches Museum Leverkusen, publisher. *Landschaft – Gegenpol der Fluchtraum*. Leverkusen, 1974: p. 72

The power of myth

The relationship to the myths of earlier cultures in the form of the use of archaic signs and symbols plays a decisive role in Land Art and, to a lesser extent, also in Nature Art in Europe. No single definition of the concept of "myth" is possible, as it belongs to the category of integrative concepts which have a great thematic diversity. Unlike the concept of "logos" – by which the Greeks understood logical thought and expression, science – myth stood for history, a living collective reality, which could not be proved by rational means.[81] Whereas, for this reason, intellectual criticism has always been unable to come to terms with the myth, it played an important role in Analytical Psychology. C. G. Jung interpreted the myth as a product of the psychological phenomenon of collective experiences which, particularly in the case of people in the archaic stage of tribal development, contributes to the inherent relationship of the individual to the community.

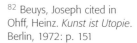
[81] Cf. Otto, Walter F. *Die Gestalt und das Sein*. Darmstadt, 1955: p. 66ff.

In the context of the situation in American society at the end of the sixties, not only the Earth as the basis of man's existence but also humanity, the community of man, were considered to be in acute danger. The integrative power of the myth was seen as an effective antidote. At the beginning of the seventies, Joseph Beuys (1921–1986), one of the most important protagonists of art to adopt a creative approach to myths, acknowledged: "We need both methods. Antimathematics must be recognised alongside mathematics, antiphysics alongside physics, antichemistry alongside chemistry. Natural science of the future will make no progress without anti-natural science, at least not without placing anti-nature = man in very grave danger."[82] At the New York gallery of René Block, Joseph Beuys celebrated anti-natural science in 1974, seeking, in the role of the shaman, the mythical relationship to the power of the Other in the shape of a coyote, with which he lived for a week in one of the gallery's rooms.[83] Beuys did not see his individual mythology as a romantically naive attempt to restore the idealised unity of man and nature, but as a question of acceptance of the opposite pole, of revival of the conscious dialogue between the Other and the Self.

[82] Beuys, Joseph cited in Ohff, Heinz. *Kunst ist Utopie*. Berlin, 1972: p. 151

[83] Performance *I like American and America Likes Me*. New York, René Block Gallery, 1974

The danger inherent in the unreflected resurrection of old myths has frequently been voiced by critics. These became particularly vociferous when "Individual Mythology" was recognised as a theme at documenta V (1972) by its director, Harald Szeemann: "Since the inclusion of a section on Individual Mythology at documenta '72 it has been apparent that the desire to escape a world which is experienced as non-social has led to the creation of illusory worlds which derive their basis and legitimacy from a return to a mythological way of life." In the same context, reference is made to the "act of negating any form of social objectivity".[84] This tendency is opposed by attitudes which insist on a clear distinction between a blind revival of old myths and an adequate contemporary and critical approach to the poetic energy of the myth.[85]

[84] Oellers, Adam C. "Landschaft zwischen Natur und Ideologie." In *Städtisches Museum Leverkusen* loc. cit.: p. 73

[85] Cf. exhibition catalogue *Mythos und Ritual*. Kunsthaus Zürich, 1981

The works of Charles Simonds (born in 1945) derive their vital qualities from the myth in a special way. In New Jersey in 1970, he descended into a clay pit and re-emerged covered entirely in clay. Lying on his side, the artist created tiny buildings made of minute clay tiles, which he fashioned by hand, for *Little People*. Simonds called this ritual *Landscape-Body-Dwelling*, thereby giving expression to his notion of the primordial myth of the creation of man. The miniature cities of an imaginary people have become well-known internationally, as Simonds initially built the transient dwellings of the invisible "Little People" – made out of 8-mm-long airbricks, small stones, sand and wood – in 1972 in demolition sites, ruins of houses and cracks in walls in New York, his place of birth, and later also in Paris. The pueblo-like appearance of the miniature cities is reminiscent of the dwellings of early cultures, which have adapted to the cycle of nature.

Charles Simonds. *Landscape-Body-Dwelling*. 1970. New Jersey.

Charles Simonds. *Dwelling P.S.1*. 1975. New York City.

In his book on Securing of Evidence – a term for a movement within Individual Mythology – Günter Metken attaches great importance to making clear that the consequence of Simonds' work is not sheer irrationalism, but has implications for society. "Simonds soon realised that his project, initially attacked as crazy, brought him into contact with people. They stopped, watched, the children joined in. The relatively rapid disappearance of the constructions, which numbered over 200, due to weathering, building development and souvenir collectors, was seen as a loss by the city's residents. Simonds, like many other young artists frustrated by the inbreeding and constraints of the gallery, felt himself to be part of a precise topographical and sociological context."[86] This formed the background to Simonds' involvement in initiatives to re-urbanise the Lower East Side.

[86] "Spurensicherung". Metken, Günter loc. cit.: p. 77–78

The use of the archetypal power of the myth in the search for a way back to the essential core of human existence is common to all art movements concerned with heightening perceptibility in nature, with the "rootedness" of man. Here the scale of the artistic intervention in the landscape is irrelevant, as Simonds' work shows. A certain tendency to the Romantic, in extreme cases to Romantic escapism, is evidently an inherent trait of mythological thinking and a potential source of danger.

Romantic Primitivism

Writing in 1938, the art historian Robert Goldwater levelled the criticism of "romantic primitivism" at the use of non-European, African and Oceanic forms of expression to give new life to meaningless contemporary art and to escape from civilisation.[87] Today many critics claim that the avant-garde of the sixties and Land Art in particular abandoned their original principles and ended up in continuing the Primitivistic tendencies of Modernism.

The writings of the French social anthropologist Claude Lévi-Strauss, who studied the symbol and coding systems of primitive cultures and made a major contribution to changing the idea of the primitive,[88] were of particular significance for the development of art in the late sixties. Lévi-Strauss not only provided convincing criticism of the arrogant attitude of modern society towards the primitive, but also regarded the tribal societies to be superior in decisive respects. His findings in the field of structural anthropology were readily taken up by an art movement keen to exercise criticism of the materialistic consumer society.

The artistic legacies of primitive culture provided a repertoire which included particularly suitable means of linking two separate concerns of Land Art. On the one hand, the "free" artist was an individualist who continued to realise his personal designs. On the other hand, Land Art attempted to bridge the gap between art and the viewer and created forms which were firmly rooted in the history of mankind as collective monumental structures. "This volatility of the collective and the personal, reason and instinct, high order and childlike spontaneity lies near the center of the particular character of contemporary primitivism," concludes the art historian Kirk Varnedoe.[89]

Art in Nature can become a dubious mixture when primitivism is combined with romanticism. Dubious because contemporary society always associates a romantic and rapturous attitude to nature with enjoyment of the trivial and an escape from everyday reality. This is not seen as being compatible with progressive avant-garde art. Modernism had – following the experience of Romanticism and its cliché-like integration into petit bourgeois tranquility – categorically rejected any articulation of aesthetic experience of nature in the medium of art.

What is Romantic about Land Art? Romantic perception of nature at the end of the eighteenth century was strongly influenced by the subjective, emotional conception and interpretation of natural phenomena, which the Romantic often saw as reflexion of his own inner nature, his desires, his feelings and his needs. Particularly in the face of menacing elemental forces, man experienced a heightened aesthetic awareness, which was described as sublimity. The sublime is still an aesthetic category today. "When danger and beauty coincide, the result is heightened beauty, which surpasses so-called normal beauty," said Walter de Maria.[90] As early as 1960 he wrote a short text entitled "On the Importance of Natural Disasters",[91] in which he declared his love of natural disasters as the sublime form of the experience of art, expressing the wish that every museum visitor might have such an experience. Many of the American Land Artists shared de Maria's love of the sublime, an attitude which their works clearly reflect.

The most impressive manifestation of a sublime experience of nature with a romantic element is *The Lightning Field*, realised by de Maria in 1977 on a remote, 2200-metre/ 6500' high plateau in the western part of New Mexico. 400 stainless-steel poles form a rectangular grid in an area measuring approximately one mile by one kilometre (its exact dimensions are 5,280' x 3,300'). The tips of the poles, which have a diameter of approximately 5 centimetres/2", form an imaginary, perfectly horizontal plane at a height of approximately 6 metres/20' above the ground. A semi-arid, flat basin, bounded

[87] Cf. Goldwater, Robert. *Primitivism in Modern Art.* New York, 1938

[88] Cf. Lévi-Strauss, Claude: *Tristes Tropiques* (1955); *La pensée sauvage* (1962); and others

[89] Varnedoe, Kirk. "Zeitgenössische Tendenzen." In *Primitivismus in der Kunst des 20. Jahrhunderts*, edited by William Rubins. Munich, 1984: p. 683

[90] De Maria, Walter cited by Hüllenkremer, Marie. "Natur als Kunst." In *Zeitmagazin*, no. 9 (21.02.1992): p. 48

[91] De Maria, Walter. "On the Importance of Natural Disasters." May 1960

to the west by a chain of mountains and known for its frequent storms, gives the work its landscape context, without which this classic Land Art project would be no more than an elaborate piece of engineering. *The Lightning Field* was, as its name implies, originally built to act as a lightning conductor during storms. Although the project is based on a rational structure, it expresses a heightened romantic perception of nature. Even without the breathtaking spectacle of a thunderstorm, *The Lightning Field* remains impressive. "The visitor may well have quivered in awe as the peasants once did at the sight of the megaliths of Carnac. *The Lightning Field* is the site of a sun-cult, albeit a modern one. Its geometric precision, its mathematics, which cannot be seen, but of which one is, nevertheless, aware, help to subdue rapturous romantic outpourings. [...] It is the intention of the artist that no more than six visitors at a time see and experience *The Lightning Field* (and remain for at least twenty-four hours). Six are actually five too many. As a place of meditation *The Lightning Field* should be experienced in solitude."[92]

In contrast to Land Art, Nature Art experiments with a new, evocative primitivism, which approaches the most fundamental forms of human creativity in a very simple and direct way. The Italian philosopher Ernesto Grassi noted: "Primitive man continues, as modern psychology has shown, to exist in each of us; no longer, however, as an intact whole, but dismembered and torn apart. Yet even this disunity still contains fragments and interacting elements of an earlier wholeness."[93] These notions of unity continue to exist in the archaic designs of patterns which, in rare moments, border on the sublime. With his reference to these dimensions the nature artist enters into a very intimate, often even playful dialogue with the viewer and with nature.

Nor is Nature Art immune to a romantic conception of nature, as Kirk Varnedoe noted in a discussion of the work of Richard Long, Michael Singer and others: "The changed parameters of recent art and new ideas of primitive culture promote [...] a newly complex sense of identification across cultural barriers. Such work evidently belies simplistic divisions between rationalist and primitivist aesthetics. But by extension it also suggests larger ways in which recent primitivism may represent something more than simple escape from, or opposition to, modern Western culture."[94]

New landscape after Land Art?

Does an examination of Land Art and Environmental Art open up new avenues for landscape architecture to overcome the serious crisis in human perception or does the subjective approach of art only lead to an aestheticising impasse? Although there are no clearly marked paths through the uncertain terrain between the disciplines, a few points of reference can be identified.

Dissatisfaction with always being given the same ecologically, socially and functionally "correct" answers for landscape design, largely devoid of any aesthetic qualities, has lead to increasing interest the experimental involvement of art in landscape and nature. Since the decline of the influence of Modernism on style, contemporary landscape architecture has been lacking any avant-garde stimulus from which it could evolve its own expressive force. Instead, a persistent, impersonal academicism is spreading. In contrast, the strongly experimental explorations of art repeatedly open up new ways of perceiving nature subjectively and experiencing landscape personally.

Nothing would seem more natural than for landscape architecture to concern itself with an art which not only addresses itself to similar themes but also works with the same materials and in the same space. As the contemporary language of a society, every form of art, from Anti-Art to Zero, deserves the attention of all planning disciplines seeing their central task as the creation of the structural conditions necessary for human life. Hence, art has an important function as a meta-language of communication between the disciplines.

However, the apparent parallels between landscape architecture and art prove to be both a blessing and a curse: on the one hand, art in the landscape creates a semantic bridge across the deep divide between the artistic world and the everyday world which the abstract art of Modernism had opened up with its autonomous system of symbols. On the other hand, there is very great temptation to trust that imitation of

[92] Gerster, Georg. "Gebärden und Geburten. Werke und Stationen der amerikanischen Land-art." *Anthos* 2/1988: p. 31–32

[93] Grassi, Ernesto. *Kunst und Mythos*. Frankfurt am Main, 1990: p. 44

[94] Varnedoe, Kirk loc. cit.: p. 692

Andy Goldsworthy. *A Wall Went for a Walk*. 1990. Grizedale Forest Sculpture, Cumbria, England.

Walter de Maria. *The Lightning Field*. 1977. Near Quemado, New Mexico. Collection of the Dia Center for the Arts, New York.

Andy Goldsworthy. *Knotweed Stalks*. 1988. Derwent Water, England.

art in formal terms will, as it were, "automatically" lead to success. One of the central purposes of this book is to counter this temptation. An uncritical, formal imitation does not produce conscious independence in landscape design, but ends in a renewed dependence on the model. It cannot simply be a question of discovering a new, universally valid blueprint for modern landscape architecture.

Three typical features of Land Art and Nature Art are of particular significance for the development of a modern language in the landscape. First, the endeavours, particularly within the Land Art movement, to return to concentration on the essential in a rejection of the designs of the consumer society wich are in terms of language and use of material. This strategy of reduction to primary, archetypal forms is most pronounced in the works of Minimal Art. What started in the gallery as a radical search for objectivity and an almost dogmatic severity became in Land Art a fascinating dialogue between the very complex, sometimes even chaotic forces of nature and the clear geometric structure of the artefact. In their meditative clarity the works of Land Art and the Japanese meditation gardens of Zen are, despite their very different cultural backgrounds, quite similar. Endeavouring to achieve expressive simplicity is still today a central concern for many outstanding artists and landscape architects and characterises their work.

The second influential feature of Environmental Art, the transience of its works, is certainly the aspect most likely to initiate fierce controversy in a society intent on acquiring, multiplying and safeguarding material possessions. Art in landscape associates different fundamental ideas with the attribute of transience: transience as resistance to the accumulation of possessions and to the traditional conception of art, as visual expression of the process of time, as a metaphor of the discontinuity of phenomena, as recognition and manifestation of the phase of decay in the natural cycle of life, as a characteristic of an open work and so forth. It seems remarkable that the potential contained in transience, the vital process of metamorphosis, has received very little attention despite its fundamental, even creative significance in landscape design. Instead, great effort goes into reinforcing ready-made (ideal) images; in a time of growing uncertainty in society, these are increasingly seen as allegedly fixed points of orientation. Only few landscape designers consciously ignore the fundamental maxims of civilised society and address themselves to the transient in an experimental way, letting the transitory take its unpredictable course. This is not to say that decline and decay are to be given free rein indiscriminately, but a more open approach to transience and the traces it leaves would, in the right place, not only help to heighten perception, but also often create new space for the spontaneous, the unexpected, the experimental. Particularly the recent dialogue with the industrial and disrupted landscapes, which are in a constant state of change and subject to the process of erosion and continually encroaching vegetation, is an indication of a new understanding of nature and, in consequence, a different approach to transience. Some of these experimental approaches and their exponents are presented here.

The third aspect, the romantic component of Land Art and Nature Art, is of particular relevance. The times when man was capable of abandoning himself to unrestrained emotional and romantic enjoyment in the park and the garden undoubtedly belong to the past. However, the question remains whether the banishment of the romantic from landscape design in favour of the rational has not led to the disappearance of essential qualities of our environment, the loss of which we are now going to great lengths to make up for. As man rediscovers himself as being able to perceive through his senses, the landscape and the garden increasingly become a symbol of present needs, hopes and yearnings, and the desire for emotive poetry and sensitive design increases. Although one of the concerns of Land Art was also to heighten perceptibility, it was, nevertheless, in danger of encouraging the regressive tendencies in the romantic understanding of nature. Instead of an escapist romanticism, perhaps it would now be possible to develop a conception of nature which is more orientated towards the complex conditions of reality and, at the same time, is aware of the true qualities of a sensitive perception of nature in a simple way. While officially banished from their vocabulary, many planners and artists privately confess that specific aspects of their work are closely linked with the spirit of the romantic. Indeed, it seems that the creation of a place of meaning and the heightening of perceptibility is not possible without the revival of certain romantic elements.

There are no rules – and not even a generally accepted vocabulary – for exploring the area where art and landscape design meet. Instead, both art in landscape and landscape design have developed a series of very different interdisciplinary approaches. The diverse ideas in landscape design are not only decisively influenced by the attitude of the individual protagonist but also by the cultural and landscape ambience of the particular project. Furthermore, there are fundamental differences between the American and the European approach to landscape. Whereas there is a tendency in Europe to follow developments in landscape and art in America particularly closely, interesting European projects are, because less striking and hence more difficult to market, easily overlooked. For this reason, this book is particularly devoted to the creative philosophy and works of members of the European avant-garde who are providing new impetus for the way in which a language in the landscape, especially in the cultural landscape, will develop in future.

All of them have entered into an intensive creative dialogue with nature in the form of landscape or garden, not treating them in the traditional manner as an aesthetic background a work of art, but as independent, sometimes even sculptural space of perception and experience. None of the protagonists portrayed regards Land Art as a universal blueprint for a modern language in the landscape. However, all are aware of the momentum generated by an artistic approach to landscape and use this awareness as a creative force to explore new strategies of design.

The selection of artists and landscape architects, representing a subjective choice, is intended to reflect the wide range of individual approaches outlined above and does not pretend to offer a complete picture of the present situation – one which is also undergoing rapid change. In addition to outstanding protagonists, whose work has influenced the international reputation of landscape architecture and landscape art in Europe for decades, the book also focuses on the unconventional, promising approaches of younger members of the avant-garde. To avoid relying entirely upon interpretation of individual works or extensive biographies, and in order to find out what individual attitudes really lie behind the theories put forward, it seemed important to let the artists and landscape architects speak for themselves, even if the spoken word was not in all cases their preferred medium of expression. The personal interviews at the office or the house of the landscape architect, in the garden or studio of the artist, at the home of the architect, in the university lecture hall or just on a park bench under the trees all took the form of a journey through an unknown, fascinating world of ideas. Perhaps the interviews will reveal that – contrary to generally held ideals – none of the individual conceptions of the world is entirely self-contained and without any discontinuity. What matters is the creative search for meaningful expression in the landscape.

The work of Isamu Noguchi deserves particular attention for a number of reasons and – on the following pages – a special position in the context of this book. Noguchi's works are a reflexion of the major aesthetic influence of Japanese art and garden art. His decisive impact on landscape design and perception of nature in the West has not so far been considered. Moreover, Noguchi's conception of space as sculpture reflects many typical elements of modern sculpture and garden art in a unique way, making his work an important milestone in the exploration of the area where visual art and landscape architecture meet.

Acknowledgements

Pieter Boersma: 20 top
John Cliett: 39 top
Dan Dancer: 28
Agnes Denes: 34 bottom
Dia Art Foundation: 16 top
Andy Goldsworthy: 19 top, 26, 38, 39 bottom
Gianfranco Gorgoni: 12 top, 22
HAWOLI: 27
Michael Heizer: 12 m., 15, 21 m./bottom, 29

Thomas Kläber: 31, 32
Nikolaus Lang: 14
Richard Long: 19 bottom, 24, 25
Nathanson: 36 top
Nils-Udo: 13
Charles Simonds: 36 bottom
Alan Sonfist: 34 top
Nic Tenwiggenhorn: 16 bottom
Udo Weilacher: 18, 20 bottom, 30

Isamu Noguchi: Space as Sculpture

Prior to Land Art, only few early twentieth century sculptors succeeded in broadening the concept of sculpture to the extent that landscape space no longer served as a background to the work, but became its subject. One of the most important sculptors in the USA, Isamu Noguchi, who was born in 1904 and died in New York in 1988, undoubtedly belongs to this vanguard. His austere, Minimalist sculptures, gardens and squares possess a supreme clarity, simplicity and timeless beauty. For many contemporary landscape architects and artists his work has had a major influence on their approach to landscape as a spatial structure.

It would do little justice to the work of Noguchi to regard it simply as Japanese art in the West. "My father, Yone Noguchi, is Japanese and has long been known as an interpreter of the East to the West, through poetry. I wish to do the same through sculpture," Noguchi wrote in his application for a Guggenheim scholarship in 1927.[1] Born in Los Angeles in 1904, the son of the American writer Leonie Gilmour and the Japanese poet Yone Noguchi, Noguchi lived a lonely life from a very early age, unable to ever feel really at home in either Japanese or American culture. His search for an identity, which took the form of extensive travel between East and West – travel which took him to Europe, to the Middle East and Asia, to New York and later to Latin America – led him to develop an independent form of artistic expression which defies categorisation. Dore Ashton, art historian and professor at the Cooper Union School in New York, describes the complex background to his impressive work in her excellent biography of Noguchi entitled Noguchi. East and West.[2]

In the course of his life the Japanese-American artist drew on very diverse sources. One of the most important influences was his meeting with Constantin Brancusi (1876–1957) and their ensuing years of friendship. Noguchi had already seen the Cubist sculptures of the Romanian sculptor at an exhibition in New York in 1926 and made use of his Guggenheim scholarship to travel to Paris in order to spend a few months at Brancusi's studio as his assistant. Many of the features of Brancusi's sculptures were later to be found in Noguchi's works. Brancusi not only taught the young artist how to approach stone – later to become the material he preferred to work in – with the sensitivity of a sculptor, but also helped him to develop his own conception of space and nature. Brancusi saw a sculpture as being defined by its base, just as a picture is defined by its frame; consequently the focus of his attention was on the base which was to form an indissoluble part of the sculpture. Hence, Brancusi saw hewn stone as being understandable only in the context of the ground it came from. A work such as the 30-metre-high, steel Endless Column, realised by Brancusi in 1937 in the small Romanian town of Tîrgu-Jiu, which, seemingly dematerialised, reaches endlessly skywards, was a clear indication of his new look at the relationship between sculpture and landscape space. Simplicity was not his real concern in art, but it was indispensable as a means of approaching the real meaning, the essence of things.

Brancusi's focus on Oceanic and African sculptures which served ritual purposes as well as on the archaic art of the advanced civilisations of the ancient world stemmed from his interest in understanding the historical origins of objects. Noguchi shared this interest and, in consequence, went on study trips to Spain, Greece, Italy, India and, in 1982, also to Peru, where he was particularly taken with the impressive stone working of the Incas at Machu Picchu. Sculpture to be Seen From Mars, a design dating

[1] Noguchi, I. cited by Ashton, D. Noguchi. East and West. Berkeley, 1992: p. 23

[2] Ashton, D. Noguchi. East and West. Berkeley, 1992

Isamu Noguchi, ca. 1941. In front of the wall is the model of Contoured Playground, a design for a playground in New York's Central Park. Like many other playgrounds designed by the artist, the project was never realised.

43

from 1947 for a giant landscape of hills in the form of a face, which was to have a nose one mile long, "is the only surviving evidence of my interest to build earthen mounds resembling those of the American Indians."[3] A few decades later, young American artists discovered their interest in structures evoking early advanced civilisations and called their geometrised mounds in the vastness of the desert "Land Art". When he was asked in 1961 what kind of art he admired, Noguchi replied, "Actually, the older it is, the more archaic and primitive, the better I like it. I don't know why, but perhaps it's simply because the repeated distillation of art brings you back to the primordial: the monoliths, the cave paintings, the scratchings, the shorthand by which the earliest people tried to indicate their sense of significance, and even further back, until you get to the fundamental material itself."[4]

It was not until 1930 that Noguchi, who in the intervening period had principally made a name for himself with portrait sculptures, returned as a young artist to the

[3] Noguchi, I. cited in The Isamu Noguchi Foundation. *The Isamu Noguchi Garden Museum*. New York, 1987: p. 143

[4] Noguchi, I. cited by Kuh, Katherine. *The Artist's Voice*. New York, 1962: p. 186

"A flight of the imagination" (Isamu Noguchi). *Sculpture to be Seen from Mars*, model in sand (destroyed), 1947.

country which he had left twelve years earlier as a child and outsider on account of his mixed descent. Japan was engaged in war preparations and confronted Noguchi, whose American background was obvious, with the nationalistic excesses of Japanese traditionalism and the pronounced patriotism of his own father. To Dore Ashton, the fact that Isamu Noguchi went to Kyoto and did a four-month apprenticeship with the Japanese master potter, Jinmatsu Uno, appears as an attempt to avoid the latent confrontation with his father.[5] Uno taught him the traditional craft of making terracotta figures, and Noguchi discovered for the first time his enthusiasm for the temple gardens of Kyoto. It was not until his second journey to Japan in 1950 – Yone Noguchi had died in 1947 –, when the old nationalistic forces had lost their influence in Japan, that he was able to devote himself to Japanese culture unreservedly. On the one hand, he welcomed the new climate of openness and greater artistic freedom in Japan; on the other hand, he repeatedly stressed the independence of Japanese art, which, to

[5] Cf. Ashton, D. 1992: p. 39

[6] Noguchi, I. cited by Hasegawa, S. *My Time with Isamu Noguchi*. Tokyo, 1951

[7] Noguchi I. cited by Hunter, S. *Isamu Noguchi*. New York, 1979: p. 154

his mind, had become subject to too much Western influence. He wrote at the time: "I sincerely wish that Japan will re-examine and rediscover its own true self in the arts."[6] Noguchi established his first studio in Japan in Kamakura and in the time that followed commuted between Japan and New York, where he continued to realise large numbers of projects and exhibit his work.

"I admire the Japanese garden because it goes beyond geometry into the metaphysics of nature."[7] At the time of his first trip to Japan, Noguchi was greatly fascinated by the famous dry Zen gardens, Ryoan-ji and Ginkaku-ji, and indeed these were to have a decisive influence on his work. The 15 stones in the Zen garden Ryoan-ji, set in the middle of white, raked sand and, although firmly anchored in the ground, seeming to float on the immaculate surface made a particularly deep impression on the artist. Noguchi understood that the wall surrounding the garden of meditation, while at the same time permitting a view of the real landscape in the background, was a crucial element in this unique conception of space. He was convinced that the creators of this garden must have had a profound understanding of sculpture. What impressed him in the dry-stone garden of Ginkaku-ji was the reflecting "silver sand-sea" ("gin-shanada") of white sand and the geometrical sand hill "platform opposite the moon" ("kogetsudai") with its characteristic play of shadows. Simplicity, the art of intimation, asymmetry, subdued colours and a highly sensitive approach to the texture and colours of individual materials were to become the characteristic features of many impressive projects of Noguchi.

Ginkaku-ji (Jisho-ji), a paradise garden in Kyoto dating from the Muromachi period (15th/16th century). Raked areas of gravel and solid mounds of gravel in front of the "Silver Pavilion" represent the sea and mountains.

Noguchi acquired his first and most important experiences of working with real and virtual space through his collaboration with the New York dancer, choreographer and ballet director Martha Graham, who commissioned him in the thirties to design sets. Martha Graham was very impressed by the first set which Noguchi created for *Frontier*. "I thought of space as a volume to be treated sculpturally and the void of theatre space as an integral part of form and action. A white rope was hung from the top two corners of the proscenium to the floor at the rear centre of the stage. This created a curious sense of dimension – an outburst into space and at the same time an influx toward infinity. A small section of log fence at the rear served as a spot for the action to start from and return to."[8]

[8] Noguchi, I. cited in The Isamu Noguchi Foundation. *The Isamu Noguchi Garden Museum*. New York, 1987: p. 2

Charging space with poetry and symbolism by means of minimal design elements and greatly abstracted characters is an approach typical of the classical Noh drama of Japan. Noguchi became acquainted with this conception of space at the time of his first journey to Japan and was very taken with the extreme reduction of the stage sets, which gave the imagination of the audience very wide scope. His main concern was a comprehensive perception of space and the unlimited sensory experience of rituals, myths and dramas. When he later turned his attention to the design of larger areas of open space, he never saw these as being sites in which isolated objects were located but as gardens in which the relationship to the whole played a vital role. Realisation of his first major garden in Paris in 1956 was – despite or perhaps because of his ambitious approach to space as sculpture – a test of Noguchi's abilities. Architect Marcel Breuer commissioned Noguchi to design a small garden for the main administrative building of *UNESCO* in Paris. When he inspected the site, Noguchi decided that he would not only design the area for which he had originally been commissioned but also the adjacent areas which link the two parts of the building. What began as the design of a linking element was soon transformed by Noguchi into a first attempt to realise the principles of Japanese garden art in the middle of a modern European metropolis and, in this way, to combine the modern and the traditional to form a harmonious whole. The materials to be used, in particular the stones, were to be imported from Japan, although there was originally no budget available for obtaining material in such an expensive fashion. Nevertheless, Noguchi succeeded in convincing the funding committee of his idea. "This ultimately led to a long and close association with my father's country and to my development as an artist. *UNESCO* was my beginning lesson in the use of stone," Noguchi admitted later.[9] With great conscientiousness he selected all the stones he needed from a mountain stream on the island of Shikoku and had eight tonnes of stone carefully packed and, along with

The *UNESCO Garden* in Paris, realised between 1956 and 1958, numbers among Noguchi's earliest attempts to combine Japanese garden art and the design principles of modernism.

[9] Noguchi, I. cited in The Isamu Noguchi Foundation. *The Isamu Noguchi Garden Museum*. New York, 1987: p. 162

Isamu Noguchi

water basins, stepping-stones, fountain stones and a stone bridge, shipped to France. Construction of the garden, which covered an area of 1,700 square metres, proved to be extremely difficult. In particular, collaboration with the experienced Japanese gardener Touemon Sanō, who came from a long tradition of gardeners in Kyoto, led to problems. The Japanese, a great admirer of the gardens of the seventeenth century, felt that Noguchi had never really understood the theory of Japanese garden art, continually violated its fundamental principles and wanted to incorporate too many design elements of his own. During the two years which it took to build the garden Noguchi, who was then fifty-two, was forced to confront these traditional ideas day after day. Whenever it was a question of where to place the sculptures or stone lanterns, Noguchi categorically refused any positions in which they were even partly covered by vegetation. Areas of water were not, in contrast to traditional rules, laid out as flowing, reflective surfaces but as motionless bodies of water. The result was a cool, modern garden, characterised by controlled biomorphic forms and cubist objects. The ground-plan of the garden evokes a surrealistic painting by Joan Miró or a relief by Hans Arp; however, in the course of time, proliferating vegetation obscured the design's original sculptural clarity. In 1988, shortly before his death, Noguchi commissioned three Japanese gardeners to carry out extensive restoration work to the completely neglected garden, which at times even had to be closed.

Despite the significance of the *UNESCO garden* as a milestone in the development

The way leading to the upper stone terrace with stone places to sit and hewn blocks of granite. *"UNESCO was my beginning lesson in the use of stone."* (Isamu Noguchi)

The stone placements and plants in the lower, landscaped part of the *UNESCO* garden are in the tradition of Japanese meditation gardens.

of modern garden art, it received no appreciative mention in either landscape architecture journals or in art journals. Art critics deemed the work to be a garden and not art, whereas landscape architects virtually ignored the garden, dismissing it as art. In the period after 1950, Noguchi created a variety of unusual sculptures, gardens and squares in Europe, the United States and Japan, primarily on the basis of commissions given by major companies. "His reputation and influence as a landscape architect, however, has been small," concluded the landscape architect Peter Walker. "Had one of the modern landscape architecture practices accomplished a project of the quality of Noguchi's courtyards at the *Connecticut General Life Insurance* (now known as CIGNA) home office in Bloomfield, Connecticut, or the Domon Ken photography museum in Japan, its position in history would have been justly secure."[10]

In contrast to stone, plants tended to play a subordinate role in Noguchi's work. This attitude is hardly surprising in view of the fact that plants do not play the same dominant role in Japanese garden art which they occupy in European gardens. Evergreen trees, bushes and perennials predominate in most Japanese gardens and are regularly trimmed to achieve austere forms. However, outside the garden, nature is allowed to develop without restraint and as "shakkei", as "borrowed landscape" becomes an essential design element. "Stones are the bones of a garden, flowers its flesh," remarked Noguchi in the context of a visit to the garden of Monet at Giverny in 1988.[11] He saw stone as being depth, as being far more directly linked with the essence of things, the

[10] Walker, P. In *Landscape Architecture* 4/1990: p. 37

[11] Noguchi, I. cited by Ashton, D. *Noguchi. East and West*. Berkeley, 1992: p. 270

Noguchi set up his second studio, which was also to become his principal one, in Mure on the Japanese Island of Shikoku in 1971. A two-hundred-year-old, restored house, once owned by a samurai, was used as a residence. Two "kura", buildings similar to barns, were added later to serve as a studio.

matter of the universe. Discussing this, the architect Shoji Sadao, who worked with Isamu Noguchi for many years and today heads the Isamu Noguchi Garden Museum in New York and is currently completing two unfinished landscape projects of Noguchi, said: "He was aware of plants as sculptural forms, and he was not as interested – or I never heard him express a particular interest – in understanding them as growing materials. [...] I think perhaps plants were a little bit too uncontrolled for him, and the ones he did choose to work with were often pretty stable."[12]

[12] Sadao, S. In *Landscape Architecture* 4/1990: p. 62/63

In 1982 Noguchi completed his last and most well-known project in public space in the United States: *California Scenario*, which he created in Costa Mesa, a town in the vicinity of Los Angeles, his place of birth. Henry Segerstrom, a successful building contractor who came from an old Californian farming family, wanted Noguchi to create a fountain for a small park. Preferring not to leave the design of the remaining area to anyone else, Noguchi suggested to Segerstrom that he be allowed to transform the entire area, which measured approximately 120 metres x 120 metres, into a sculpture garden.

California Scenario, located in the middle of a commercial complex, is almost entirely enclosed by two glass-fronted office buildings and by two 12-metre-high, white-rendered walls which are part of an adjacent car park. The entire area, an austere, introverted space, is paved with rough stone slabs. Noguchi's design draws on the full

The *Sunken Garden* at the Chase Manhattan Bank Plaza in New York was realised between 1961 and 1964 and is clearly in the tradition of the Ryoan-ji Zen garden in Kyoto. In summer water flows from concentric rings of fountain jets, transforming the *Sunken Garden* into a shallow pool.

repertoire of his many years of experience of Japanese garden art, stage design and sculpture to create a place of timeless beauty and profound imagery. He used space like a stage to give expression to the compelling dialogue between nature and culture, employing the fundamental materials stone, plants and water in a reduced, archetypal manner. Stone, which Noguchi always insisted on selecting personally, occurs in both its unworked elemental force as a flat or upright boulder and in the form of an idealised Platonic body. A stream flows from a free-standing, triangular wall of natural stone, reminiscent of the observatory at Jaipur, plunges down a narrow watercourse and meanders across the area to finally disappear under a reclining stone pyramid. The highly-polished granite surface of the pyramid reflects the sky like a mirror and evokes an ancient Japanese myth, according to which a mirror was used to entice the sun goddess out of her cave so that she would restore light to the universe.

California Scenario is, as its title implies, reminiscent of the impressive natural landscape of California. *Desert Land* is a small round mound of earth with a sparse covering of cacti, agaves and bushes, a metaphor of the forbidding charm of the deserts of California. Opposite lies *Forest Walk*, a grass-covered ramp, surrounded by sequoias, a reference to the impressive forests of these giant trees along stretches of the coast of California and in the Sierra Nevada. The other major elements of the project are *Land Use*, a mound of grass bearing a granite slab with the title *Monument to Develop-*

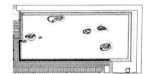

Ryoan-ji, Japan's most famous dry Zen garden at Kyoto, was created in the Muromachi period, late fifteenth century.

ment and a small grove of trees, which provides a concave-shaped bench with shade. *Monument to Development* is Noguchi's ironic criticism of the uncontrolled building boom in California, for which huge expanses of fertile arable land had to be sacrificed. *The Spirit of the Lima Bean*, a group of fifteen large, almost unworked granite stones, precisely interlocked to form a sculpture, is, in formal terms, a reference to Noguchi's impressions of Machu Picchu. Noguchi intended the sculpture to evoke the origin of California's wealth: prior to its being sold as land for development, farmers cultivated the land, their chief crop being beans.

The skyline of Costa Mesa and neighbouring Irvine is today dominated by sophisticated office buildings, symbols of the seemingly unlimited growth possibilities of California. *California Scenario* greets the visitor like an oasis, not a place of empty stillness but of meditative tranquillity. All the components of the space are interlinked and create a unique, compelling spatial structure, through which the beholder moves as if on a stage. "Gardens led me to a deeper consciousness of nature and stone. The natural hard rock boulders – basalt, granite and the like – which I use now are a petrification of time."[13] Noguchi uses the watercourse to break through the petrified time. The flowing body of water is evocative of the symbolic power of the element, a symbolism which is not confined to Shintoism and Buddhism. The white boundary wall is reminiscent of the walls which enclose a monastery garden of meditation, making the sky a "borrowed landscape".

[13] Noguchi I. In *Wiener Festwochen*, 1990: p. 142

To the Issei, a two-part basalt sculpture, is today the main focal point of the *Japanese-American Cultural and Community Center Plaza*.

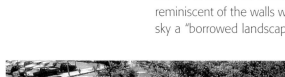

Originally, Noguchi was only to create a sculpture for the *Japanese-American Cultural and Community Center Plaza* in Los Angeles, California. Instead he designed the entire open area of over 4,000 square metres, between 1980 and 1983.

Western landscape architecture has long been trying to adapt Japanese garden art in such a way that its sensuousness, its timeless beauty and profundity of meaning contribute to an open space design which, despite its distinctive character, is accessible without any knowledge of Shintoism. However, actual practice usually results in superficial designs which, at best, reflect the Japanese garden in formal terms. Moreover, practical considerations predominate in urban space, and purely functional planning produces open space devoid of any meaning whatsoever. If simplicity is proclaimed, contrary to the maxim of Constantin Brancusi, to be an objective in itself, it tends to end up in rigidity and unimaginative monotony. In contrast, Noguchi succeeded in creating an open work in a rationally defined, urban context, its enigmatic nature, its archaic symbolism and economy of means evoking a meditative, almost mythical atmosphere. *California Scenario* is rooted in the tradition of Japanese cultural history and, at the same time, is a contemporary conceptual reinterpretation of existing reality.

American landscape architects criticised the plaza, pointing out that the absence of anywhere to sit, the lack of shade and the unusual proportions made it a place where people would not choose to spend time.[14] Noguchi was well aware of such functional requirements but, nevertheless, he uncompromisingly decided to disregard purely functional aspects in favour of creating a place of significance. The exceptional environment addresses the visitor directly and stimulates his imagination, its ultimate

[14] See *Landscape Architecture* 4/1990: p. 63

Isamu Noguchi

[15] Noguchi, I. cited by Beardsley, J. in *Landscape Architecture* 4/1990: p. 50

[16] Noguchi, I. cited in The Isamu Noguchi Foundation. *The Isamu Noguchi Garden Museum.* New York, 1987: p. 286

deciphering being no more possible than a definitive interpretation of the Zen gardens of meditation.

In 1949 Noguchi wrote that "a reintegration of the arts towards some purposeful social end is indicated in order to enlarge the present outlet permitted by our limiting categories of architects, painters, sculptors and landscapists".[15] In the final analysis he did not care what label was put on his work: "Call it sculpture when it moves you so."[16]

Ground-plan of *California Scenario* in Costa Mesa, California, 1980–1982. It is composed of the following elements (clockwise from top left): *Energy Fountain, Forest Walk, The Spirit of the Lima Bean,* the reclining pyramid where the watercourse ends, *Desert Land,* a free-standing wall containing the source of the stream, *Land Use* with the *Monument to Development,* grove of trees with curved bench.

A triangular sandstone wall, approximately nine metres high, is the source of the watercourse of *California Scenario.*

The watercourse disappears under a reclining pyramid of polished granite, which reflects the sky. The thickness of the sandstone pavingstones increases almost imperceptibly between the source of the watercourse and its end.

Isamu Noguchi

Desert Land, a mound planted with cacti, is a reference to the deserts of California.

The reflective glass façades of two bank buildings and two 12-metre-high walls of a car park enclose the site of *California Scenario*, which is 120 metres by 120 metres.

The Spirit of the Lima Bean is a sculpture composed of fifteen, precisely interlocked blocks of granite. It is a reference to the family of Henry Segerstrom, who commissioned *California Scenario*. His family had used the site for agricultural purposes for fifty years.

Energy Fountain, a metaphor of the thriving economy of California, is composed of a stainless steel cylinder and a cone of rough granite.

Isamu Noguchi

The *Isamu Noguchi Garden Museum* was opened in Long Island City, New York, in 1985. Over 200 of Noguchi's sculptures are exhibited at the Museum.

„The museum garden here provides an intimate setting for viewing sculpture, but it is not the subject of the museum" (Isamu Noguchi)

Noguchi was commissioned to plan *Bayfront Park* in Miami, Florida in 1978. The site extends over approximately eleven hectares and Noguchi was able to realise about three-quarters of the park during his lifetime. After his death, the park was completed by Fuller & Sadao, architects, Long Island City. Typical features are a large amphitheatre, a stone garden and a tower equipped with laser.

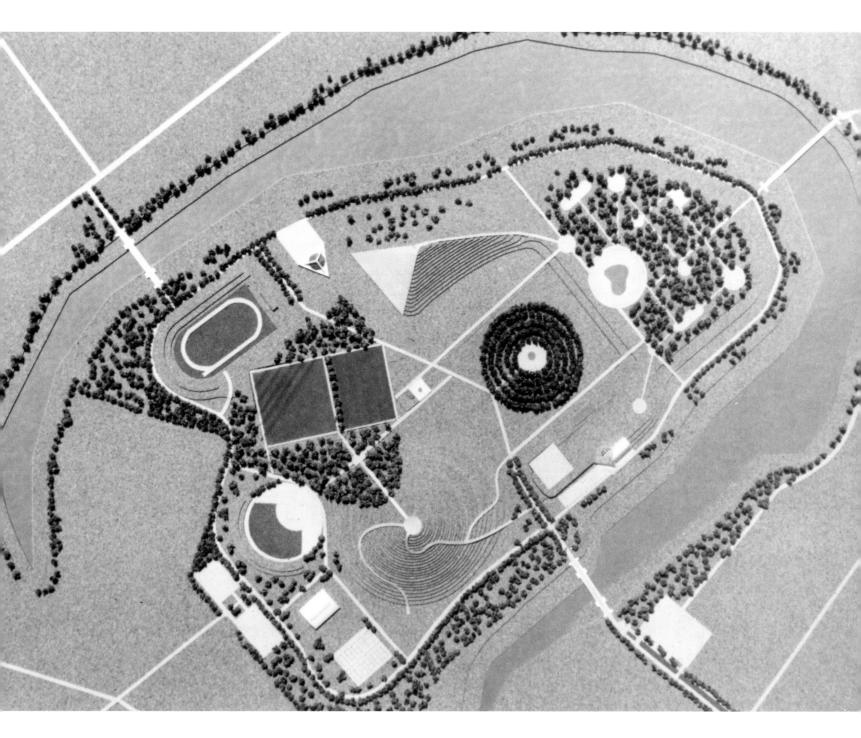

Model of *Moere Ken Park* in Sapporo, Japan, which extends over an area of 162 hectares. Noguchi was commissioned by the city in 1988 to plan the park located on the city's northern edge. Fuller & Sadao plan to complete the project by 1997.

Isamu Noguchi

Biography and Selected Works

Isamu Noguchi was born in Los Angeles in 1904, the son of the Japanese poet, Yone Noguchi, and the American writer, Leonie Gilmour.

1923–1926	Student of art at Columbia University and training in sculpture at Leonardo da Vinci Art School. First own studio
1927–1929	Guggenheim scholarship for visit to the Middle East, visit to Paris. Assistant at Constantin Brancusi's studio for several months. First one-man exhibition in New York
1930–1932	Visits to Paris, Peking and Japan. Studied brush drawing with Chi Pai Shih in China and learnt to work with clay under Jinmatsu Uno, a master Japanese potter. Exhibitions and first work on stage sets in New York
1933–1937	First designs for public squares, monuments and playgrounds. First set for *Frontier*
1942–1948	Design and production of furniture and lamps. Intensive theatre work
1949–1952	Travels through Europe, Central East and Asia; drawings and photographs. Establishing his own studio in Kamakura, Japan
1952–1956	Divided time between New York and Japan
1956–1961	Establishing studio in Long Island City, New York
1971–1979	Establishing studio in Mure on the Japanese island of Shikoku
1980	Establishment of the Isamu Noguchi Foundation, Inc.
1981–1985	Establishment of the Isamu Noguchi Garden Museum in Long Island City, New York
1984	Honorary doctorate from Columbia University New York State Governor's Art Award
1986	Representative of the USA at the Biennial in Venice
1987	National Medal of Arts awarded by the President of the United States

Isamu Noguchi died in New York on 30 December 1988.

Selection of realised and planned projects in open space:

1933	*Monument for the Plogh* (not realised)
1938	*Ford Fountain* for the World's Fair in New York, 1939–1940 (destroyed)
1947	*Sculpture to be Seen From Mars* (not realised)
1951–1952	Two bridges for the Peace Park at Hiroshima, with Kenzo Tange, architect
1952	Monument in memory of Hiroshima's dead, with Kenzo Tange, architect (not realised)
1956–1957	Gardens for the Connecticut General Life Insurance Company, with Skidmore, Owings & Merrill, architects, Bloomfield, Connecticut
1956–1958	Garden for UNESCO in Paris, with Marcel Breuer, architect
1960–1964	Sunken Garden for Beinecke Rare Book and Manuscript Library, Yale University, New Haven, Connecticut
1961–1964	Sunken Garden for the Chase Manhattan Bank Plaza, with SOM, New York
1964	Gardens for IBM Headquarters, with SOM, New York
1960–1965	Billy Rose Sculpture Garden, Israel Museum, Jerusalem
1970	Fountain for EXPO '70, Osaka
1972–1979	Philip A. Hart Plaza, Civic Center, Detroit, Michigan
1978–1986	The Lillie and Hugh Roy Cullen Sculpture Garden, Houston Museum of Fine Arts, Houston, Texas
1979	Piazza, Finanziaria Fiere di Bologna, with Kenzo Tange, Bologna, Italy Commencement of Bayfront Park project, Miami, Florida.
1980–1982	*California Scenario*, Costa Mesa
1980–1983	Japanese-American Cultural & Community Center Plaza in Little Tokyo, Los Angeles, California *Constellation* (for Louis Kahn), Kimball Art Museum, Fort Worth, Texas
1983–1985	Shikoku Garden Museum, Kagawaken, Japan
1984	Domon Ken Museum Garden, Sakata, Japan
1988	Commencement of the approx. 1.2 hectare Moere Ken Park, Sapporo, Japan.

Numerous exhibitions at all major international museums of art

Selected Bibliography

Noguchi, I. *Isamu Noguchi: A Sculptor's World*. New York, 1968

Isozaki, A. *Isamu Noguchi, Space of Akari and Stone*. Tokyo, 1985

Noguchi, I. *The Isamu Noguchi Garden Museum*. New York, 1987

Grove, N. *Isamu Noguchi Portrait Sculpture*. Washington D.C., 1989

Grove, N./Botnick, D. *The Sculpture of Isamu Noguchi: A Catalogue*. New York/London, 1990

Ashton, D. *Noguchi: East and West*. New York, 1992

Apostolos-Cappadona, D./Altschuler, B. *Isamu Noguchi: essays and conversations*. New York, 1994

Acknowledgements

By kind permission of the Isamu Noguchi Foundation Inc., New York: 43, 44, 52 bottom, 53
Shigeo Anzai: 52 top r.; Gary McKinnis: 51 top; Kevin Noble: 52 top l.; Isamu Noguchi: 45 bottom, 46, 48 m., 49; Michio Noguchi: 47
as well as:
Kiichi Asano: 45 top; South Coast Plaza: 51 m./bottom; from Sutherland Lyall, Künstliche Landschaften, Basel/Berlin/Boston 1991: 50

Himmelstreppe (Sky Stairway)
is a seemingly archaic clay
structure in the Moroccan
plain of Mârhâ to the south of
the High Atlas. The distinctive
structure was created between
1980 and 1987.

Signs of Remembrance – Hannsjörg Voth

The project artist Hannsjörg Voth, born
in 1940, is a trained carpenter, graphic
artist and painter and, above all, a landscape artist. His work is not, however,
readily associated with garden art, but
seems to be much more closely related
to early Land Art in America and to
sculptural interventions in desert landscapes, far away from any form of civilisation and characterised by an unmistakable tendency towards the
monumental. Since the end of the sixties this loner, who shuns publicity, has
gone to the limits of his physical abilities to realise projects for the outside
space. He has developed a form of dialogue with nature, landscape and civil-
ization which clearly stands apart from
the pioneering works of Land Art on
account of its remarkable sensitivity,
semantic complexity and close links
with European cultural history. Voth's
works, which his wife, Ingrid Amslinger,
documents in breathtakingly impressive
photographs, are undoubtedly some of
today's best examples of landscape art
in Europe. The artist's almost meditative
treatment of the four elements, water,
earth, fire and air, provides revealing

insights into the potential force of artistic interventions in the complex relationship between landscape and natural environment.

Voth's creativity has always been characterised by the desire to investigate the elementary relationships in nature and their fundamental connections with man. Whereas in his youth he had hoped that archaeology or zoology would provide him with the answers he was seeking, as a young artist he spent an increasing amount of time making drawings to analyse the complex structure of landscape. The drawings he did between 1972 and 1974, entirely utopian in character, depicted implanted geometric figures in marked contrast to the topography of imaginary ideal landscapes. Actually realising them was not yet under discussion. However, Voth developed a feeling for the formal and spatial relationship between the artefact and the ideal pristine landscape. Later, Voth found traces of this original landscape or, as he likes to call it, "zero landscape" on the sea and in the desert.

Feldzeichen (Field Marks) was Hannsjörg Voth's first project in the natural environment, which he realised in 1975. In a field near Ingelsberg, a small town just outside Munich, Voth used voluntary local helpers to erect four thirty-metre-high poles, the ends of which were bound with white linen cloths. "The poles were driven into the landscape not only as positive markings, as a definition, but also as stigmas, as lances thrust into the body of the earth which had so often been tormented and abused," wrote the art historian Lothar Romain. "The four poles placed on a hillock in the middle

On 13 April 1975 Hannsjörg Voth erected the fourth pole of *Feldzeichen (Field Marks)* on an arable field in Ingelsberg near Munich with the help of local labourers.

[1] Romain, L. In Deutsches Architekturmuseum Frankfurt 1986: p. 40

of a field mark removal of the normality with which the environment, which has long since been altered and divided up into lots, is still presented as part of the natural order and preserved as such."[1] As an integral part of the project, it was intended to spend a year observing and documenting the way that the field marks withstood natural erosive forces, recording the metamorphosis of the marking in its environment.

In addition to the semantic relationships between a seemingly archaic work and exploited agricultural land, *Field Marks* revealed a social dimension which has meanwhile become an important element of Voth's art. It was only possible to realise

the project with the support of the public; something which was not just a question of the complicated process of obtaining permission from the local authorities. The poles were erected by means of the technique which is traditionally used for maypoles. Although the helpers perhaps did not fully understand the artistic implications of Voth's project, *Field Marks* were, nevertheless, instrumental in bringing about a direct dialogue and the shared experience of having created something together. The archetypal image of signs placed in the landscape, be they of military, religious or magical origin, or, as here, the work of an individual artist, formed the basis of collaboration and communication with the local people. However, this process was not able to prevent the poles from being sawn down by persons unknown only a short time later. The field marks were, despite or indeed because of their ambivalent possibilities of interpretation, probably experienced as disconcerting, frightening or provoking.

Voth makes a sharp distinction between the projects which he was commissioned to do and the often visionary actions which he has realised at his own risk and with the utmost tenacity and persistence. Included in the latter category are Voth's most impressive projects such as the sensational raft journey *Reise ins Meer (Journey to the Sea)* on the Rhine in 1978, the 1981 action *Boot aus Stein (Boat of Stone)* on the Ijsselmeer in the Netherlands and *Himmelstreppe (Sky Stairway)*, which the artist built in 1985–1987 on the fringes of the Moroccan desert. He still lives there during the winter months.

Four thirty-metre-high poles mark a place on arable land which has been cleared. The intention was to observe and document the changes to the bindings and the reactions of the villagers and the visitors for a one-year period. *Field Marks* was sawn down by persons unknown only a few weeks after it was completed.

Hannsjörg Voth lives in *Sky Stairway* for a few months of the year. View from the working area to the entrance.

Design drawing of *Himmelstreppe*, 1984.

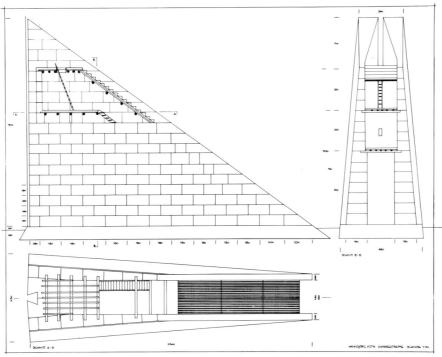

Hannsjörg Voth

With *Himmelstreppe* Hannsjörg Voth invokes the genius loci of the desert. The triangular clay structure, which is 23 metres long and 16 metres high and contains areas for living, working and sleeping, seeks formal confrontation with its surroundings, marking a place in the seemingly infinite expanse of the desert. For Richard Serra such a building serves as a barometer by means of which the landscape can be interpreted. It does not represent, but redefines its location. Resembling the great archaic calendar structures, the steps, which seem to lead into an endless distance, symbolise the link between the finiteness of earthly things and the infinity of the cosmos. Yet the symbol is transient: the clay which was trodden in the traditional manner will not be able to withstand the erosive force of the desert indefinitely. The special place will only live on in the tales of the nomads, with whom Voth has a special bond of friendship.

It was only recently that Hannsjörg Voth realised *Goldene Spirale (Golden Spiral)*, which can be seen from *Himmelstreppe*. The choice of this form was, as he says, a project he had always particularly wanted to do and which had long been taking shape in his mind. The artist considers the spiral to be the most important archetypal form for the dynamic growth of all living things. This indicates the particular importance of the project, which assimilates the sum of all earlier experience, desires and insights. After two years of preparation, the ritual search by a Moroccan diviner for the right place to build

Himmelstreppe was built in the traditional clay with the help of Moroccan labourers.

Himmelstreppe, drawing on transparent paper, mixed technique. 1985, 45 x 62 cm.

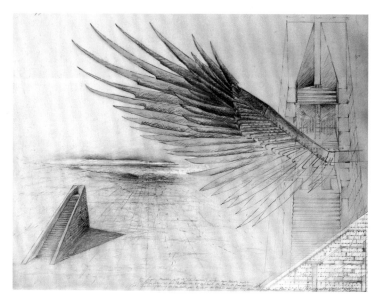

Himmelstreppe, drawing on transparent paper, mixed technique. 1985, 45 x 62 cm.

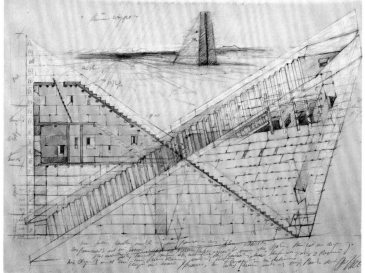

a "hassi", a well, marked the start of building work. A well is vital for the survival of the nomadic desert tribes. For Voth the source of life, which is reached 22 metres below ground by means of a spiral stairway, forms the structural centre and the conceptual core of the site, which, like *Sky Stairway*, was built with the help of Moroccan labourers, using the traditional method of clay building. Whereas Robert Smithson's *Spiral Jetty* is an anti-clockwise spiral, symbolising the destruction and end of the world, Voth built his spiral in a clockwise direction according to the aesthetic principle of the golden section, thus creating a symbol of hope. The wall surrounding the site is the boundary of a gradually ascending ramp, which is 260 metres in length; this wall achieves a height of 6 metres at the inner end of the spiral, the entrance to the complex. In contrast to *Sky Stairway*, *Golden Spiral* does not seek a strong formal contrast to the environment. From the entrance, the spiral staircase descends 27 steps to two areas for working and living. On a level which lies one hundred steps below, Voth celebrates – almost a little too emotively – the cosmic-divine element, the beginning, the latent elemental force by means of an archetypal boat, an ark of precious metal, which, protected by a shrine, floats on the surface of the water.

The fundamental geometric structure of *Sky Stairway* and *Golden Spiral* evoke the classical ideal architecture of the Revolutionary architects, Etienne Louis Boullée and Claude Nicolas Ledoux. Like those of Ledoux, Voth's structures combine geometric

The nomads named the well adjacent to *Himmelstreppe* after its builder: "Hassi Romi", the well of the European. Today they call the well "Hassi Hanns".

severity with a Romantic understanding of nature. These two of Voth's projects are like dissimilar siblings, created by a Romantic visionary with ambivalent, in part even contradictory ambitions. Whereas *Sky Stairway* refers to the cosmic and gives expression to the desire of the individual to transcend his own limitations, *Golden Spiral* is rooted deep in the earth and immersed in meditative contemplation of the origin of life. Both projects seek to make the invisible visible, to make reference to the metaphysical dimensions of life, to reveal the rootedness of man.

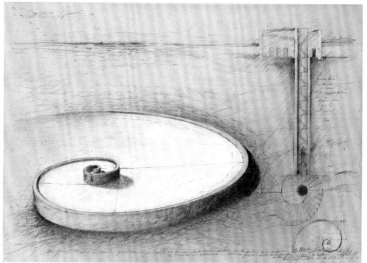

Goldene Spirale, drawing on transparent paper, mixed technique, 1994, 60 x 90 cm.

One hundred steps descend from the core of the *Goldene Spirale (Golden Spiral)* to the water level deep in the well.

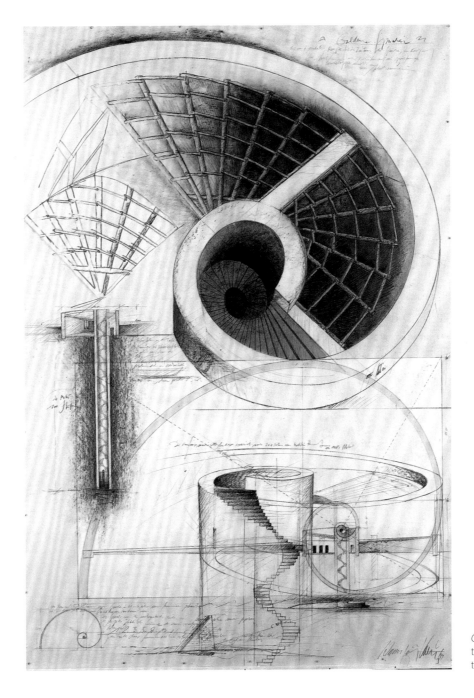

Goldene Spirale, drawing on transparent paper, mixed technique, 1994, 170 x 120 cm.

Hannsjörg Voth

All of the projects which you have realised so far have involved enormous amounts of organisation and financial outlay. Where does this tendency to do things on such a large scale come from?

There are two reasons. First of all, there is a tendency not to give very much thought to this aspect at the very beginning of the work. But as soon as you go to the actual site, you realise that it dwarfs everything and that proportions are clearly distorted. The works have to have certain dimensions or otherwise they are simply swallowed up by the surroundings. There are not very many artists whose work in the natural environment is successful. It's something which requires experience and a bold approach to dimensions as well as technical knowledge and a grounding in economics. When I carried out the action *Journey to the Sea*, many people took exception to the size of the raft and the figure. "Are you suffering from delusions of grandeur?" was the question people kept asking me. The raft was 32 metres long and the figure was around 20 metres in length. Today, every convoy of barges on the Rhine is over 150 metres long! In other words, my raft was one of the smallest on the river. Criticism of art becomes particularly loud whenever the economic purpose of such large projects is not apparent.

The system of values we have today means that economic aspects are the principal criteria of evaluation.

Hannsjörg Voth

The other reason that the projects are so elaborate and demanding is that I have to experience myself during the work on the project. Sometimes I push myself to the limits of my physical and mental abilities. I want to have a conscious experience of the world and of life. Of course, as I get older this is something I won't be able to do to such an extreme. Perhaps I would then have to delegate more of the work, but I know that this won't satisfy me. I'm sure it would be intolerable for me if I weren't able to play an active role in all phases of the project.

Do you see yourself as working in the tradition of Land Art?

When I work in the natural environment, I certainly see myself as working in the tradition of Land Art. The American sculptor Michael Heizer is probably the person whose work is closest to my own; in contrast, my work has little in common with that of Christo, although he has certainly made a decisive contribution to making art in public space popular.

When in 1975 I used bindings for *Field Marks*, my first project in outside space, people kept trying to find parallels to Christo. My bindings had a great deal to do with bandaging a wound, whereas Christo wraps in order to reveal. This is not an aspect you will find in my work. I am concerned with aesthetic principles.

Realising projects in the desert is often interpreted as a way of escaping the restricting conditions of the Central European cultural landscape or of escaping society.

For me both factors play an important role. On the one hand, our Central European landscape is suffering from over-use. There aren't any natural landscapes left here. Everything has been ploughed, cultivated and is, in the end, one vast garden divided into individual lots and criss-crossed by cables of every conceivable kind.

I can't find any ambience for what I am seeking in such an environment. Elements of this ambience existed on the Ijsselmeer, where I did *Boat of Stone* in 1981. Another possibility is to work in countries where the natural environment has not been developed to the same extent as it has in Central Europe. The Moroccan desert is one such example.

My work has also very clearly got something to do with escaping from people. Today people no longer seem to be capable of approaching nature and creative work with respect. The trend today is to drive to the ends of the earth and then to destroy everything there. I like to call this the "Hellabrunn" [after the name of the Munich zoo] effect. Ever-growing numbers of people would like to see wild animals at close quarters, but they don't want to give any real thought to the nature of these creatures or, for that matter, to the nature of the landscape.

Nevertheless you are, to a certain extent, dependent on public attention.

That's true. It's difficult for me to come to terms with this schizophrenic mixture of escape and dependence. On the one hand, I'm a social being and so I'm dependent on recognition. In addition, I have to survive financially and that's only possible if I communicate with my social environment. This creates considerable tensions. The people who really support my projects are individualists who are not only convinced by my work but are also prepared to bear a substantial part of the risk and provide the projects with financial guarantees from the outset.

They are my most reliable partners and they are people with whom I enjoy discussing my projects. These people not only support me financially, but also socially. I can't expect such support from the general public. That's why I prefer to maintain a distance from the general public. The media enable me to communicate my ideas and projects, something which is very advantageous. This doesn't mean that I create art for the mass media. I create my art entirely for myself.

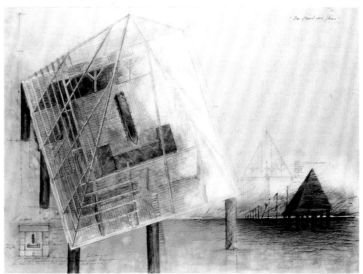

Boot aus Stein, 1980, drawing on transparent paper, mixed technique, 70 x 100 cm.

In 1981 Voth erected a temporary pyramid-shaped pile-structure, which had an area of 14 x 14 metres and a height of 12.50 metres. It was his intention to live on the sea for a year and chisel a four-metre-long boat out of stone. The foundations of the structure were destroyed by drift-ice in January 1982. The *Boot aus Stein (Boat of Stone)* sank to the sea-bed.

Hannsjörg Voth

Voth's *Reise ins Meer (Journey
to the Sea)* started on the
Rhine near Ludwigshafen on
30 May 1978 and ended in
the North Sea near Rotterdam
on 5 June 1978. Position on
30 May 1978: the gravel
works near Mainz-Wiesenau.

Most of your works are of a transient nature and are destroyed by time. Have you any ambitions to realise lasting projects?

Of course, I am not immune to the notion, and this is why I'm not able to dispense with documentation of my transient projects. These are usually my own and not those I was commissioned to do. Theoretically, I could exclusively realise works which would, in the way that sculpture is traditionally understood, last beyond my death. However, my primary concern is to realise an idea, not to preserve an object. That's why I try, as far as it is possible, to preserve my projects in other forms, such as film, photographs, tapes or books.

Sometimes you have even deliberately destroyed your work, a move which has not always found general acceptance. Why do you do this?

Journey to the Sea was, as were a large number of other projects, seen as a provocation. It was not my intention to provoke and it wasn't until much later that I became aware that I had done something which provoked people. The main reaction to the burning of the figure was a complete lack of understanding. Two and a half years of work and DM 300,000 were, after a short journey which only lasted ten days, burnt within just ten minutes. 150 tonnes of material went up in smoke, and people didn't approve at all. By destroying the work, I wanted to make it clear that our fossilised society expends a lot of energy on preserving and increasing values. However, this way of thinking, which is entirely aimed at restoring and preserving, prevents the development of anything new. It's my belief that it's always necessary to go back to a zero point in order to develop new approaches and new motivation. "Why don't you just keep the figure or the raft?" was the question I was asked at the time. "The raft, for example, could be turned into a pub." When I replied, "Yes, why not? Take the raft, you can have it," it was suddenly realised what the consequences would be. The raft would have had to be serviced and looked after, a berth would have had to be found and probably paid for. For the rest of its life, energy, time and money would have had to be invested in an object which had already served its purpose, instead of something new being started. Destroying the raft may be seen as a provocation by many people, but for me its preservation just didn't make any sense.

Art has basically – like religion – always been a means of overcoming fears. Abstract, not tangible things were given artistic form. The ensuing objects were used in rituals. Whoever was best able to give material form to these fears was an artist. In other words, artists only gave visual expression to what was culturally and existentially necessary for people. This interaction can be traced through the history of all religions. Today, the artist no longer primarily satisfies universal

needs, but works egoistically on whatever he is obsessed with, occasionally presenting the results to the public. But most people still see art as being something sacred. They feel cheated and provoked by today's art, often experiencing it as blasphemous.

In 1992 you realised the project *Zwischen Sonnentor und Mondplatz* (*Between Gate of the Sun and Court of the Moon*) in the street area which links different parts of the building of the European Patent Office in Munich. Was it your first project in public urban space?

It was my first project in urban space which is so frequented by people. Perhaps I have preferred working in the natural environment because I grew up in a small town and still feel most at home in a rural setting. I consider living in the country a great privilege; I have lived in a city for over twenty years because it's the city which can provide the artist with the cultural environment which he is dependent on.

With *Sonnentor und Mondplatz* I was working in urban space which is used daily by passers-by. Here, at the link between Theresienwiese and Hackerbrücke, passers-by are forced to look at my work. I didn't originally want to do the project because I didn't have any experience in working in an urban context. I was aware that I was taking a great risk as I had to concern myself with architectonic proportions which I had not been confronted with in any of my previous work. When working in the natural environment, I adopt a far more intuitive approach; I take the scale I want as my starting point, but which, as works progresses, usually proves to be difficult to realise both technically and financially. I reduce the scale of the design several times in succession until its realisation becomes possible. Here it was quite different. I began with a model in order to get an idea of the situation and the proportions. I always had people in mind, people moving around in this public space. I had to respect people as, here, passers-by don't, in contrast with my earlier projects, have the freedom to decide whether they want to come into contact with my work or not. These considerations had to be repeated over and over again to prevent the dimensions of my sculpture from becoming unreasonable for people.

Despite the reservations and problems you have described, *Between Gate of the Sun and Court of the Moon* is typical of your work and uses a large number of archetypal images.

The site with the two cosmic symbols, the sun and the moon, is primarily an urban space for access and communication. I wanted people to be able to experience the cosmic dimensions of time and scientific and technological progress here. I wanted to show the existence of an order in which the earth and people have a place and which is experienced and interpreted by all cultures. If I always use symbols, meta-

Journey to the Sea. 5 June 1978. At the "Industriebank-West" station, North Sea. 9.30 p.m.: burning of the figure.

Hannsjörg Voth

The *Court of the Moon* is a water-basin, 34 metres in length and 4 metres in width, containing 28 circular granite slabs which depict the phases of the moon. *Gate of the Sun* and *Court of the Moon* are linked by a stone ridge, through which water flows.

Zwischen Sonnentor und Mondplatz, drawing on transparent paper, mixed technique. 1992, 188 x 120 cm.

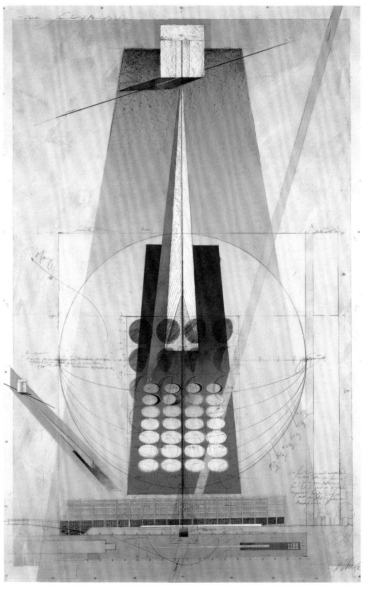

Only the sun passes through the *Gate of the Sun*, built in light granite and measuring 4.60 x 4.00 x 0.40 metres. At the "real middle of the day" it casts its light through a narrow aperture onto the meridian line of black granite. *Zwischen Sonnentor und Mondplatz (Between Gate of the Sun and Court of the Moon)* was realised adjacent to the European Patent Office in Munich in 1993.

phors and archetypal forms in my work, I do so in the awareness that very specific cultural structures and corresponding forms of behaviour and meaning have been passed on to all people since the beginning of history. But these are, on the whole, buried in our unconscious. In the history of mankind the sun was the supreme being until the time that other systems of belief manifested themselves. The sun cults of, for example, the Aztecs, the Egyptians, the Indians, the Greeks and the Germanic peoples, bear this out and are still part of our heritage today. Whenever I'm with people who are still rooted in tradition, I'm always reminded how much these old structures still live on.

Realisation of your projects is hardly possible without the help of engineers.
I had a lot of contact with engineers during work on *Reise ins Meer* and *Boot aus Stein*. Of course, I work entirely on my own during the design phase in order to prevent a project idea from being dismissed at an early stage. It's only when I have precise formal ideas that I consult technical people and, in consequence, have to correct individual details. The experts take these questions concerning details very seriously because I consult them in their capacity as specialists in their own particular field. I try to give them the latitude they need for their work. Of course, the question which I am always asked is what my art actually means; in fact the technical side is a good stepping-stone to get to what I want to say. It's my experience that in our society these are people upon whom only one-sided demands are made. The consultants I work with become fully involved in the project as the work progresses because it is never entirely only a question of details. Working with landscape architects can certainly lead to problems, something which I have already experienced in connection with horticultural exhibitions. But this is understandable in a way, as an artist often places his work in a landscape which has already been designed, and the landscape architect has come to terms with this. As a rule, it's better if artist and landscape architect work together right from the beginning. Whereas working with engineers hardly ever presents any problems, the procedures involved in obtaining official permission to do things are often a great test of my patience. Dealings with politicians and bureaucrats are not always smooth, and this situation is by no means easy to resolve.

What is it about your projects which makes them so dangerous that politicians and public authorities often oppose them?
No politician today wants to be held responsible for an unpopular art project which will cost him the support of voters. *Field Marks* was not, for example, accepted as art and therefore attacked by local politicians. I think that our education system is also partly to blame for the lack of understanding of present-day art. In contrast with mathematics and orthography, it's not sufficient to only teach art for a few years; people can only understand art if they confront it continually. This doesn't go so far as to say that people have to like art, but at least today an artist is not just expected to paint beautiful landscapes. People who are still not jaded and in touch with their traditions have more direct access to my art. When I built *Field Marks* in a field outside Ingelsberg, I explained to the farmers that my work was something which was a part of everyday life. I reminded them of the wayside crosses and maypoles which people once used to erect and this comparison was one which they understood. People who have no relationship to traditions fall back on fragmentary textbook knowledge, something which usually produces lack of understanding and opposition.
The many administrative and insurance regulations are an additional major problem as far as realisation of projects is concerned. Our laws and building regulations are so unnatural that nobody can afford to take even the slightest risk. At the same time, the regulations leave hardly any scope for creative work in the outside space. Only once, it was when I installed the 21-metre-long *Himmelsleiter (Sky Ladder)* in Freiburg in 1983, did someone, in this case the chief planning officer, who was also chairman of the art society, have the courage to accept responsibility for the action and the risk that went with it. Normally the ladder would have had to have been fenced off to stop anyone from climbing it. The chief planning officer remarked aptly, "Anyone who is brave enough to climb up will make sure that he doesn't fall off!" *Field Marks* was also opposed on safety grounds. Fears were expressed that the 30-metre-high poles could fall over in a storm and kill somebody. The farmers just laughed and said, "I'd like to see the person who goes and stands under a tree during a storm and waits for it to fall down and kill him!"

Many of your projects give the impression that your purpose is to convey specific messages.
This is something I wouldn't rule out for any of my projects. I believe that every artistic statement also contains a message. But it would be wrong to think that I am mainly interested in conveying a message. I am primarily interested in the egoistic realisation of my own ideas. I don't see why I have to provide a visual work with words of explanation. I presuppose a certain basic understanding and I'm disappointed every time that this is not the case. If I submit an entry to a competition, I can understand if an explanatory text is required; the people who have to make the decisions usually use words to arrive at their evaluations and what is purely visual is not very accessible to them. The very existence of a title of a work of art is a statement and can be important information for the beholder. Paul Klee, Joseph Beuys and many other artists devised wonderful titles for what they created.

The archetypal forms which occur in your work frequently evoke earlier places of cult worship.

I'll have to go back a bit in order to answer this. I began to work publicly as an artist at the age of thirty, but many of my ideas had already been in existence for a long time. While I was growing up, I tended to be an "outdoor type", who had no time for school. At that time I was very interested in observing nature and I wanted to convey my impressions. One day when I had skipped school again, I returned home with a young birch tree. I laid a circle of stones, which had a diameter of around three metres, in the garden, dug a hole in the middle and planted the birch tree. The stone circle has disappeared, but the birch tree is still there. That's just one of the many stories from my childhood. As an adult I repeated some of these obsessions. I built the *Boat of Stone* out of peat as a child, and the raft is also a creation from my early youth. When today I express metaphors in symbols such as a circle or a square, this has partly something to do with the images from my childhood, but is also connected with geomancy. I believe that these archetypal images lie in the consciousness of many people, but the key to decoding them has been lost. The human race is not an invention of the modern age. Millions of years ago our ancestors internalised necessary cultural structures as well as forms of behaviour and meaning which are still in us today. It's particularly when I'm in contact with people who have not lost their traditions that I notice that certain things are understood intuitively very quickly. I don't copy the archetypal structures, rather they confirm what I do. I choose forms which present themselves in my consciousness and which have a spiritual meaning for me. These are forms which are an indissoluble part of the whole. It was not until the emergence of the major religions that man began to set himself above nature. The expulsion from Paradise began with the biblical instruction "Subdue the earth and have dominion over it …"

In other words, interventions such as the building of the *Hassi Romi* in the desert are more than just functional interventions which are needed for people to survive?

The well next to *Sky Stairway* in Morocco was indeed initially built for entirely practical reasons. I needed water in order to build the steps. I could have used another well close by, but I didn't want to get involved in any disputes with the nomads who used this well to water their animals. That's why I decided to build my own well. It wasn't until later that I found out that neither water nor a well is considered to be the property of any one person by Islamic culture and that a person who builds a well is seen as having obtained a place in Paradise. The fact that such great value is placed on water in the desert, while here it is wasted irresponsibly and political agitation is needed to make people

aware that it is essential to life, is something which has made a lasting impression on me.

In the light of what you have just said, it's surprising that it's particularly nature conservation organisations which can't get along with your art.

I consider the environmentalists' fears that our natural resources will run out to be justified, but I feel they don't go far enough. A broader view would not only recognise natural networking, but also spiritual and intellectual connections and necessities. The creative act and, in consequence, art would be taken far more seriously. At any rate, I consider that it's important to realise that the nature of art is metaphysical rather than serving the purpose of material survival.

Can you imagine working in a devasteted landscape?

This is a new question to me. At least it's a problem I've never had to face so far. I am very disturbed when I see devasteted landscapes and greatly saddened when I learn the reasons for their devastation. I'm afraid that I would cover up something with my art, would do something which was only on the surface and, while people would feel reassured, the underlying causes of the devastation would still remain.

Where does the inspiration for those of your projects in which childhood experiences don't play a role come from?

This is a question I've often asked myself. Desires develop inside me of their own accord. When you notice that during the course of your life certain themes keep coming up, it's only natural that you start investigating them to find out more. You visit places where something similar has happened. Like all creative people, I know what it feels like to go round in circles without getting anywhere. I have experienced the fear of getting stuck. After all, nobody wants to just keep copying and quoting himself. There was a time when I wasn't able to explain these fears and it helped me when I realised at some time or other that lots of other people had the same problem. And the problem is always the same: an artist sits in front of a blank canvas and doesn't know what the result will be. That's why you can't ask an artist what he's going to paint on his canvas tomorrow or the day after. That's the risk that goes with being creative. Despite all my fears, I have so far always found a way of continuing my work.

Do you have a vision, a project that you want to realise no matter what?

It seems that I have already managed to do all the things I really wanted to as I realised my projects in very quick succession. If you look at the projects *Field Marks*, *Journey to the Sea*, *Boat of Stone* and *Sky Stairway* in terms of the longings which find expression in them, I admit that I have to ask myself what longings still re-

Himmelsleiter (Sky Ladder), realised in Freiburg in 1983, towered to a height of 21 metres, an early indication of the artist's desire to escape the constraints of the Central European cultural landscape.

In the winter of 1986/1987, Voth fashioned iron feathers with the help of Moroccan craftsmen and assembled them to form a winged object with a wing-span of 3.50 metres. These wings, which are kept in the *Sky Stairway*, bring to mind the wings of Daedalus and Icarus and lead weight to the interpretation of the structure as a mysterious take-off position.

main. What primary experiences can follow those on the sea and in the desert? That's not an easy question to answer. In fact there is still a project that I would very much like to realise, but this will very much depend on whether I find the right place and the right environment and also still have enough energy. I would like to create a work on a mountain. What I envisage is an elevation in a wide landscape where I build a habitable project where I can live beyond the reach of the outside world. The form that I envisage is the archetypal spiral. The spiral is an important form for me as all living things have to follow the course of the spiral of growth. I need a lot of time to realise a project on a scale such as this. The form has to be developed to its logical conclusion, I have to choose the right material, establish what method of construction is suitable, secure financing and, most important of all, find the right place. This is always my greatest problem as there are no places left in

have lived in a community instead of living alone in the desert. But then I'd have been confronted with such familiar forms of behaviour that I'd have had to conform too much.

Do you equate commission work with loss of freedom?
Yes, but by accepting commissions I earn the money which I need to realise my independent projects. I carry out commission work in accordance with the terms of my commission and as efficiently and as well as I can, and after that the project is finished for me.

Can you still realise your artistic potential sufficiently when you do commission work? How great are the restrictions which you face?
I haven't been doing commission work for very long. So far my experiences have been varied. I have, on the whole, been able to realise most of my ideas. My opinion is that, in addition to my own ego-trips, I should also do projects in the public space of my own surroundings. Art has become an insider business and I find it very regrettable that the visual arts have isolated themselves to such a degree and, on the whole, only still find expression in museums and galleries.

Do you feel that interest in art in public space has increased tangibly?
Yes, I would go so far as to say that there is great interest. Increasing secularisation of the world in which we live is accompanied by a growing demand for art in public space. Of course, politicians have also acknowledged this deficit and have become more often willing to support artists, but only for as long as sufficient money is available. This attitude has made art a luxury. I find this regrettable as it reveals a lack of understanding that art is a vital part of our lives.

Central Europe which guarantee me the freedom I need. The kind of environment I'm looking for is an ideal landscape which hasn't been manipulated. Another aspect is that I am all too familiar with the mechanisms of Central European life-style and need to involve myself with a completely different cultural group. Perhaps Morocco would once again be a possibility, or Mongolia, although that would be very difficult from the point of view of logistics. What's more, I would no longer be able to realise a project in Central Europe from the financial point of view. I don't want to lose my freedom by getting into debt.

Freedom means a great deal to you, but financial and spatial freedom are not enough for you?
No, I also need a cultural environment which allows me to give full expression to my own understanding of culture. In Morocco, I could

Hannsjörg Voth

Biography and Selected Works

Hannsjörg Voth was born in Bad Harzburg in 1940.
He and his wife, Ingrid Amslinger, a photographer of architecture, live and work in Munich.

1955–1958	Apprentice carpenter in Bremer-vörde
1961–1965	Studied painting and graphic design at the Staatliche Kunstschule in Bremen
1966/1967	Graphic and layout designer for an American advertising agency in Frankfurt
1968	Art director of various advertising agencies, drawing and painting work in Munich
since 1969	Free-lance painter and sculptor

Except where noted, locations are in Germany

Numerous awards, including:

1973	Bavarian Award for Painting
1977	First prize in painting awarded by Philipp Morris International
1978	Prize awarded by the Norwegian International Print Bienniale, Fredrikstad, Norway
1980	"Arnold Bode" award, Kassel
1982	"Kunstfonds" grant, Bonn

Projects which have been realised in open space:

1973–1975	*Feldzeichen*, Ingelsberg near Munich
1975/1976	*Platz der Macht*, Neuenkirchen, Lüneburger Heath
1977	*Steine leben ewig*, Neuenkirchen, Lüneburger Heath *Neubepflanzung* for two rose-beds, Colombi-Park, Freiburg im Breisgau
1976–1978	*Reise ins Meer*, Ludwigshafen – North Sea
1978–1981	*Boot aus Stein*, Ijsselmeer, Netherlands
1978–1982	*Erdkreuz*, International Horticultural Exhibition (IGA), Munich
1980–1983	*Himmelsleiter*, Freiburg im Breisgau
1980–1984	*Steinhaus mit Seelenloch*, Federal Horticultural Exhibition (BUGA), Berlin 1985
1980–1987	*Himmelstreppe*, plain of Mârhâ, Morocco
1988/1989	*Lebensbogen*, sewage plant at Dietersheim near Munich
1990–1992	*Scheitelhaltung*, Rhine-Main-Danube canal near Hilpoltstein
1991–1993	*Zwischen Sonnentor und Mondplatz*, European Patent Office in Munich
1993/1994	*Wachstumsspirale*, Freising-Weihenstephan near Munich
1994	*Pegel Insel Ried*, Donauwörth
1993–1996	*Arche II*, Glonn near Munich
1993–1997	*Goldene Spiral*, plain of Mârhâ, Morocco

Since 1967	Numerous one-man and group exhibitions, including:
1987	*Zeichen der Erinnerung*, Deutsches Architekturmuseum, Frankfurt *Bateau de pierre*, project drawings. Goetheinstitut, Paris
1988	Project drawings. Galerie De Room, Oslo, Norway and Galerie Skala, Copenhagen, Denmark
1990	*Himmelstreppe*, water-colour. Institut für moderne Kunst, Nuremberg
1991	Drawings. Galerie Nouvelles Images, The Hague, Netherlands
1995	Hannsjörg Voth. *Zeitzeichen-Lebensreisen*. Übersee-Museum, Bremen

Selected Bibliography

Institut für moderne Kunst, editor. *Feldzeichen*. Nürnberg, 1975 (catalogue)

Kunstverein Göttingen, editor. *Voth – Projekte – Zeichnungen 1974–80*. Göttingen, 1980 (catalogue)

Institut für moderne Kunst, editor. *Boot aus Stein*. Nürnberg, 1983 (catalogue)

Deutsches Architekturmuseum. *Voth. Zeichen der Erinnerung. Arbeiten von 1973–1986*. Frankfurt, 1986 (catalogue)

Institut für moderne Kunst, editor. *Hannsjörg Voth/Hassi Romi*. Nürnberg, 1989

Voth, Hannsjörg. "Zwischen Sonnentor und Mondplatz." In *Daidalos*, no. 47 (1993), Berlin

Masiero, Roberto. "Scheitelhaltung, Rhein-Main-Donau-Kanal." In *Domus*, no. 750, Milano, 1993

Voth, Hannsjörg. "Scheitelhaltung." In *Daidalos*, no. 49 (1993), Berlin

Thomsen, Christian W., editor. *Hannsjörg Voth. Zeitzeichen-Lebensreisen*. Munich, 1994 (catalogue)

Acknowledgements

All illustrations were kindly provided by the artist.
All photographs: Ingrid Amslinger

Environment for Peace.
Florence, 1978

Harmony and Doubt –
Dani Karavan

Dani Karavan, who grew up in the pioneering spirit in the Tel Aviv of the thirties, not only has seemingly inexhaustible creativity and unerring composure, but is also capable of conveying the kind of enthusiasm which is probably indispensable for an artist to work as creatively as he has been doing for over thirty years. Dani Karavan's extensive work is characterised by a strong desire for tranquillity and harmony. This desire for harmony is undoubtedly a consequence of the fact that his life was, from the very beginning, influenced by war and destruction in the state of Israel.

His first major landscape project, an environment which today is still considered to be a masterpiece, was a monument to the soldiers of the Palmach Brigade, which stopped the Egyptian offensive in the Negev in 1947: the *Negev Monument*, a sculpture village to the northeast of Beer Sheba. This work, created between 1963 and 1968 on an area of approximately 10,000 square metres, was the first to reveal the typical repertoire of Karavan's artistic language. What makes his projects so powerful is their simple, clear geometric forms, the deliberate use of number symbolism and a specific understanding of the laws of nature. For Dani Karavan "obeying the laws of nature" does not mean acting according to principles of science and ecology, but integrating form, material and texture of the work in the context of the particular place. This not only means paying careful heed to natural and urban structures but also being aware of the particular nature of the materials used, be it wood or concrete. "The book of nature", Galileo Galilei declared in the Renaissance, "is written in the language of mathematics and the letters are triangles, circles and other geometric forms." It seems appropriate to link Karavan's clear, geometric formal language with the way that the Renaissance understood nature, particularly in view of the early enthusiasm which he developed for Renaissance art during his studies at the Academy of Art in Florence. It is particularly the precision in the creation of space and the harmonious proportions of structure and space which he sees as being closely linked with the idea of universal harmony.

Although he is of the opinion that his art is not essential for people, Karavan does want to help people to define their identity. Cultural identification of people with their town is the theme of what is so far his largest and most complex project, which he has been working on in the satellite town of Cergy-Pontoise near Paris since 1980: the *Axe Majeur (Great Axis)*. Cergy is one of the "villes nouvelles" which were planned on the periphery to accommodate the overspill from Paris; Pontoise, the nearby old town is, at least as far as a name is concerned, to provide Cergy with an identity. However, the satellite towns around Paris either grew too slowly or started to sprawl. In Cergy-Pontoise the town planners are attempting to halt the sprawl: with a three-kilometre axis along which the artist has located twelve stations. "Twelve," Karavan wrote when the project was announced in 1980, "is the number of time, of the year, of the day and the night, in other words it is the number which determines the rhythm of an individual's life, individuals for whom this axis is to be designed."

The *Negev Monument* in the seclusion of the desert landscape around the Israeli town of Beersheba. The sculpture village of concrete, desert acacias, wind-chimes and water elements was realised between 1963 and 1968 and covers a square area of approximately 10,000 square metres.

The twenty-metre tower of the *Negev Monument* can be see from afar. However, the desert sands have silenced the tower's wind-chimes.

Place Belvédère, the starting point of the axis, is marked by a 36-metre-high tower. The postmodern design with its neoclassical forms is by the Catalonian architect, Ricardo Bofill, known for his grandiose designs inspired by Baroque architecture. The axis proceeds to an orchard, a reference to the way that the landscape was once used, and, crossing the large plateau of the *Esplanade de Paris*, arrives at the *Place de l' Ombre des Colonnes (Place of the Shadow of the Columns)* with its twelve columns. From here there is a magnificent view of the countryside around Paris, stretching across green terraces and the valley of the Oise. The axis is, although not yet completed, a popular place to walk along. A footbridge is planned to provide a link with the *Ile astronomique (Astronomic Island)* in the nearby lake, where astronomic instruments and calendar structures are to be displayed. At night the axis is marked by a laser beam which originates from the *Tour Belvédère*.

Passages, an environment in memory of the philosopher and writer, Walter Benjamin, has a considerably clearer political message. It is located at Port Bou, a small coastal town on the Franco-Spanish border, where Benjamin, threatened with deportation to France and extradition to Nazi Germany, committed suicide on 27th September 1940 after fleeing across the Pyrenees. When the project was inaugurated in May 1994, Dani Karavan made it clear that he did not see his work as a monument but as a hommage to all individuals who had crossed the border here during the Spanish Civil War and the terror of the Third Reich in order to flee from a totalitarian regime. The power of Karavan's work at Port Bou lies in the simplicity of his interventions. They harmonise

The project *Passages*, an environment in memory of the philosopher Walter Benjamin, was built on the steep coast near the village of Port Bou on the Franco-Spanish border.

"It is more arduous to honour the memory of the nameless than that of the renowned. Historical construction is devoted to the memory of the nameless." Walter Benjamin

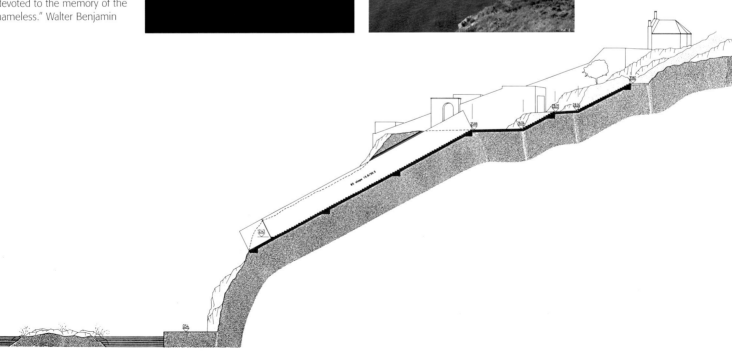

73　　　　　　　　　　　　　　　　**Dani Karavan**

with the natural landscape to create an unforgettable atmosphere evoking both hopelessness and meditative tranquillity. The Passage is cut into the steep coast at a point where a lone olive tree is lashed by the sea wind in its fight for survival. Steep steps lead down a narrow, dark, square iron shaft and continue between two high steel walls towards the infinite expanse of water beyond, almost as far as the spray of the surf. It ends abruptly at a glass wall, in which the words of Benjamin are engraved: "It is more arduous to honour the memory of the nameless than that of the renowned. Historical construction is devoted to the memory of the nameless."

All of Dani Karavan's works in the outside space have in common that their content and form are deeply rooted in the genius loci, in the context of the natural environment. As a child, Karavan learnt how to interpret landscape and nature from his father Abraham, called Abi. Abi Karavan was a gardener and created public gardens and parks in Tel Aviv in the thirties.

Passages. The final escape route leads down through a shaft of steel.

Steel plate, fence and view across the sea, evoking the yearning for freedom.
Passages, 1994

Your father was a landscape gardener. What role has the profession of Abi Kara-van played in your life and your work?

When my father was still alive and I was still a young man studying painting, I didn't have any direct relationship to his work. On the contrary, I even criticised it to a certain extent because, to my mind, he was not designing landscape, but merely copying what was there. He believed his job was to create landscapes which would disappear again as a result of the insatiable appetite of the goats. At the time, Tel Aviv essentially consisted of sand-dunes and sparse, yet beautiful desert vegetation. He wanted to recreate the natural landscape and always said: "When I have repaired nature, you can design it."

What do you associate with the concept of "nature" today? What does working in the natural environment mean to you?

I was born in Tel Aviv at a time when nature there was still very much untamed. I lived in a small place in the dunes, surrounded by the power of nature. Nature was always all around me, not least on account of my father's profession. I can't really put into words what nature is for me, as it's a part of me.

Do you see natural materials as being special materials to work with?

Not really. In my first environment, which I realised in the inner courtyard of the Palace of Justice in Tel Aviv in 1963, I used very low plants as artistic material in the same way that I used stone and other materials. When I built the *Negev Monument* (1963–1968), I only planted very few trees and used plants like any other material in the context of the surroundings. I also use weeds, water, sunlight and so on, in other words materials which all undergo changes due to the passing of time and the influences of weather and changing seasons. Each material requires its particular kind of use as a reflexion of its own particular energy and its inherent possibilities. Obviously, I can't use sunlight in the same way as stone or iron, but I use each material in its own specific way: stone is different from iron, concrete is different from marble, marble different from concrete. Each material has its own significance, and the purpose of the work is to intensify this significance. I use each material when I need it. I don't have any set ideas about this. What I primarily try to do is to carry out my work in a way which has the agreement of the client and is in line with the budget and the available time. For me it is particularly important to take the user into consideration; that's why I attach particular importance to using materials which people know from everyday life. Incidentally, this was also a practice during the Renaissance, the principles of which have had a strong influence on my work. While I was studying fresco-painting in Florence in 1956, I realised that the material which was used to build roads and houses was also used to create sculptures. For example, if

you go to Florence and visit the church of San Michele near the Palazzo Vecchio, you will find sculptures by Donatello in the niches and these sculptures are of the same material as the floor. This is a mode of working which is very important to me.

Is the durability of your work also something very important to you?

No. I have also created works of a transitory nature, for example during the exhibition in Florence (*Environment for Peace*, 1978); projects of this kind are also very important to me. All that remains of them is photographs and memories. People still talk to me about the Laser Installation in Florence. "I was there. I was young then. It was beautiful," or: "I didn't like it," or "I came to look at it every night. I spent all my

money to be able to see it." These people were often young artists then. This is a phenomenon which has continued up to the present. The project in Florence has grown in size and importance over the years. The further it lies in the past, the more monumental it seems to become. It is considered to be one of the best projects ever to have taken place in Florence.

Is there a contemporary art movement to which you feel a particular affinity?

I have an affinity with many different art movements, Minimal Art, Concept Art and Land Art, to name a few. However, I think that I use elements from these movements in a completely different way. Land Art has used landscape as an object, as a gigantic art object. The enlargement of the object plays an important role. For

Dani Karavan installed the *Environment for Peace* using white concrete, wood, olive trees, lawns, water, windchimes and an argon laser, at the Forte di Belvedere in Florence, closely linking it to its urban context.

Dani Karavan on the Tour Belvédère, view along the *Axe Majeur (Great Axis)* to the south-west.

Dani Karavan

◁ p. 76/77
The laser beam temporarily links Brunelleschi's dome with the Forte di Belvedere. "Line of light in homage to the science of the Renaissance." Dani Karavan, 1978

example, the *Spiral Jetty* by Robert Smithson was not primarily created to be used by people or experienced physically. Although I sometimes use the same formal language, I work in a way which is completely different. When I realised the *Negev Monument*, I had absolutely no idea that the Americans were experimenting with Land Art somewhere in Arizona. Generally, my work is created for people to use. My art cannot exist without people. My work is not there to be looked at but to be experienced.

The *Axe Majeur*, the Great Axis at Cergy-Pontoise near Paris is the largest of your current projects. It is said that you want to give the satellite town an identity by creating an axis which extends over several kilometres. Is a symmetrical axis really a contemporary form of landscape design?
I have to make it clear that the *Axe Majeur* was not my idea. The only reason that I'm doing this project is that I was asked to do so. I was

Most people who are familiar with the site at its present stage of development find it very hard to believe that the artist worked on the project before the architect. Normally, it's the other way round. I originally had other ideas for this place, but when I started work with Bofill I made changes. He also changed some of his ideas and so we were able to work together very successfully. I think that working with other experts and finding solutions to the related problems is one of the most important things I do.

Was the axis the only solution that you were able to envisage for the site?
There were, of course, plenty of alternatives. Before the clients contacted me, they had already worked with architects, town planners and landscape architects in order to try and find a solution, but none was convincing. The idea of a line which was to form the backbone of a natural amphitheatre existed long before I was commissioned to carry out the project. Of course, this idea influenced my work on the

View across the *Esplanade de Paris*, towards the *Tour Belvédère*, sixty-three metres in height and the starting-point of the *Axe Majeur* of Cergy-Pontoise. The neoclassical architecture is the work of the Catalonian architect Ricardo Bofill and shapes the character of the axis.

asked to realise an axis which was to be three kilometres in length; as I knew nothing about Cergy-Pontoise and the problems of the satellite towns around Paris, I didn't initially react to the inquiry. I had never felt the need to realise such an enormous project. When, despite all my misgivings, I went to look at the site, it became clear to me how beautiful the landscape was and I started to understand what the people wanted.

Did the architect Ricardo Bofill influence your design idea?
No. Bofill wasn't involved until much later. I had already been working on the project for two years when Ricardo Bofill was brought in. Originally the clients even wanted me to design the façades of the surrounding architecture, but I'm not an architect and so I explained to them that it would be very difficult to continue working on the project without knowing what the architectural context would look like. The result was that an eminent architect was commissioned to perform this work.

axis. All other details were derived from this basic idea and are characterised by a certain symmetry. Nevertheless, certain counterpoints and breaks are necessary. There are small details which defy symmetry: for example, the line of the trees, which is defined by a strip of concrete, or the large solitaire tree opposite, which has yet to be planted. The line I just mentioned will be diagonal to the solitary tree and mark a line which is exactly north-south. This means that after passing through the Bofill building you come to the first break in the symmetry. From here you proceed to the two squares, where a lone tree has also deliberately been placed asymmetrically. Incidentally, the squares are to be designed as basins, conveying the impression that the water is flowing uphill. The same principle is used in the Baroque garden of Le Nôtre, the only difference being that it is asymmetrical in my design. The large *Esplanade* also has a diagonal incision, a reference to the railway which once was here. Most of the breaks in symmetry are the result of the natural topography, such as the north-south line; others, such as the reconstruction of the railway lines, are derived from the idea of tracing the archaeology of the emerging industrial age. The *Twelve Columns* lead to the large garden on the hillside, where counterpoints which were already present are repeated: supporting walls, remains of buildings, fruit-trees and so on. All these traces will be preserved. All I will do is add the axis and underline some details by giving them a context. The *Astronomic Island* also has a completely irregular shape, and the sculptural elements on the island won't be symmetrical either. To a certain extent, I use small elements to break up symmetry as I feel that this is sometimes more effective than using large elements.

In what way is your approach similar to that of Le Nôtre?

I didn't know anything about him when I started work on the project. I was given the commission and went to Florence. That is where I created the first large model of the project, which is on a scale of 1:2000. This model contains the complete idea, as it were, the entire script of the axis, based on the idea of the urban planners. They originally wanted to build a large stadium on the site of what is today the grande esplanade. In my opinion, this would have been a catastrophe as such an edifice would have blocked the view and people would also have been sitting with their back to the landscape. I wanted a design which was very open. The *Esplanade* is a gigantic body of earth, which had to be banked up on the hillside. There were heated discussions with the clients, who asked me "What on earth are you doing? You're using a lot of money to build something which was there anyway. The view afterwards will be the same. Why do we have to stand on a level which is six to eight metres higher?" I explained to them that it was nature which required this measure. My work is a large sculpture. It needs this large bare space as a counterpoint to the lushness of nature. The beholder first has to cross the large geometric platform before arriving at a point from where he can survey the vast, overwhelming wealth of nature. I didn't have Le Nôtre in mind when I was in Florence in order to work on the design. I haven't seen very many of his works. Although I've been to the park of Versailles and to the Tuileries, I don't know Vaux-Le-Vicomte and Saint-Germain. I don't usually do any research work in preparation for my projects and so I don't know any other works of Le Nôtre from what I have read. I want to work with my senses and feelings. Later on, when I started to understand Le Nôtre's philosophy of creativity, I found many points of reference. I corrected certain points, studied details and tried to use some of the typical detail contained in his work. For example, water which seems to be flowing upstream; the large pool which leads off the Oise is intended to create such an effect. Concept Artists and Land Artists never use such elements. I feel at

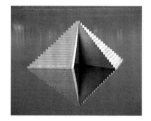

The *Pyramid in Water*.

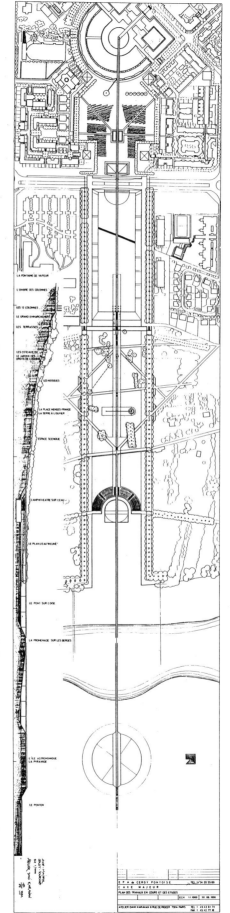

Plan of the three-kilometre *Axe Majeur* at Cergy-Pontoise near Paris, which has been under construction since 1980. Twelve stations are located along the axis: the *Place Belvédère* with the *Tour Belvédère*, the *Jardin des impressionistes Camille Pissaro*, the *Esplanade de Paris* with the remains of an old railway line and the fountain of steam, the twelve columns of the *Place de l'Ombre des Colonnes*, the terrace, the park *Jardin des droits de l'homme Pierre Mendès-France*, the *Gérard Philipe Amphitheatre*, the pool, the bridge, the *Ile astronomique* and the *Pyramid in Water*, the motorway intersection and the laser beam.

Dani Karavan

home in such a tradition, as I work in a kind of flow which has a long history.

Does your awareness of the history of civilisation also explain your work with archetypal forms?
Yes, it does.

Your projects are often strongly influenced by architectural means of expression. Many artists who work in a similar way to you find it difficult to cooperate with architects as the latter also often see themselves as artists.
My collaboration with architects has always been good, and I have always seen them as being of valuable assistance. The people who have always promoted my work or encouraged me to realise certain works or present my ideas have never been curators, museum directors or art critics, they have always been architects. When Christian de Portzamparc was working on planning for the Esplanade Général de Gaulle in La Défense, he was told that the regulations required that between one and two per cent of the building costs be used for art and that it was intended to commission an artist, namely Dani Karavan, to design a work or an environment. "If you're going to commission Dani Karavan", the architect replied, "then he shouldn't be commissioned just to create one object or environment, but to design the whole Esplana-

A thermal spring feeds the fountain of steam on the *Esplanade de Paris*.

de, the entire outside space in the context of my design." In Cologne the architects wanted to work with me at all costs and made sure that I was given the commission. The architect defended my work when problems arose in connection with building the North-Rhine-Westphalian parliament building. Nor would Nuremberg have been possible without the architect. He was one of the people who insisted on continuing the work despite the financial problems, and he was the person who was determined to find a solution. I have always been held in high regard by the architects. They have always sought to work with me and held the view that my work would be a valuable contribution to the overall design. The Cologne architects Peter Busmann and Godfrid Haberer also hope that our collaboration will continue in the future. My experiences have all been very positive.

Richard Serra sometimes claims that his works are to be understood as criticism of architecture. Do you feel it is justified to interpret your work in this way?
Claims can be made about lots of things, many interpretations are concerned with theory and sometimes also with questions of belief. For example, Bruno Zevi wrote in the 1978 exhibition catalogue in Florence that my work was architectural criticism. But that was never an issue for me. It was said of the *White Square* in Tel Aviv that it was to be interpreted as criticism of Tel Aviv. Tel Aviv is a somewhat chaotic city, and my project was interpreted as the ideal of the organised city. However, I never realise a project with such aims in mind.

Dani Karavan's projects are sometimes reminiscent of the metaphysical paintings of the Italian painter, Giorgio de Chirico. From the twelve columns the steps descend to the park *Jardin des droits de l'homme*.

It has sometimes been said that there is a connection between Isamu Noguchi and you. What links you with Noguchi's work?
I met Isamu Noguchi at the beginning of the sixties when I was designing a set for Martha Graham in New York. I was impressed by his work, which I had already seen on stage in 1950. Noguchi was extremely important to me in the early years. Later on, I went my own way, but I'm sure that his work has had a major influence on me. I can't really say exactly what this influence was. Perhaps the fact that he realised projects which were to be used by people and not just looked at; also the fact that he made vegetation an integral part of his work, but not in the sense of Japanese garden art, definitely not, only in conceptual terms.

You don't have any strong affinity to Japanese garden art?
It's the Japanese who see a relationship between their art and mine. The first time I went to Japan and saw the Zen gardens, it was clear to me that, although I worked with similar materials, I gave them a completely different meaning. Sand and gravel are as different from each other as bronze is from marble. A tiny stone can be just as beautiful as Michelangelo's David. The same intellectual vibration and tension can also be achieved using minimum means.

View across the park *Jardin des impressionistes* and the *Esplanade de Paris* towards the twelve columns and the *Ile astronomique*. Paris-La Défense can be seen in the distance.

Pierre Restany writes in his book on your work that semiotics plays an important role in your work. Do you work with semiotics consciously or is the semiotic interpretation just another approach to understanding your work?

I always want to find a reason for what I do. I can't just do something just because I somehow feel like it. I have to find a reason. I find reasons in many different areas. Semiotics is a great help here. Numbers play a particularly important role in my work. I believe that the numbers which we use daily, such as hours, days, months and so on, are closely linked with the rhythm of life and the relationship between man and the universe. When I use the number twelve or six or the mythical number seven, it's a question of this relationship for me. For example, it says in the Bible that you should work for

The site of the twelve columns at the end of the *Esplanade de Paris* affords a view across the terraced *Jardin des droits de l'homme Pierre Mendès-France* to the *Pyramid in Water*.

six days and rest on the seventh. This has something to do with rhythm. Why not three, twelve or ten days? Perhaps we still have some energy left after six days and need to stop before we use it all up. All these things have been preserved for mankind over the centuries. Incidentally, I have a very close relationship to the Bible, certainly not for any religious reasons, but because of the wisdom and poetry contained in the Bible. This culture is part of my life. None of the characteristics of my work which are emphasized by Pierre Restany originated from a concept. There is nothing in my work which is a prefabricated, fixed idea. What I try to achieve is a kind of harmony. My work doesn't criticise. Peace is important to me, not in the sense of my political vision of peace, but more as a feeling. The feeling of creating a relationship, a dialogue between the elements which I encounter: between sunrise and sunset, between

the many ways that water manifests itself, between the invisible below the ground and the visible above the ground.

The first time I came to Cergy-Pontoise and was shown the axis, I asked: "Why have you chosen to realise it at this particular place? You are not touching anything specific on the horizon. The Eiffel Tower, La Défense and many other elements are in relationship to each other, but the axis just runs into the distance. We have to find a reason for it." And so we started to study the surrounding area and found out that, by extending the axis, we would come to a small island in the Seine called Ile de Chatou, the Island of the Impressionists. And it is at this point that we intersect the major historical axis of Paris. Although this is something which can't be seen at the beginning of the axis, it creates a conceptual link between the *Axe Majeur* and the great axis of Paris, and, at the same time, it underlines symbolically the historical meaning of Pointoise for the surrounding area.

What is the function of art in the public space today?

I don't think that it's art in the outside space which is particularly important. Rather, I consider all kinds of art to be important. Every kind of creation is important. Everyone should realise his way of entering into dialogue with others. When I give talks on my art, I am in the habit of stressing that this is my kind of art. It is not the only kind of art. It is one of an endless number of possibilities. I don't do what I do in accordance with some kind of preconceived idea. It's much more the constant search to find a way; a search which is influenced by encounters, sometimes by projects which are planned or have already been realised, by reactions to my work. People will judge my work, today and in the future. It will continue to exist or not, that's something I don't know.

In one respect I feel that I have a special responsibility: as long as I work in my studio, my art is my private affair. Once I receive public funding and build for the public, I have a responsibility towards the public. I am, in this respect, in the same situation as architects and landscape architects. On the other hand, I am still a sculptor who designs usable objects which are judged by the criteria of form, material, light, shadow and the interaction of these aspects.

As an artist, do you encounter particular difficulties when you create usable objects? I am thinking, for example, of all the statutory safety requirements which have to be complied with.

I certainly try to keep to all the legal regulations. I'm often told that this or that detail will be impossible to achieve, and I prove that it can be done. When I installed the large set of steps at "documenta 6" in Kassel in 1977, I was very worried that someone would fall off as there weren't any railings. The organisers tried to prohibit visitors from ascending the steps and cor-

The thirty-six metre *Tour Belvédère* is the starting point of the *Axe Majeur*. The square tower of 3.60 m side lenghts illustrates, as do many other elements along the axis, Karavan's use of number symbolism.

At night the course of the *Axe Majeur* is marked by an argon laser beam.

Dani Karavan

doned off the access, but people just simply removed the barrier and climbed the steps. "documenta" was on for one hundred days, and there were always people on the stairs. I asked the people in Kassel who were responsible for the exhibition. "How many people fell over on the streets of Kassel during this period?" "A lot", was the reply I got. "Why don't you close the streets then? People didn't fall off the staircase, they fell over on the streets." When building a design, it's my responsibility to make sure that nothing happens to people. For example, people can walk on the *Negev Monument* and there are points where they could easily fall. This is something people realise and they're careful.

Of course, I do have problems with fire safety regulations and other kinds of laws. I don't see these as being serious restrictions, I think they're okay. No artist and no form of art is entirely free from restrictions. Even a piece of paper is a restriction. You are restricted by the colours you buy as you won't, for example, ever find the shade of red which you instinctively feel is the right one. If you want to be absolutely free, you can't create art. I think you need certain limitations. If you don't want to accept them, you'll have to try and overcome them. You will have to try to tear up the paper or cut it into small pieces or look for a new piece or try to change its form. After a while, you may decide to create the best you can using the given format.

I have a lot of problems of this kind, far more than some other artists, as I have to work with so many different institutions. In terms of Cergy-Pontoise this means municipal authori-ties, politicians, the ministry of cultural affairs, the French president and the people who are carrying out the work for me – the firms which won the bidding for a particular piece of work: they don't have anything to do with art, they just want to earn money. They don't under-stand that three millimetres are sometimes important for my work. I have to work with all of them, have to explain to them what matters, have to find a way to argue with them and, at the same time, to keep them on my side.

In this respect the difference between working in the natural environment and working in the city is not so great. I'm never completely free. I was possibly free when I created the *Negev Monument* because nobody interfered when I was creating the form. Nobody asked me if it really was possible to realise this project. The only problems I had were of a financial nature. I was working with a group of people who were determined to go for it.

The spatial situation in the natural envir-onment is not the same as in the confined space of a city. Doesn't this affect the way you work?

Definitely. Spatial integration is one of my most difficult tasks as an artist. It's not so easy to find the right answer to this question and to the requirements. The reason for this is that many different reactions are possible.

Are there other landscape artists whose work you think particularly highly of?

Yes, I believe that the work of Newton Harrison and Helen Mayer Harrison is very important. I have perhaps even been influenced by the ecological approach of their art. They have given me more freedom because they showed me that it's possible to realise such things. Another artist whom I met in New York is Agnes Denes.

She works with nature a lot and created the *Wheatfield Battery Park City* in Manhattan in 1982.[1] I like many of the nature-based works of Robert Morris – and Robert Smithson should be mentioned here, and of course Michael Hei-zer. I like some of the work of James Turrell a lot, especially his *Roden Crater* project in Ari-zona. I liked the works which George Trakas, Richard Fleischner and Alice Aycock did as part of "documenta 6".

[1] Cf. p. 34

Have you ever worked with any of these artists?

Yes, a few times. I worked with them at "documenta 6" and at the sculpture park of the Villa Celle, which is near Pistoia in Italy. Maybe you know the project in Tuscany. It's a beautiful private sculpture park by Giuliano Gori which contains a large number of excellent works including, for example, some fine pieces by Richard Serra.

How does an artist from another cultural background come to terms with the situation in Europe?

Of course, here my Jewish heritage plays an important role. I belong to a culture which was forced to move from one part of Europe to the next over a period of two thousand years. The attempt to assimilate to the way of life in each individual country is as much part of this culture as is the flexibility to adapt to the immediate environment in question. My family also moved around a lot until they eventually came to Central Europe. My father was born in Galicia and the family moved to Manchester when he was one year old. His parents spoke Polish, German and Yiddish, but his mother tongue was English. He heard all these languages at home. He returned to Poland before the First World War when Poland was still part of the Austro-Hungarian Empire, and, at the age of eighteen, he arrived in Israel. I feel that this information is stored in my genes. Perhaps this makes it easier for me to understand different cultures and to feel at home in them.

How do you come to terms with German-Jewish history when you work in a place like Nuremberg?

Actually, I never wanted to work in Germany. I refused to work in Germany until 1977 when Manfred Schneckenburger invited me to take part in "documenta 6" in Kassel. I took part without really knowing why – perhaps it was the prospect of working in the international art scene. Then I got my first commissions in Germany. It wasn't easy for me, as I wasn't sure if I was invited because I was a good artist or because I was Jewish and people wanted to ease their conscience. Is it just attractive to have a Jewish artist from Israel working in Germany, or are people really convinced by my work? This is a doubt which will be with me all my life – despite the fact that I know in some way that they are convinced by my art.

At the time I didn't want the Nuremberg commission at all. I don't normally take part in competitions, and I hoped that my design wouldn't win. But I was given the project and I am very glad that I had the opportunity to realise it, because I feel that it is an important project. Nobody called on me to do something on human rights as this was not the issue; each artist was free to decide what he wanted to do. Human rights were not the first thing that came to my mind in Nuremberg. I was mainly con-

cerned with finding a formal solution for the street. It was only then that I had the idea of human rights for Nuremberg.

Despite being happy that the project was realised, I still have doubts as to whether it hasn't, after all, helped the Germans to ease their consciences. Perhaps I shouldn't have done it. It is not my job to ease other people's conscience.

I don't intend to realise a Holocaust Monument in Germany. It wouldn't matter what the commission was, I wouldn't accept it, because I don't think it is something I'm supposed to do. And I will always have my doubts, just as I have my

doubts about all my work. Not just on account of my Jewish background. I have my doubts as to whether Cergy-Pontoise is good, whether I have done the right thing, whether I should have done things differently. There are very many things that I will always have my doubts about. I will leave this world with doubts and questions, not with answers.

Dorfplatz (Village Square), an environment in Horgen, Switzerland, was realised in 1995 as part of a project to convert a farm into a communication centre. The unconventional site is in marked contrast to the style of the farmyard. The neon-lit column to measure time, the watercourse of strict architectural proportions and a small amphitheatre in light concrete are unmistakable elements of Dani Karavan's formal repertoire.

Biography and Selected Works

Dani Karavan was born in Tel Aviv on 7th December 1930.
He lives and works in Tel Aviv and Paris.
He studied painting in Tel Aviv and at the Bezalel Academy in Jerusalem.
Member of a kibbutz until 1955.

1956–1957 Studied fresco technique at the Accademia delle Belle Arti in Florence and drawing at the Académie de la Grande Chaumière in Paris

1960–1973 Designed sets for several theatre and dance groups in Israel and Italy and for the Martha Graham Dance Company in New York

Selected projects realised in outside space:

1962–1964 Wall relief in concrete for the Weizmann Institute of Sciences at Rehovot, Israel

1962–1967 Wall reliefs and design of inner courtyard for the Palace of Justice in Tel Aviv

1963–1968 *Negev Monument*, environment of concrete, desert acacias, windchimes, sun lines and water, Beersheba, Israel

1965–1966 Wall relief in stone for the plenary chamber of the Knesset, Jerusalem

1969–1970 Environment of stone, metal balls and olive trees for the square in front of the Danish School in Jerusalem

1972 Monument to the victims of the Holocaust, Weizmann Institute of Sciences, Rehovot, Israel

1976 *Environment for Peace*, Israeli Pavilion, 38th Biennial in Venice

1977 *Environment of Natural Materials and Memories*, documenta 6, Kassel, Germany

1977–1988 *Kivar Levana*, environment in Wolfsohn Park, Tel Aviv

1978 *Two Environments for Peace* and laser installation, Forte di Belvedere, Florence, and Castello dell'Imperatore, Prato

1979–1986 *Ma'alot*, environment in front of the Wallraf-Richartz-Museum/ Museum Ludwig, Cologne

1980 Commencement of work on the *Axe Majeur* of Cergy-Pontoise

1989–1994 *Weg der Menschenrechte*, Germanisches Nationalmuseum, Nuremberg

1990–1994 *Passages*, environment in memory of Walter Benjamin at Port Bou, Spain

1994 Memorial in honour of the inmates of the Gurs concentration camp, Southern France

1995 *Dorfplatz*, environment for the further training centre of the Schweizerische Kreditanstalt in Horgen, Switzerland

1993–1995 Environment for UNESCO, Paris

Selected Bibliography

Barzel, Amnon. *Art in Israel*. Milano, 1988
Bott, Gerhard, editor. Dokumentation. Germanisches Nationalmuseum, Nürnberg, 1989
Duby, Georges. *Cergy-Pontoise 1969–1989, "L' Axe Majeur."* Paris, 1989
Kampf, Avram. *From Chagall to Kitaj – Jewish Experience in 20th Century Art*. Barbican Art Gallery, London, 1990 (catalogue)
Restany, Pierre. *Dani Karavan*. Munich, 1992
Schneckenburger, Manfred. "Dani Karavan." In *L' Art et la Ville. Urbanisme et Art Contemporain*. Secrétariat Général des Villes Nouvelles, editor. Genève, 1990
Töpper, Barbara. "Dani Karavan und Frédéric Bettermann." In *Bildhauerzeichnungen des Wilhelm-Lehmbruck-Museums Duisburg*. Duisburg, 1991 (catalogue)

Acknowledgements

Kindly provided by the artist:
Andreas Heym: 83 l.
Constantinos Ignatiadis: 81
Michel Jaouën: 83 r.
Dani Karavan: 72, 74
Kumasegawa: 75 l., 79, 80 l.
Roman Mensing: 84
Gil Percal: 73, 75 r.
Alex Rubinschon: 85
Peter Szmuk: 71, 76/77
as well as:
Rita Weilacher: 78, 80 r., 82

Mare Nostrum, the name the Romans gave to the Mediterranean. "Large trees fill *Little Sparta* with the sound of the sea." Ian Hamilton Finlay

Poetry in Nature Unredeemed – Ian Hamilton Finlay

At the time when Ian Hamilton Finlay and his wife Sue moved into the small ruined farmhouse of Stonypath near the Pentland Hills in the Scottish Lowlands, the overgrown property of over one and half hectares was surrounded by bleak moorland. Today visitors walk along an uneven track and, after climbing three gates and passing the grazing land for the sheep, emerge into a lush, paradise-like garden. The finely balanced composition of works of art and magnificent displays of flowers immediately captivate visitors. Over a period of three decades, Ian Hamilton Finlay, who was born in 1925 and 30 years ago already had an international reputation as an exponent of concrete poetry, has created a very personal and intricate poetic garden. With the passing of time and as a consequence of passionate battles against total secularization of our culture, his garden has assumed neoclassical features.

Finlay's neoclassicism is far from being a superficially aesthetic imitation of classical forms, but is the consequence of his programme for "Neoclassical Rearmament", which dates back to 1978 and which he considers to be crucial in view of the serious general decline in our cultural values. For Finlay the classical tradition is essential as it is based on the conviction that man as a cultural being may not submit to untamed nature. It was at this time that Stonypath was renamed *Little Sparta*. In a figurative sense, this name stands for opposition to the fashionable superficiality of much of today's art. Finlay lives this opposition with convincing seriousness, and he does not shrink from any confrontation when it is a question of adopting a clear stance against the widespread trend towards political correctness. The persistence with which he defended *Little Sparta* in 1983 in his dispute with the local inland revenue office, which wanted to tax his garden temple as a building used for commercial purposes, is evidence of the unshakeable determination of the artist to resist secular forces.

The art of this dissenting artist draws on the entire repertoire of European cultural history. In particular he regards the French Revolution as a perfect example of the

The Garden, Little Sparta

1 Entrance to Front Garden
2 Roman Garden
3 Henry Vaughan Walk
4 Sunk Garden
5 Mare Nostrum
6 Raspberry Camouflage
7 Sundial (Fragments/Fragrance)
8 Julie's Garden
9 'Das grosse Rasenstück'
10 Temple Pool
11 Temple of Philemon and Baucis
12 Lararium
13 Allotment (Epicurean) Garden
14 Pacific Air War Inscribed Stone
15 C. D. Friedrich Pyramid
16 Claudi Bridge
17 Xaipe after J. C. Reinhart
18 Grotto of Aeneas and Dido
19 Hypothetical Gateway to an Academy of Mars
20 Hillside Pantheon
21 'Silver Cloud'
22 Virgil's Spring
23 Upper Pool
24 Middle Pool
25 Apollo and Daphne
26 Nuclear Sail
27 Lochan Eck
28 Hegel Stile
29 Midway Inscription
30 'The Present Order ...'
31 Laugier's Hut
32 Saint-Just's Column
33 O Tannenbaum
34 Tristram's Sail (Sundial)
35 Garden Temple
36 Monument to The First Battle of Little Sparta

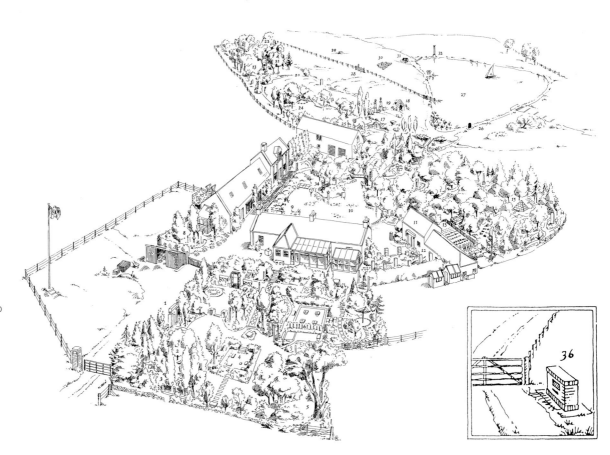

dialectic of culture and nature, of reason and terror. As a poet, Ian Hamiliton Finlay contributes his own layer of meaning to the landscape by adding to the garden context poems, aphorisms and quotations cut in stone — metaphors meant to create associations and interpretations on the part of the visitor. For example, he had the words of the French revolutionary, Louis-Antoine Saint-Just, cut in individual blocks of stone word for word: *THE PRESENT ORDER IS THE DISORDER OF THE FUTURE SAINT-JUST*. The work was executed by the sculptor Nicholas Sloan. Anyone able to move the stones would be in a position to keep changing the meaning of this quotation. In the sense of an open work, this game enables the beholder to keep changing the perspective, to experience new meanings, to understand "revolution". The conventional standpoints of contemporary thinking are suddenly no longer unalterable. However, Finlay rejects intellectual indoctrination and does not force the visitor to enter into dialogue with his works; he merely offers a possibility for critical reflection.

Finlay's garden *Little Sparta* is like a luxuriant, verdant island in the middle of the sparse vegetation of the moors and grazing land of the Pentland Hills in Scotland.

THE PRESENT ORDER IS THE DISORDER OF THE FUTURE SAINT-JUST
A quotation of the French revolutionary, Louis-Antoine Saint-Just (1767–1794), cut in blocks of stone in 1983, with Nicholas Sloan.

Plan of the stone monument *The Present Order*. Finlay's instructions: "Cut around out-lines. Arrange words in order."

Ian Hamilton Finlay

Ian Hamilton Finlay's garden contains a few examples of military symbolism, caustically revealing his contemporary interpretation of Arcadia: a small sculpture of an aircraft-carrier evokes the Second World War while serving as a harmless bird-table. In the charming setting of Lochan Eck *Nuclear Sail* emerges: a stone replica of the conning tower of a nuclear submarine, a symbol of the huge threat which lies beneath the surface. Finlay is not afraid to use symbols of the Nazi dictatorship, employing them to express that beneath the visible surface of the pastoral tranquility of Arcadia lies a battlefield upon which not only death, but also violent death and murder once held sway. What matters to Ian Hamilton Finlay is open discussion of the social taboos of our time. He goes to the very heart of the problem zones of a society in which repression and amnesia are practised, in which the traditional mechanisms of enlightenment are no longer effective. It is hardly surprising that this kind of open criticism meets with rejection as it threatens to shake the foundations of the bourgeois weltanschauung.

Nuclear Sail, the conning tower of a submarine, cut in stone, was created in 1974 in collaboration with John Andrew. The small lake Lochan Eck had been dammed a few years earlier.

The works which Finlay has been having realised throughout the world for many years reveal the unmistakable characteristics of his poetry. They increase our perceptive ability, also in as far as our own cultural history is concerned. One of the early and most impressive projects outside *Little Sparta* is the work *Five Columns for the Kröller-Müller*, which came into being in the sculpture park of the Kröller-Müller Museum near Otterlo in the Netherlands in 1982. Here, in conjunction with Sue Finlay and the sculptor Nicholas Sloan, the artist provided five existing trees with half-section column bases, which had the effect of transforming the living trees into neoclassical columns. Each plinth bears a name which, for Finlay, is closely associated with the French Revolution: *LYCURGUS*, the legendary lawmaker of Sparta; *ROUSSEAU*, the philosopher who paved the way for revolution; *MICHELET*, the historian; *ROBESPIERRE*, the advocate of revolution; and *COROT*, the impassioned neoclassical landscape painter. Yet *Five Columns for the Kröller-Müller* has two further levels of meaning, to which Finlay makes reference by giving the work a fur-

The NAUTILUS submarine emerges among the hostas in the *Roman Garden* at *Little Sparta*.

ther two titles. The second title *A Fifth Column for the Kröller-Müller* interprets the work as a subversive contribution to modern sculpture and modern sculpture parks. The third title *Corot – Saint-Just* is an expression of Finlay's ideal of the indissoluble link between artistic vision and visionary politics, between aesthetics and ethics. Thus Finlay's installation is not only an example of a cultural appropriation of nature which puts the scientific, rational view of the world into perspective. The Sacred Grove is also a contemporary monument to heroes by a self-confessed adherent of classical ideals. *Five Columns for the Kröller-Müller* is closely linked with the spirit of Stowe, the Temple of British Worthies by William Kent.

Little Sparta also contains references to classical garden art: as in the case of the English landscape garden at Stourhead, where in the eighteenth century Henry Hoare used the ideal landscapes by Claude Lorrain and the poems of Virgil as his model, Ian Hamilton Finlay makes visible images which are rooted in the mind of the beholder and influence his thoughts and actions.

"So what can garden art in general learn from him? Our conventional gardens are, as it were, naive," concludes Swiss sociologist Lucius Burckhardt. "Because flowers are beautiful, they are planted en masse; because ponds and hills are delightful, bulldozers

Five Columns for the Kröller-Müller or *A Fifth Column for the Kröller-Müller* or *Corot – Saint-Just*, Rijksmuseum Kröller-Müller in Otterlo, 1982, with Sue Finlay, stones with Nicholas Sloan. Half-section column bases of classical proportions have been placed against trunks of five trees. Each column base bears a name which has a connection with the French Revolution: LYCURGUS, ROUSSEAU, ROBESPIERRE, MICHELET and COROT. "Tree column base" is Finlay's name for these neoclassical columns. They represent subversive criticism of modern sculpture and modern sculpture gardens, hence the title *A Fifth Column*. The third title *Corot – Saint-Just* reveals Finlay's idealized link between aesthetics and ethics.

are brought in and flat ground turned into minigolf topographies. In contrast, what Finlay teaches us is reflective gardening: gardening must be based upon a theory of landscape. [...] Before any first cut of the spade, the attempt should always be made to understand landscape without any gardening intervention. This understanding is not spontaneous and naive: our perception is culturally predetermined, and it must be guided onto the right track by intervention. This can take the form of a word or a sign: the intervention in terms of gardening is not directed towards the garden, but to our minds."[1]

[1] Burckhard, Lucius. In *Anthos* 4/84: p. 7

Ian Hamilton Finlay

When I read that you came to Stonypath in 1966, I wondered why you came to live in this relatively remote place.

My wife Sue, who I was still with at that time, and I lived at that time in a tiny house at Easter Ross, north of Inverness. We had a baby and there was no running water in the house. In those days nappies still had to be washed as there weren't any disposable ones like today. This was very difficult in a house without running water. Sue's father owned all the land around here and told us that we could live here if we wanted to. The farmhouse was in a terrible state because it had been empty for so long, but it did have running water.

Moving here obviously changed your whole life a lot.

Yes, that's true. The land around the house was still a wild moorland, where sheep grazed. But

very gradually. When I began, I had no intention of making a garden which would be renowned and which people would want to come and see. This is something which still amazes me today.

The next stage began in the early seventies when the garden was gradually taking shape. Jürgen Brenner of Brenner and Partners, a firm of architects in Stuttgart, just happened to spend his summer holidays in Scotland. He already knew my poetry because every year he published a kind of anthology of art and poetry and had included some of my works in it. So when he came and saw the garden he told me about his design for the *garden of the Max Planck Institute in Stuttgart* and asked me if I would like to do something for the garden.

I said that I would love to, and I designed the works together with my friend Ron Costley. Jürgen Brenner had all the works made in

Ian Hamilton Finlay

Inscription at the *Temple Pool*, 1969, with the sculptor Maxwell Allan.

Garden Temple and *Temple Pool* at *Little Sparta*. Finlay sees the *Garden Temple* as being in the tradition of the "Musaea" in ancient Greece and of the garden temples in the great English Landscape Gardens.

whatever situation one is in, one should make the best of it and use the possibilities that exist in that particular situation. Had we been in another situation, I can imagine I'd have done something totally different such as writing books, making films or something. I knew nothing about gardening. In fact, I was more ignorant and naive than you can possibly imagine. Yet once I began with the garden, I was gripped by a kind of vision, although I can't really say where it came from. It was like something outside of me which came into me and was very engrossing. The idea of placing artefacts in the landscape seemed to complement my interest in concrete poetry.

We were incredibly poor then and, for a long time, all that I had was a spade. Even now we're still greatly hindered by lack of money. Everything had to go along very, very slowly. In a way this was perhaps fortunate because as long as I was still learning it was quite good to proceed

Germany by German craftsmen. This commission was a big step forward for me. A few years later the director of the *Kröller-Müller Museum* in Otterlo came to see me and invited me to create something for the garden of the museum.

What were the first steps you took towards creating your garden?

You have to imagine how desolate it was, there was only one tree and, although there was running water, there were no pools or anything. So I began by digging a square hole in the front, which became the *Sunk Garden*. I dug an irregular hole at the back, which eventually became the *Temple Pool*. I added things whenever I could find the money. The garden proceeded as a series of what I call corners and little areas. Usually each little area gets a small artefact, which reigns like a kind of presiding deity or spirit of the place. The artefact was sometimes very small, but it had a part to play in the composition. My understanding is that the work is not the artefact, the work is the whole composition.

Until the Second World War a garden was understood as an amalgam of plants, trees, art and architecture. The problem now is that everything is split up. And that's why today there is a ghastly phenomenon called the sculpture park, and then there's the posh plant garden or the botanical garden or a diluted neo-Impressionist garden with a lot of coloured flowers. But these are not really satisfactory as compositions. The decisive feature of traditional gardens was, in my opinion, the existence of disparate elements to work with. Of course, when you have these elements, you don't always need to compose in the same way. The language used in a garden can vary greatly.

When I started to put the inscriptions and artefacts into the garden, it was very difficult for me because I just didn't know how to do it. I used to spend wet afternoons going through the Yellow Pages, hoping to find someone who knew how to do it. But I never found anybody. And then when I started working with lettercutters, I thought that they would know, but they didn't. They knew how to make a tombstone for a client, but they had no further interest in what happened to their work after it left their workshop. I was left with the baffling feeling that there must be a set of rules or somebody to guide me. Sometimes I was literally not able to sleep for worry, and I used to go into the garden in my dressing-gown at three o'clock in the morning and desperately wonder how I would ever find the right way of doing it.

Anyway, little by little I learned how to do it on

One of the many sundials at *Little Sparta* which bears an inscription. Finlay sees sundials as being a successful linking of philosophy, poetry and crafts.

Have you ever concerned yourself with classical garden art at any time?

I've never had the possibility of seeing these famous historical gardens. When I started the garden here, I tried to learn from books on gardens, very few of which were in existence then. Another way I came into contact with gardens was through my father. He was from the country near Edinburgh, and my grandfather was the forester or the head of the sawmill, I'm not sure which, on the estate of Hopetoun House, which is a famous classical building set in magnificent neoclassical gardens. My uncle was night-watchman at the big house, and I used to go there sometimes to stay with my aunt. I would suppose that I gained my first impressions from this place. Anyway, the idea of the neoclassical garden was always quite easy for me to understand. It somehow seemed to be a part of me.

my own, then came the vexed question of how to put language into nature. I started with sundials because nobody would ever question the presence of words on a sundial. Then I realised that you could also put words on benches because people often donate benches to parks and have their names inscribed on them. Gradually, I built up a kind of language. The plaque on the tree was a further possibility which I discovered. Then came the tree-column base, which like the half-section column base is placed at the foot of the tree. I don't know if there are any historical precedents for this; maybe one day I'll read a book on Roman garden art and see that this has already been done by somebody. It seems such a natural thing to me. And once you have discovered something, you can expand it. In other words, it's really only a question of building up a language.

A comparison of your garden with classical landscape gardens reveals certain parallels. As far back as the eighteenth century the works and sculptures in a garden were an indication of the political affiliations of its owner and his conception of the world.

Yes, that's true. It was a question of a certain political programme. You have to remember that many of the people who designed the great English gardens were exiles and that's why they created their gardens. For example, they were people who had been thrown out of parliament or disgraced or were against the regime. The garden might not have had a revolutionary character, but it was certainly an expression of op-

As in *Adam und Eva* by Albrecht Dürer, the *Woodland Garden* contains a plaque in the boughs of the trees which bears the initials "AD". 1980, with the sculptor Nicholas Sloan.

Elegiac inscription at the *Upper Pool*, 1975, with John Andrew. "See" Poussin is a reference to the well-thought-out architectural and natural forms in Nicolas Poussin's paintings, whereas "Hear" Lorrain underlines the lyrical elements which are characteristic of the classical landscape paintings of Claude Lorrain.

position. The garden wasn't, in a political sense, a reflection of contemporary culture, but in an aesthetic way it was. Perhaps that's why it's so difficult today. After all, modern art doesn't fit into gardens very well because hard-edge art doesn't fit into gardens well. Taking the example of the *Kröller-Müller Museum*, I know that they have to do an enormous amount of restoration work on the sculptures every winter. At Stowe and in other landscape gardens this is not so much a problem as the works are of a kind which can assimilate weathering.

The crisis of our age is the crisis of secularisation, where everything is reduced to a banal level. This has happened to the garden, too, and has led to the splitting up of the elements

Ian Hamilton Finlay

I already referred to. Sculpture parks are usually badly composed and run by people who come from museums and have no idea that outdoor space is not the same as indoor space. The works are put on top of the ground and not in the landscape. This degree of ignorance never ceases to amaze me. And yet our age considers that it is environment-conscious. I don't think any age has ever understood the environment less than ours.

The way in which you have realised your garden in the midst of what was once a desolate area conveys the impression that yours is an idealised counter-world.

My purpose was to create something harmonious and serious, but, of course, also something with wit. It occurs to me that classicism is a problem for people. Yet I can't see it as a problem. For example, when people talk about the French Revolution, they talk as if it's something which has absolutely nothing to do with them, not only because it took place so long ago. I don't feel this at all. Even when I read the Pre-Socratics such as Heraclitis or Parmenides, I don't have the feeling that I'm reading something which was written nearly two thousand years ago. To me this is something which is still very much alive and present, whereas what is uppermost in most people's minds is that this is very far away and different.

I have the same feeling about art. I don't know if it's still this way today, but when I was younger, people in Scotland used to worry about being artists. They kept asking what is art and how can I justify being an artist. I never had such worries. I have always understood what art is, that it's something very powerful and real and natural to people. So if something is not a problem for you, it's very difficult to explain it.

Ten or fifteen years ago I was obsessed with the idea of having to fight the complete secularisation of our culture. My life seemed to consist of a series of battles. Now that the secularisation has been achieved, it's everywhere. Ten or fifteen years ago it was at a much earlier stage, and it was possible to isolate the problem and talk about it. But now that it's everywhere, I don't feel the same way. The fact that it is everywhere seems to mean you can't do anything about it any longer. It was from this awareness of problems that my great battle with Strathclyde Region came about. They're taking me to court this month. Actually, I wish they'd taken me to court ten years ago. Then it was all real to me, but now it's something which is over. I had the feeling that I won this battle, but they didn't concede defeat. And there's nothing more difficult than trying to win a battle twice. You see, you can only seriously fight and win battles which are crucial to you.

What are the problems which do matter to you today?

The problem for me is the realisation that you can't speak about the problems of our time.

And if you could speak about them, you'd be condemned. Apart from this, our time hasn't actually got any vocabulary for speaking about our problems. Political correctness is a vocabulary which has usurped the true vocabulary with which we could speak about our own time. Political correctness is like a substitute or the secularisation of morality, in a certain way it's even the end of morality. We'll probably only be able to speak properly about our own time twenty, thirty or forty years from now. But what I'm sure about – and I can only say it in this clichéd way – is that we'll speak about the trivialisation, the vulgarisation, the secularisation of everything. What has happened in our culture and our society is what I call the destruction of piety. Not only in terms of our behaviour, but even the whole concept of piety.

So what would you say are the most important ingredients in your garden?

Tact and a certain ability to compose. Unfortunately these things are never talked about, as harmony as the content of something is very difficult to write about. After you've said something is harmonious, what else can you say? Harmony may be the most important thing, but it's easier to write about things which are seemingly problematical. Then it's easier to find lots of words.

Coming back to nature, how do you define your own idea of nature?

On the one hand, for me nature is the realm of the tragic, of destruction but, on the other hand, it's what Rousseau understood by it. It's interesting that Rousseau never really defined nature, but only used it as the opposite of the artificial. He used it as a way of exposing the artificial and condemning the artificial, it's the good which he set against the bad. I feel the same, I can use nature like Rousseau or as the raw material of an ideal landscape. But nature is also the realm of the tragic and normally I oppose nature and culture. Of course, there's quite a lot of nature in my garden. In contrast with the way a lot of people nowadays use it, nature is not, for me, the ultimate expression of the good.

Many new kinds of trees which are surprisingly heterogeneous are being planted in your garden. Why is this?

The basic idea of my garden is a grove, which for me is a kind of Platonic form. The garden is organized in such a way that you first have to go through the front garden and then the woodland garden before you suddenly come to the open landscape. This effect is very important, and I'm quite aware of it, but I haven't deliberately created this experience. I just make use of the natural landscape.

For me the grove is a basic element of the garden as it gives you lots of possibilities for composition. The trees are clearly nature, but the

Moss-covered stepping-stones and marsh marigolds in flower at the *Middle Pool*. One of the first stones bears an inscription which resembles a dictionary entry: RIPPLE, n. A FOLD, A FLUTING OF THE LIQUID ELEMENT.

grove isn't nature, it's cultural. The grove has a long cultural history. What I find so sad about suburban gardens is that they never include a grove. You can have a grove in even a very small garden, and it will give people great pleasure. There is something about a grove which is really wonderful, perhaps it's this Platonic concept. So in my garden nature becomes part of the art, and it's also still present as nature, but only on condition that it is incorporated into the art.

So would it be possible to place your artistic installations in a natural landscape, thereby defining the natural landscape as a cultural landscape?
Yes, it would. Taking the example of adding a stone plaque to a tree, when you put the plaque against the bark of the trunk, you become very conscious of the stone and its formal aspect, and you become equally aware of the bark and leaves of the tree. The objects give each other definition, and then it's no longer just a question of nature.

On the Path of Language, Little Sparta, 1990, with the sculptor Keith Bailey.

As we have hardly any untouched nature left in Central Europe but mainly only cultural landscape, it is difficult to be clear about the precise differences.
A famous example of this confusion is Julie's garden in the "Nouvelle Héloise" by Rousseau. Was this garden nature or not nature? It certainly looked like nature, but it wasn't nature because it was something made to look like nature. This should be the great model for European landscape architects. Today you sometimes see works of so-called art and they look as if they are untouched by human hand, and this seems to me utter nonsense. It is a complete renunciation of culture in favour of nature.

Lucius Burckhardt likes to describe your garden as the grammatical context for your one-word poems.
The point about the one-word poem as I define it is that it consists of a title, which can be of any length, plus one word. It's not just one word.

You can't make a poem of one word, there has to be a relationship. I can imagine putting a one-word poem in the garden, but I've not done it so far. It's conceivable that, instead of the title, you could use pine-trees or something similar, but the word always needs a relationship, and culture has to be the point of reference.

The objects in your garden attract attention and, in particular, the language and words communicate to visitors directly.
People always think that the work is the artefact, but that's not right: the work is the artefact in its context. The work is a composition and the composition is not an isolated object, but an object with trees, plants, flowers, water and so on. This should be clear, but what happens is that everybody always points their camera straight at the artefact. This always reminds me of a story about Mondrian in which somebody asked him about right angles in his works. His reply was: "Right angles? I see no right angles!"

Reading about the way your garden has changed over the decades gives the impression that the dispute with Strathclyde Region, which began around 1970, marked a very decisive turning-point. For example that was the time that Stonypath was renamed *Little Sparta*.
When I began doing things away from the garden, it became clear to me that every work turned into a battle to try to get it done properly. Everybody only thought about money and time. I was horrified that nobody cared about standards. I was driven quite frantic by the fact that things were just not done properly. It was at this point that I thought what we need is a revolution to make people think.
Then I thought about what revolutions had already taken place and I happened to find "The French Revolution" by Thomas Carlyle in the house. I became fascinated by this event, and so I started reading as much as I could about the French Revolution. I found Saint-Just very congenial to me because there was no discrepancy between his thinking and what he did. He spoke like an axe and he acted like an axe. I also found Robespierre congenial. He had to be eliminated because he was convinced that democracy couldn't exist without spirituality and piety. I became aware of a universal problem, namely that intellectuals, who were able to understand something, had no idea of how to put their ideas into practice. In other words, you couldn't count on them in any way.
I experienced an example of this when a London publisher wanted to publish a third edition of my poems. After I'd signed the contract, he told me that he wanted to publish the book as a first edition. I told him quite clearly that the book was a third edition and not a first edition. And he just laughed and told me he could make more money out of a first edition. It took me eight years and a lot of effort to get this fraud brought out into the open. I've never been

forgiven. I had done something which was awfully wrong, nobody really knew what it was, but it was something awful. It was at this time that I became aware that my garden and my work were profoundly at odds with the prevailing culture.

It was at this time that I converted what had been cow-sheds into a gallery, so that I could show visitors works that I couldn't present in either the house or outside. Then I realised that the word gallery had taken on a meaning that it didn't use to have: now it's associated with making money and the tourist industry. So that's why I called it a garden temple; this changed the nature of the building, so that instead of being a place which housed the works, the works which were present defined the place – which is something entirely different. I asked the Region if the name could be changed from gallery to garden temple and was told that this wasn't possible because "garden temple" were not words they had in their computer. You can't really laugh at bureaucracy because it's such a clichéd thing to do, but anyway I said that this was a ridiculous statement. After all, any reputable history of Western gardens contains the word garden temple and it's not put in italics or quotation-marks.

If the festivals and manifestations which David held for Robespierre could be considered to be religious ceremonies, something which is generally agreed, then my building could be considered to be a religious building. I told the Strathclyde Region that the building was exempt from tax because the law states that buildings which are used wholly or partly for religious purposes and supported by a public body are exempt from tax. I said that the public body was either the Revolutionary, neoclassical tradition as such or the Saint-Just Vigilantes, which was a partly real, partly mythical organization. Of course, this caused consternation, but I was very serious about it because I wanted to show that the whole concept of piety had disappeared from culture. Anyway, I stood my ground and, of course, I received threatening letters and then some of my works were seized and so on. The art critics were not willing to write about any of this. Nobody wrote about it in a way which revealed that what had happened had a deeper meaning, which had to be elucidated and understood.

In other words, the conflict with the Strathclyde Region was not a one-off event, but something inherent in the culture of our time.

Right. That's why I changed the nature of the garden and the building in order to be explicit. The heroic emblems appeared and I chose the name "Little Sparta" as a contrast to "Athens of the North", which is the popular name for Edinburgh. Just as my temple was intolerable to Strathclyde Region, Robespierre's piety was intolerable to many of his contemporaries. This was also the reason why he failed. Here we're

Ian Hamilton Finlay, *Apollo in George Street*, drawing by Ian Appleton for the exhibition *The Third Reich Revisited*, 1982.

very similar. I think we can all understand ourselves better through the French Revolution. The Revolution dramatised ideals and problems in a way which was real. This is something which is all very vivid to me, not at all academic.

You often make use of the symbolism of the French Revolution to represent culture and sometimes you use Nazi imagery to represent nature.

Yes, but there's nothing obscure about this. Death represented by an old man with a scythe has ceased to have any meaning for us at all. That's why I used the SS lightning flash because it has a meaning for us, but evidently more

meaning than people are willing to tolerate. I don't intend to let myself be dictated to by political correctness or fashion. Every age knows taboos from history, but it never knows what its own taboos are. Our age treats the existence of any form of power as taboo. But power is a universal principle and, while you can suppress all mentions of power, the fact of power remains.

I used to build a lot of models and if I put a swastika on the tail of a plane, nobody thought anything of it. It's only in the world of intellectuals that these signs are negated. The point is that the signs have a present-day content. That's why I substituted a submachine gun for Apollo's bow and arrow. The bow and arrow

OSSO, three pieces of marble, inscribed in collaboration with the sculptor Nicholas Sloan. The work was shown at ARC, Musée d'Art Moderne de la Ville de Paris, in 1987 and sparked off a defamatory press campaign against Finlay.

Ian Hamilton Finlay

was a very serious weapon for the Greeks, and Apollo did not have such attributes as a joke or ornamentation. Apollo stood for the spirit and innerness and this is represented by the lyre. He also stood for the other things which we don't want to see as existing in the world. We're not willing to admit that they do exist, and we don't know how to handle them. To some extent I've been aware of taboos all my life, but I've never allowed myself to be dictated to by them.

This is, of course, a risky approach. When Osso was exhibited in Paris in 1987, this sparked off a heated debate, which ended in your not being able to realise your design to commemorate the Bicentenary of the French Revolution.

I had extensive exhibition space at my disposal, which I found difficult to fill, so I built a sequence, which ended with big cubes which were associated with neo-Platonism, and began with *Osso*. *Osso* symbolised unredeemed nature, in terms of Neo-Platonic philosophy. *Osso*, which is the Italian word for bone, consists of three pieces of marble, the middle flank of which bears the SS lightning flash. So *Osso* is a broken bone. To me the SS is pure nature, unredeemed by culture, while the cubes represent the highest level of culture. This was made perfectly clear by the exhibition catalogue, but this one word was the one that stuck in people's minds.

The work was exhibited again at the Liverpool Tate Gallery in 1988, and not a single person complained about my work or raised any questions. The *Osso* which caused all the problems didn't exist, it had been invented. First it was claimed that the work consisted only of the SS sign and nothing more. Later when the exhibition went off smoothly, it was maintained that there were two *Ossos*: one which was in France and one at the Tate, but the photograph shown in the Tate catalogue is of the *Osso* in France. So why all this fuss. The same people talk about my garden as if it were full of swastikas, and they even accuse me of anti-Semitism in order to destroy me and my works.

Certain things are taboo and this depends on a very primitive mechanism. If a thing is taboo, intellectuals will not see it as part of art. Its meaning is only what is outwardly visible. For certain people a nude figure is always something pornographic. For example, Botticelli's *Venus* is nude, and therefore she's pornographic. What fascinates me is that, in my experience, ordinary people don't have these problems with taboos, it's only intellectuals. And this is very strange. Anyway, the majority of people who were accusing me knew very well that they were inventing their accusations.

Visitors to your garden are confronted by an enormous diversity of philosophical ideas and cultural references. Do you perhaps make it a little too difficult for people to understand what you mean?

No, not at all. It's only intellectuals who have problems with the garden. I assure you that many of the ordinary people who visit my garden because it's in the Good Garden Guide never have any difficulty because what they don't understand they just leave. People go to gardens expecting to be pleased. It's not the same as going to exhibitions. They don't have any problems with the garden, if they find something in Latin and they don't understand Latin, they just ignore it. I'm always amazed how pleased ordinary people are by the garden. They often leave, saying now they're going to go away and change their own gardens completely. They don't mean that they're going to put inscriptions in their gardens, but they're going to organise them in a different way.

The language of my garden is on a very democratic level, it's extremely accessible. The *Grotto of Aeneas and Dido* is actually very easy to understand. Aeneas and Dido fell in love. She was a great queen, she laid on a hunt on a hillside, there was a terrible thunderstorm, they took shelter in a cave and there they made love for the first time. This is all very easy to explain, but if it's a question of a solid cube or something, what do you say?

The more elitist, the more democratic – this is the paradox of it. Admittedly, people say there are two figures – a red one and a green one –, the red one is chasing the other one and people think the red one is Pan. I tell them that it's not Pan but Apollo, who is chasing Daphne. The beautiful nymph asks her father, the river god, to help her escape, and he turns her into a tree. This is very easy to explain, but, of course, here Apollo is very often equated with Saint-Just. So here he's not just Apollo but he's also Saint-Just chasing the ideal of a virtuous Republic, but with too much rigour, too much desire. In consequence, the ideal republic is lost and returns to nature. It's very very easy.

Although you have realised many projects all over the world, *Little Sparta* is considered to be your main work. I know you don't like this label very much.

That's right, I don't like it. I attach the same amount of importance to all my works, but of course there's not such a wealth of my works anywhere else. People always want to categorise me, so that they can say: "That's the bloke with the garden." Then that's it, and nobody thinks about your other works. I would hate to be classed as one of those fanatical people who, in a naive way, make their gardens into their whole life. I don't want people to think about me in this way. I would still like to add to my garden, if I can find the money to do so.

How do you finance your garden?

By the things that I do in other places. But I always have great trouble with money. It's very expensive to run the garden. I regret that I don't get any help from the world.

The *Aeneas and Dido Grotto* at *Little Sparta*.

APOLLON TERRORISTE, 1988,
with Alexander Stoddart.
At *Little Sparta* Apollo often
represents the French revolutionary, Saint-Just.

*IHR HOLDEN SCHWÄNE
TUNKT IHR DAS HAUPT*, from
Hälfte des Lebens by Friedrich
Hölderlin. One of nine per-
manent works for the Re-
gional Horticultural Exhibition
in Schloßpark Grevenbroich,
1995, in collaboration with
Pia Maria Simig and Horst
Ottenstein.

Ian Hamilton Finlay

There are many more pieces in your garden than I originally thought. How much more can the garden accommodate?
There's a large field which has still to be developed. It'll probably take me the rest of my life. You can achieve a great density of works if you do it tactfully. Of course, in the great English gardens there's a lot of rhetorical space, space between the individual features. This doesn't exist here. But if you do the planting judiciously, it's surprising how intricate you can make the result.

Your works are often shown in combination with the works of other artists. Are there other artists who are congenial to you or even have a similar approach?
Generally, I don't like public art very much at all. You probably know the book "Earthworks and Beyond" by John Beardsley. A lot of the works in this book are deplorable, because they don't have any sense of design. Nor do they have any sense of scale. They're just huge, without any inspiration.

really find words to describe our time. Words such as beauty, order, decency, goodness, purity are nowadays scorned all over the world as sentimental. What ever has happened?

Perhaps today people are trying to accept that all the breaks and contradictions in life are typical features, maybe even exciting ones?
The thinking behind this is that harmony has no content, but harmony is a content.

Don't lots of your artefacts depend on disharmony between form and content, or between the work and its context? I'm thinking, for example, of the warship, something you wouldn't expect to find in a garden.
You might find it unusual, but for ordinary people it's not, believe me. For ordinary visitors warships are part of the world. Tanks are part of the world. One of the main sculpture themes in

Miniaturised aircraft carriers, submarines and fighter planes characterise the ambience in the *Roman Garden* of *Little Sparta*. Work in stone in collaboration with John Andrew, 1980.

Does this mean you're not happy to be in the context of Land Art?
My work hasn't got anything to do with Land Art. The works of Richard Long are okay because they're either very ephemeral or quite modest in scale. I see myself in the tradition of the landscape garden and the garden; a big problem of modern landscape architecture is that it's not at all lyrical, and this hasn't really got anything to do with the inscriptions and so on.
I have great faith in the power of art and poetry. I was even able to make art out of the battle with the Strathclyde Region. I saw the possibility that art could impose something lyrical on this incident. Lyricism means relating things to each other in a certain kind of way. That is the art. Something strange has crept into the culture of our time. It teaches people to hate instead of to love things, to be dishonest instead of honest, to be impure instead of pure. Everything which was once of value has been discarded. I can't

Roman gardens was the Roman war-galley. War imagery was part of many historical gardens, but it's not recognised as such any more. I would say the quantity of warlike imagery in my garden is miniscule compared with the pastorale. Then again, you have to ask what a warship means. A warship is not necessarily just a warship, and a tank is not just a tank. In the *Roman Garden*, which is right next to the gate, there are lots of aircraft carriers and similar things. The point is that I wanted to make a chamber-music version of one of the great Italian gardens, a miniature. Of course, I don't have a Roman war-galley in my garden, that would be too corny. The aircraft carrier is much better because only imperial nations can afford to have them. It's the modern equivalent of the war-galley. In terms of political correctness the aircraft carrier is bad. For bird-lovers a birdtable is something good. So we have something which is both good and bad. If you put crumbs on the aircraft carrier in winter, the little birds come and then they become little planes. This is a kind of mimicry, which in the seventeenth century would have been recognised as wit. This is a work which is a crossing point for a lot of layers of meaning and ideas. I have a kind of hypothesis about this, which is not entirely serious, but it's partly serious: that camouflage for military vehicles is the ultimate form of classical landscape painting because it represents the general and not the particular. I once had a wooden model of a tank and on it

ary people are, which means a certain willingness to be pleased, or if you wish to be an intellectual, you have to really be an intellectual and not put your whole education to one side.

Sometimes things are not miniaturised, but enlarged. At the *Hypothetical Gateway to an Academy of Mars* there are two grenades on top of the pillars.

These are finials, an ornamental way of crowning a pillar, and they have their own tradition in garden history. They have very different forms, such as a simple ball, or fruit, pineapples in particular. In many eighteenth-century gardens columns were topped with pineapples. So I just added one small element, namely a ring, and I had the pineapple grenade. Seeing it in philosophical terms, it's a Heraclitean image that nature is a harmony of conflict and war is the king of all things. In terms of today's political correctness, I'll probably be accused of advocating sales of armaments. This is not what concerns me. You can still see that in nature there is a constant conflict. As soon as you start to garden, you see that every little plant is an imperialist and wants to take over the whole place. Harmony is always the precarious balance between the different elements. And you can also see the grenades in this way.

What impression of your garden should people take with them?

Most people have the impression of paradise, they experience the garden as perfectly tranquil and pleasing. If this is the impression that people have of my work, I'm more than happy.

"Et in Arcadia ego" is an indication that not everything is paradisiacal.

As you know, it's quite possible to argue about how to interpret this quotation: Poussin's painting gives expression to the elegiac aspect. Of course, you can describe my garden as being very elegiac, and even this people find peaceful. No, my problem is the intellectuals, who seem to be in a position to deny their understanding of culture. Culture is beginning to despise culture.

Hypothetical Gateway to an Academy of Mars was created at *Little Sparta* in 1991 in collaboration with David Edwick.

was painted a copy of a landscape by Poussin instead of the typical camouflage. I had another model which had a water landscape on it. One day an intellectual from Germany was here. He looked at them and told me: "I cannot stand all these 'panzers'." This is such an absurd response. Normally, it's quite true that this is a tank, but I wanted a tank because it's normally camouflaged. I liked the idea of classical landscape painting being a kind of camouflage. You either have to be open to the work in a way that ordin-

Et in Arcadia Ego, 1976, stone, 28,1 x 28 x 7,6 cm

Ian Hamilton Finlay

Biography and Selected Works

Ian Hamilton Finlay was born in Nassau, Bahamas, in 1925.
He studied at the Glasgow School of Art for a brief period in the early nineteen forties before doing national service; since then he has worked autodidactically.
After 1945 he became a shepherd and farmer on the Orkney Islands and started writing. He wrote short stories and plays.
He moved to Edinburgh, Scotland, in the late fifties and wrote his first poems around this time. Since then he has had numerous publications. He has lived and worked at Stonypath near Dunsyre, Scotland, since 1966.

Selection of projects realised in outside space:

1974–1976	Series of projects with Ron Costly; garden of the Max Planck Institute in Stuttgart, Germany
1980–1982	*Sacred Grove* with Nicholas Sloan, Kröller-Müller Museum, Otterlo, Netherlands
1983	*The Present Order is the Disorder of the Future, Saint-Just*, Stonypath, Scotland
1984	Tree plaques with Nicholas Sloan, Merian-Park, Basle, Switzerland Maritime Village, Swansea and Villa Celle, Italy
1985	*Black and White* with Nicholas Sloan, Schweizergarten, Vienna
1986–1991	Installations and plaques with Nicholas Sloan and Bob Burgoyne, Stockwood Park, Luton, England
1987	*A View to the Temple* with Keith Brookwell and Nicholas Sloan, documenta 8, Kassel, Germany *A remembrance of Annette* (von Droste-Hülshoff), sculpture projects, Münster, Germany Inscribed stone *F. Hodler*, Furka Pass, Switzerland
1989	*Stone Drums* with Michael Harvey, entrance to the Harris Museum and Art Gallery, Preston
1995	Nine works for the Regional Horticultural Exhibition in Grevenbroich/Schloßpark, Germany
Since 1966	Continual development of the garden *Little Sparta* in collaboration with various artists.

Since the late fifties numerous international one-man and group exhibitions, including:

1968	First one-man exhibition, Axiom Gallery, London
1972	Restrospective exhibition, Scottish National Gallery of Modern Art
1980–1981	*Nature Over Again After Poussin*, travelling exhibition
1984	*The British Show*, travelling exhibition by the British Council, Australia
1985	*Little Sparta & Kriegsschatz*, Espace Rameau-Chapelle Sainte Marie, Nevers, France and Eric Fabre Gallery, Paris *Reflections on the French Revolution*, Graeme Murray Gallery, Edinburgh
1987	documenta, Kassel, Germany
1988	*Contemporary British Sculpture Show*, Tate Gallery, London
1990	Kunsthalle Hamburg, Kunsthalle Basle, Switzerland *Von der Natur in der Kunst*, Messepalast, Vienna
1991	*Rhetorical Image*, Museum of Contemporary Art, New York Philadelphia Museum of Art *Konfrontationen*, Museum der Modernen Kunst, Vienna *Die Sprache der Kunst*, Kunsthalle, Vienna *Metropolis*, international exhibition, Berlin *Virtue and Vision*, Royal Scottish Academy
1992	London Institute of Contemporary Art
1993	CAYC, Buenos Aires.
1995	*Ian Hamilton Finlay. Works in Europe 1972–1995*, Deichtorhallen, Hamburg

Selected Bibliography

The best idea of the work of Ian Hamilton Finlay in the field of the visual arts is, in addition to the numerous international exhibition catalogues, provided by:
Abrioux, Yves. *Ian Hamilton Finlay. A visual primer*. London, 1992 (2nd edition)
The book also contains a very comprehensive bibliography, compiled by Pia Simig.
Further recommended reading:
Finlay, I.H. *Heroic Emblems*. Calais, Vermont, 1976
Foundation Cartier, editor. *Poursuites Révolutionnaires*. Paris, 1987
Graeme Murray Gallery, editor. *Ian Hamilton Finlay & The Wild Hawthorn Press: a catalogue raisonné, 1958–1990*. Edinburgh, 1990
Galleria Acta, editor. *Catalogue of Finlay Exhibition*. Milano, 1990
ICA London, editor. *Instruments of Revolution*. London, 1992
Bann, Stephen. "The gardens of Ian Hamilton Finlay." In Mosser, M./Teyssot, G. *The history of garden design*. London, 1990.
Chapman. Scotland's Quality Literary Magazine no. 78–79. "Ian Hamilton Finlay". Edinburgh, 1994
Crowther, Paul. "Ian Hamilton Finlay. Classicism, Piety and Nature." In Academy Group, editor. *Art and the Natural Environment*. London, 1994
Zdenek, Felix/Simig, Pia, editors. *Ian Hamilton Finlay. Works in Europe 1972–1995. Werke in Europa*. Ostfildern, 1995

Acknowledgements

Kindly provided by the artist:
Robin Gillanders: 87, 90 l., 95 r.; Werner J. Hannappel: 91, 101 bottom; Tom Scott: 103 r.; W. P. Wood: 93 l.
as well as:
Udo Weilacher: 89 top/m., 90 r., 92, 93 r., 94, 95 l., 97, 98, 100, 101 top, 102, 103 l.;
from Yves Abrioux, Ian Hamilton Finlay, A visual primer, London 1992: 99

Un air rosé, 1965. Minimal
intervention alters perception.

The Invention of Espace Propre –
Bernard Lassus

The projects which dominate contemporary French landscape architecture are
flamboyant, extravagant in both financial
and formal terms. Most of the new
parks and gardens – particularly those
in prestige-conscious Paris – were
already impressive at the design stage
on account of their artistically designed
drawings and stylised details. Much of the
ballast of traditional ideals of garden art:
economical, ecological, functional and
sociological constraints, seems to have
been cast aside. Many of these gardens
present themselves to visitors to Paris
as carefully tended jewels which *bon gré
mal gré* have to suffer daily use.
Landscape architect and artist Bernard
Lassus, professor at the Ecole Nationale
d'Architecture La Villette, has little interest in a park which is an elaborately
styled *objet d'art* created by a particular
designer. The eloquent landscape theor-
ist and "only garden thinker of our time",
as the American expert on gardens Bob
Riley called him, is far more concerned
with discovering the everyday place as a
special one. A tabula rasa place does not
exist for him. For Bernard Lassus, landscape – like *millefeuille* – consists of

many historical layers and levels of meaning superimposed upon each other, making any place potentially unique. It is a consequence of the cultural and age-related heterogeneity of our society that the individual increasingly only perceives particular levels of meaning of the garden and the landscape. Thus, the fundamental problem facing the designer of a public garden is that he has to make different ways of interpreting it possible, has to develop a complexity which enables a lover of flowers, a child at play and an expert on garden history to become aware of what makes this a special place. However, the result should neither be a superficial theme park landscape, nor should it permanently eliminate the wide variety of possibilities of the place.

Following his studies of art, his work in the studio of the painter Fernand Léger in the fifties and his kinetic works and environments in the sixties, Bernard Lassus increasingly turned his attention to a detailed analysis of the history of landscape development. His intention was to understand the basic principles of landscape perception. From the very beginning Lassus was particularly interested in the imaginative motifs of the gardens of workers and allotment holders. His teacher Léger had also been interested in the life of the worker in the beginnings of Modernism. Lassus believes that these gardens clearly express the relationship of the individual to his environment and his inner picture of nature. In the course of a study which was conducted over a number of years at the beginning of the eighties, Lassus decoded the design language of the hobby gardener, enabling him to establish some of the most important theoretical principles of his landscape architecture. Since then, the creation of an envir-

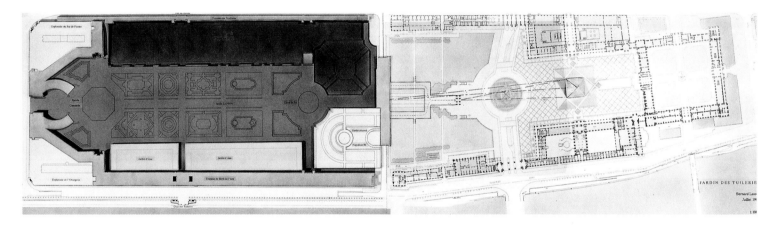

The 1990 design entered in the competition to redesign the *Tuileries* in Paris is a sensitive approach to the discordance between the axis of the Louvre and that of Le Nôtre's garden. *Axe mythique* and *axe sensible* were to be relinked.

onment with a wealth of sensuous experiences and as little intervention as possible has been one of Lassus's most important aims.

Whereas in France there is a tendency to reject this unconventional provocative thinker, many outstanding landscape architects outside France have recognised the feasibility of the strategy of "minimal intervention" and make deliberate use of it by employing gentle intervention to develop a comprehensible landscape from an accumulation of unrelated landscape fragments. Lassus considers detailed knowledge of the historico-cultural principles of landscape to be an essential prerequisite for the proper application of this principle.

The concept of stratification of landscape and Lassus' excellent knowledge of the principles of garden design are revealed in his ideas for the rehabilitation and *Redesign of the Tuileries Gardens*, which were developed in 1990. Today the major axis of Paris extends from the Arche de La Défense to the Louvre glass pyramid, designed by the architect I. M. Pei, and integrates the Tuileries Gardens into the structure of Paris in a new way. Since the demolition of the Château des Tuileries in 1882, the Gardens have been in danger of losing their identity in the shadow of grand architectural gestures. The design which Lassus entered in the competition focused on the fractures between different time levels and on the continuous metamorphosis of the garden. It was intended to enable visitors to trace the garden's development. For this purpose, an archaeologist's approach was to be adopted in order to uncover five different strata of the garden at different levels:

- the stratum of the sixteenth century, when Catherine de Médici had the magnificent garden laid out (80 cm under the present ground surface);
- the stratum of the garden during the time of the royal gardener of Henry IV, Claude Mollet (20 cm under the present ground surface);
- the stratum at the time of Le Nôtre (present level);
- the stratum of the nineteenth century (50 cm above the present level);
- the stratum of the contemporary era (170 cm above the present level).

As historical documentation of the different designs is often fragmentary, Lassus proposed adopting three strategies: restoring the parts of the garden which had been preserved or were well-documented, rehabilitating the oldest stratum for which only fragmentary documentation is available, and the coherent reinventing of the parts of which nothing is known any more or of which nothing is yet known – for example the contemporary stratum, which is to provide space for a broad range of activities. What Lassus was aiming to do was neither to create a perfectly restored garden to be put under a preservation order, nor was he interested in a design which completely

Bernard Lassus planned the *Tuileries*, which lie between the Arc du Carrousel in the foreground of the perspective view and the Arche de la Défense, as a *jardin stratifié*. Historical strata of garden art were to be restored, rehabilitated or reinvented.

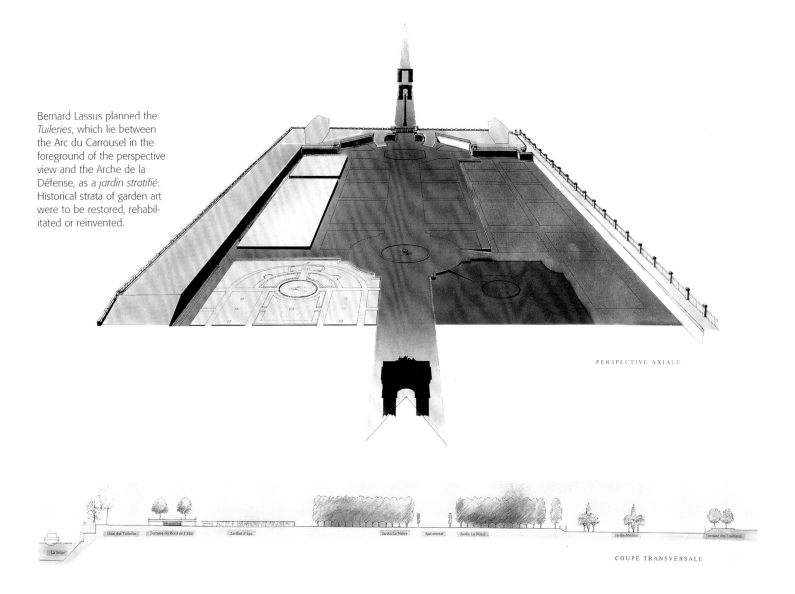

PERSPECTIVE AXIALE

COUPE TRANSVERSALE

transformed the site. Visitors were to have the possibility of experiencing directly the diversity and inner structure of the temporal and spatial intertwining of the strata, the garden's unique potential as a cultural monument and contemporary space. Lassus's plan was not selected despite, or perhaps because of its ambitious nature.

Stephen Bann considers Bernard Lassus to be the only artist who has succeeded in developing a new poetics of landscape.[1] Lassus has demonstrated the implications

[1] Bann, S. "From Captain Cook to Neil Armstrong." In *Projecting the Landscape*, edited by J. C. Eade. Canberra, 1987

Bernard Lassus

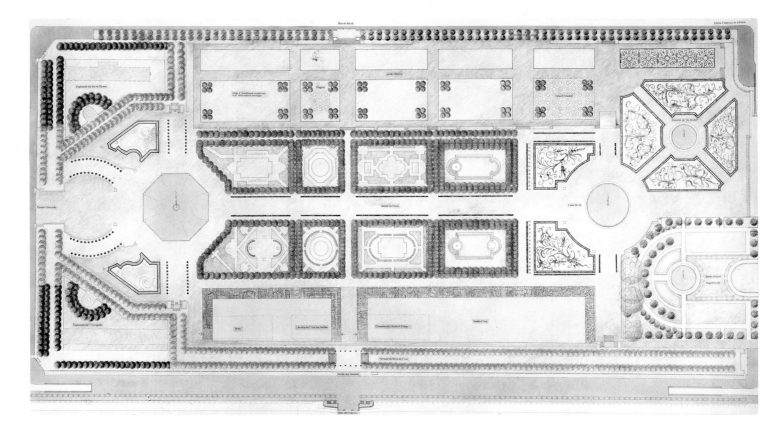

of his theoretical conception in many designs entered in competitions and proposals for projects and has won numerous national and international awards. The acknowledged originality of the projects, however, prevented their actual realisation in many cases. Realisation of the competition design for the *Parc de la Corderie Royale* in Rochefort-sur-Mer is thus something of an exception; the *rest area of Nîmes-Caissargues* is another of the very few major designs of the last ten years to be actually realised and shows the range of landscape design issues which Lassus addresses in practice. However, the real strength of his work lies in his intensive theoretical study of the phenomenon of natural environment and landscape. He has laid important foundations for the future of garden art.

The vision of Bernard Lassus: The *Tuileries* as an archaeological window revealing the history of the place with the addition of elements of modern garden art. The design which was entered in the international competition held in 1990 was not chosen.

Professor Lassus, you had a strong relationship to art when you began your career. You studied painting under Fernand Léger in 1950 and today you work as a landscape architect. How do you reconcile the dichotomy between art and landscape architecture?

It's quite simple. Art and landscape architecture are the same thing for me. There's no difference. The problem which many landscape architects have is that they lack any training in aesthetics. They don't know what an invention is; in order to understand the nature of invention, you need training in aesthetics. Garden artists such as Le Nôtre had training in painting. William Kent, the great English garden artist, was a painter, and so was Roberto Burle Marx. Many good landscape architects have excellent aesthetic training. Of course, theoretical knowledge and social awareness are also important. Someone who has never had the possibility of understanding the nature of open spaces which are of social relevance cannot become a landscape architect, because what a landscape architect does is develop the open spaces which society needs for its activities.

Landscape architecture is a profession in which it's important to master a lot of different techniques. This is undoubtedly one of the particular difficulties facing our profession. Twenty or thirty years ago, I discovered that landscape would become the place of inventions. That's why I moved from art to landscape design. We are forced to be inventive, as tomorrow's landscape is a mystery and yesterday's landscape is not something we can just simply reconstruct. It's no longer painting and sculpture which make inventions, but garden art. The garden is the place of inventions of our age.

Recognising the problems and asking the right questions is the most difficult part of any new task. That's why I used the *analyse inventive* to find out where the problems lay. The project for the *Park of Duisburg-Nord*, which was part of the Emscherpark International Building Exhibition in Germany, was one of the first projects to make this need for invention clear to me. The *Park of Duisburg-Nord* is not a project which you can simply publish in a magazine, it is an invention. Inventive analysis enabled me to understand important parts of the overall problem facing the Duisburg project. The project can be realised once you have invented the analysis.

What significance does the ecological approach to landscape design have for you?

Environmental protection safeguards the basis of our existence, but we're not conservationists in the normal sense of the word. To see us in this way would, I feel, be a serious misconception. On the one hand, it's certainly good and important that landscape architects concern themselves with conservation of the landscape, but this doesn't go far enough as conservation is not the answer to the real problems. Keeping water clean, noise protection and so on are scientific

and technical problems, important tasks in the field of environmental protection, but they are not problems of landscape design. These are differences which need to be properly understood.

Your theoretical approach to landscape perception played an important part in the realisation of the *Frankfurt Green Belt Project* in the summer of 1990.

Most people think that theory doesn't matter in landscape design. Tom Koenigs, who was chief environmental officer in Frankfurt at the time, understood the importance and complexity of landscape theory. He invited me to Frankfurt as he knew that I'm one of the people in France who really understand the theory of landscape design. I made a contribution towards realising the project in my collaboration with him and the landscape architect Peter Latz. It was important to formulate the theoretical background as the rational and conceptual basis for creating the green belt. A green belt doesn't come into being because landscape architects plant trees at random or because two streams are cleaned up somewhere. The question it was important to ask was: What significance does a green belt have for the city of Frankfurt and how does it work? It's necessary to make clear to the people involved that the Green Belt actually consists of very diverse, heterogeneous landscape elements. The Green Belt is neither a French garden nor is it an English landscape park. But what the landscape architects saw in their mind's eye was the ideal picture of a green belt, rich in a diversity of vegetation and fauna. Furthermore, the parliament of Frankfurt couldn't support a plan which required the demolition of houses, allotments and factories just for the sake of creating areas of grass. That would have been ridiculous. That's why I had to develop a theoretical system, which I then used to convince those whose job it was to make the decisions. I see this as being proof of the strength of a coherent theory which, in this case, redefined the network of the individual elements and their relationships.

How do you define landscape?

I go along with the generally accepted definition of landscape – that it is a concept which serves to identify a part of our environment. Landscape as such doesn't really exist, it is, if you prefer, a cultural phenomenon. Planting lots of trees and creating small streams doesn't have anything to do with landscape, not even in historical terms. I'm quoting Christian Cay Laurenz Hirschfeld, the great German garden art thinker. The great philosopher from Kiel wrote "Geschichte und Theorie der Gartenkunst" in 1779. I don't think it's possible to be a landscape architect in Germany or to understand German landscape design if you haven't read Hirschfeld's theory, if you don't know what the theory of Friedrich Ludwig von Sckell is, if you haven't read Leberecht Migge. The existence of the concept of landscape makes it possible for

Bernard Lassus

us to say that a mountain is beautiful. Two hundred years ago people thought mountains were ugly. And garden artists thought the same way. Today the mountain landscape is admired. So what is landscape? It's the means we have to read reality. Landscape means the ability to interpret, the ability to call things by their name. If you don't understand this, you don't understand what landscape is.

There are obvious similarities between your theories and ideas and those of both the Swiss sociologist Lucius Burkhardt and the Scottish artist Ian Hamilton Finlay.
There are also differences in our views and, in my opinion, the Dutch garden artist Louis G. Le Roy has also discovered very important aspects. He discovered how spontaneous vegetation can be used to achieve a new design, something which is rarely talked about today. However, at present there are some landscape architects working in France – Gilles Clément for example – who can certainly be described as pupils and

to be aware of where ideas originate from and who has taken them further. I believe that it's essential to understand Le Roy's concept in order to be able to talk about a particular kind of garden art today. Good landscape architects, and in the context of Germany I am thinking of, for example, Arno Schmid, Peter Latz and Jürgen von Reuß, are familiar with the historical and theoretical foundations of their profession. I can imagine that ten years from now we may well

The design called "The day before yesterday, yesterday, today and tomorrow", entered by the planning team of Bernard Lassus et Associés in the competition to find a design for the *Duisburg North landscape park* on the site

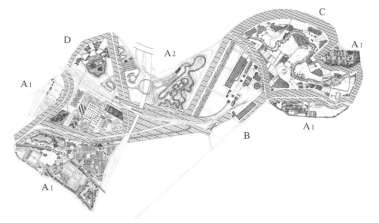

The zone of the *Duisburg North landscape park* called "The Day Before Yesterday" was to be a reconstructed section of idyllic countryside, through which the Emscher – which was still a factory canal – was to meander picturesquely.

see the history of garden art from a very different angle, and perhaps we'll realise how stupid it is to separate the history of the French garden from the history of the English garden. People will realise that there are approaches which are far more interesting. In my opinion, the debate on the English and French gardens was over about two hundred years ago. The remaining points of contact with the present are of a purely intellectual nature.

which was once the location of the blast-furnaces in Duisburg-Meiderich, 1991.
Rows of trees were to serve as temporal pens and separate the different islands of time from each other.

imitators of Le Roy. Le Roy reintroduced the old concept "circus games". The Romans had wild animals and gladiators fight each other to amuse the populace. This practice still exists in Spain today and, so that the fight in the arena takes longer, the picador weakens the bull by thrusting a banderilla into the neck muscles of the bull. Le Roy does the same thing. He stages a fight betweeen plants and, to make the fight last longer, he cuts the vegetation back from time to time. And this is the point which is often not understood: the free choice of means is an important factor. The person who intervenes in the fight between plants can choose the means with which he intervenes. The position adopted by Le Roy in this game is a classic one. It is classic not only in terms of garden art but also in terms of our Western history, indeed of the entire history of mankind.
The fact that so little is known about Le Roy particularly in the young profession is, to my mind, an indication of the poverty of landscape design which has no cultural awareness. It's important

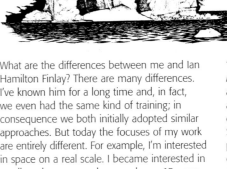

What are the differences between me and Ian Hamilton Finlay? There are many differences. I've known him for a long time and, in fact, we even had the same kind of training; in consequence we both initially adopted similar approaches. But today the focuses of my work are entirely different. For example, I'm interested in space on a real scale. I became interested in small gardens very early on and over 15 years ago I wrote an article in which I explained that Finlay's approach was very similar to the method of "minimal intervention". He is a specialist in miniaturisation. He does not work in real space but in imaginary space. He designs imaginary

"Tomorrow" in the *Duisburg North landscape park*: In addition to research gardens and laboratories, the artificially created zone "From Ice to Steam" is intended to allow people to experience the extreme conditions of water and demonstrate how much man is able to influence his environment by technology.

space by proceeding from fixed points, from objects. This is a very simplified way of explaining what he does, but it is, in essence, the underlying principle of his work.

Miniaturisation is a phenomenon which we know from garden art. The model of the classical "Roma Triumphans" in the garden of the Villa D'Este is just one of many examples. I have already examined this problem in my study of workers' gardens[2]. The relationship between Finlay's strategy and the design of workers' gardens with their arsenal of figures, rich in associations, is clear. The decisive difference is that Ian Hamilton Finlay has a large garden at his disposal and can choose whether he wants to work with miniaturisation or not, whereas workers have no choice in their small gardens.

Finlay uses miniaturisation to simplify things, while I work with both dimensions, the miniaturised and the real. Take for example the *Labyrinthe des batailles navales (Labyrinth of Naval Battles)*, which was planted in Rochefort. The space of the labyrinth is on a real scale: if there is one square metre, I want it to remain one square metre and to be experienced as one square metre. What interests me is the connection between real and abstracted space. This dimension of my work on what I call *espace propre* it is something which many people are not aware of. To become aware of this dimension they have to visit the places. Photographs are unsatisfactory as actual space cannot be broken down into individual photographs. This was an incredible obstacle for a long time as nobody was able to understand what really mattered to me.

I had an exhibition on *espace propre* at the Coracle Gallery in London a few years ago. I hung strips of yellow paper from the ceiling of the gallery, suspended a plumb line next to a wall and put a spirit-level on the floor. I did this in order to destroy the notion that rooms are exact geometric forms. You see, people believe in geometric forms. And this is the big mistake in many present garden designs. They see a whole series of geometric drawings with angles, straight lines and so on, but in fact these don't actually mean anything. They're just drawings. I wanted my work, a purely geometric system, to show that no room is completely vertical or exactly horizontal. I enjoy such projects as they ask important questions. It's a matter of destroying

misconceptions and examining what seems to be reality: I assume that the room is not a parallelepiped. I might draw it as such, but I know it's not really this way. It's not possible! For me geometrically exact rooms are fakes, camouflage. People who always believe what they see are a problem for me. Autosuggestion is our arch-enemy. That's why we need to fight against misconceptions, false geometry, everything which is false. As Finlay proceeds from imaginary proportions, he doesn't need to bother about destroying misconceptions. He doesn't need real space, that's not his problem. He creates his garden, but I have to work in real space. That's why I try to achieve clarity: 21 centimetres is 21 centimetres for me and not 22 centimetres. With his miniaturised ships, Finlay turns part of the garden into the sea. I say: "The sea's the sea, and 21 centimetres is 21 centimetres."

I'm interested in the relationship between the imaginary components and the real components. An artist sees others as being no more than spectators, whereas for me it's important that a person can read a newspaper, take off his shoes, stretch his legs out and so on in the space. At the same time, he should have the possibility of thinking of the sea. A landscape architect who is not aware of both components is not, in my opinion, capable of designing landscape. If he can think of the ocean and the element water and, at the same time, senses that the air is pleasant, the water is clean and tastes good,

Miniatures of warships are displayed in the *Labyrinthe des batailles navales (Labyrinth of Naval Battles)* in the *Parc de la Corderie Royale*, a labyrinth of hedges cut in a wave-like pattern.

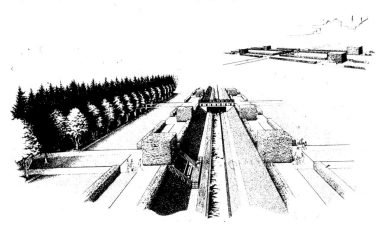

The character of the Emscher as an industrial canal was to be preserved along parts of its course through the *Duisburg North landscape park* in the competition design 1991.

2 Lassus, B.: *Jardins imaginaires*. Paris, 1977

Bernard Lassus

then he can work with landscape. In real space I'm interested in motor cycles and motorways because, if there's no space for traffic, an accident will happen. This doesn't have anything to do with functionalism but with appropriate space. When I redesigned the *rest area of Nîmes-Caissargues* on the A54 motorway, I tried to link the imaginary with the real. The rest area is bounded by an avenue of trees, which is 700 metres in length and intersects the motorway. Is it the avenue which intersects the motorway or is it the other way round? The colonnade of the old theatre of Nîmes stands at one end of the rest area and, slightly to one side, I had two belvederes built of metal; they are a reflection of the profile of the historical Tour Magne in Nîmes. There is a stone maquette of the Tour Magne mounted on each of the steel belvederes so that visitors will understand the connection. The belvederes afford a view of the real tower in the town, and from the town it's possible to see the belvederes at the rest area.

At night they are illuminated. Nothing like this has ever been done at a rest area before, but people still react very positively to the design. I didn't want this parking area to look like a parking area, so what I planned was an avenue, and the cars park along the avenue under the trees. It's as simple as that. I'm very satisfied with this project, and people are beginning to understand it. It's a new kind of work, which is part of the motorway and challenges people to reflect on it.

How has your work changed since the sixties when you were still working as an artist?

Many people see my supposed transition from artist to landscape architect as a discontinuity. But, for me, my development since the sixties hasn't been a discontinuity but a continuous process. To understand this, it's vital to realise that it's not possible to separate landscape architecture and art.

The motorway *rest area of Nîmes-Caissargues*, 1992. A carpet of green, 700 metres in length, bounded by avenues of trees, crosses the motorway between Arles and Nîmes.

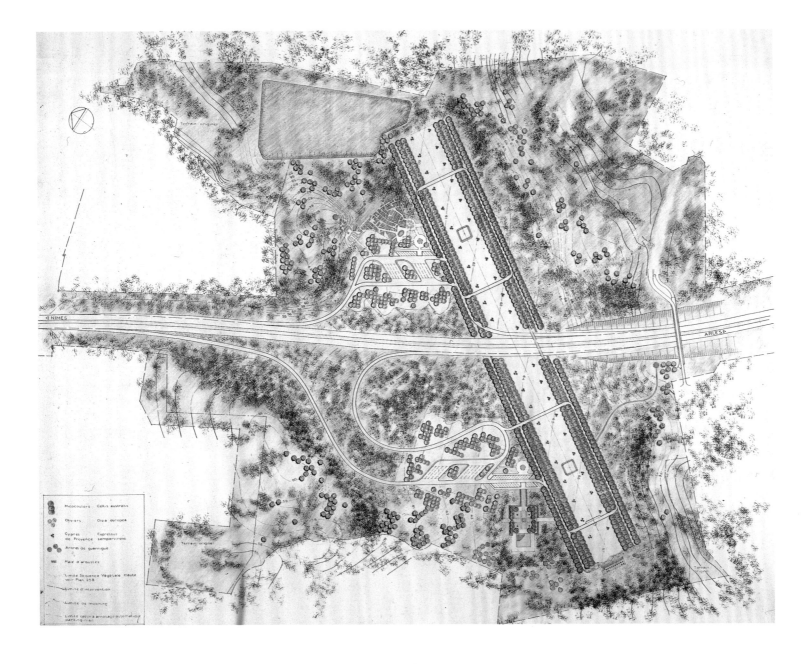

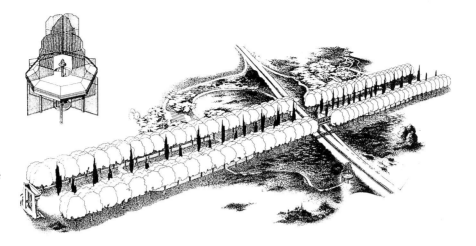

The dominant structural element of the rest area is the colonnade of the old theatre of Nîmes, which had to be demolished on its original site in the town. Lassus had the remains of the nineteenth century building re-erected at the motorway *rest area*.

To make the references clear, a maquette of the *Tour Magne* in Nîmes has been placed inside each of the belvederes.

113

Bernard Lassus

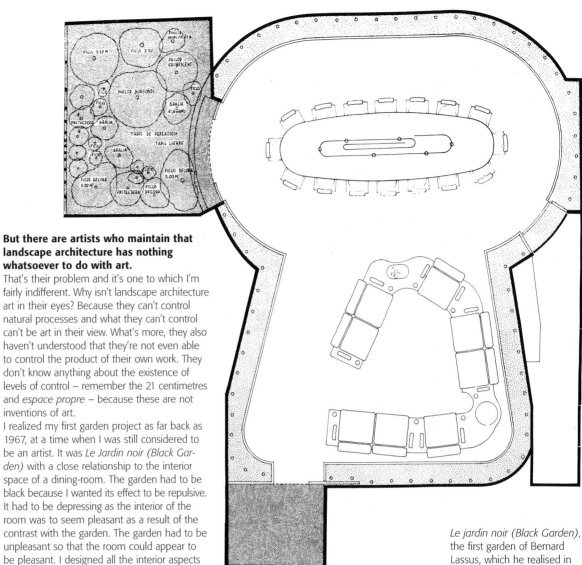

But there are artists who maintain that landscape architecture has nothing whatsoever to do with art.

That's their problem and it's one to which I'm fairly indifferent. Why isn't landscape architecture art in their eyes? Because they can't control natural processes and what they can't control can't be art in their view. What's more, they also haven't understood that they're not even able to control the product of their own work. They don't know anything about the existence of levels of control – remember the 21 centimetres and *espace propre* – because these are not inventions of art.

I realized my first garden project as far back as 1967, at a time when I was still considered to be an artist. It was *Le Jardin noir (Black Garden)* with a close relationship to the interior space of a dining-room. The garden had to be black because I wanted its effect to be repulsive. It had to be depressing as the interior of the room was to seem pleasant as a result of the contrast with the garden. The garden had to be unpleasant so that the room could appear to be pleasant. I designed all the interior aspects of the room, paying special attention to the light. It was essential that the room seemed pleasant although it was made of plexiglas and lit by artificial light. I was very pleased with this garden. In 1967 a negative garden had nothing to do with what was then accepted as art. Stephen Bann included the garden in an art book which was published in 1970 and was very much criticised for this. The *Times* wrote: "Why does the book include a dining-room between Vasarély and Giacometti?" Bann was perfectly clear that this was no ordinary dining-room. He had understood that a dining-room can also be a work of art. The book was a success and had a major influence on the ongoing discussion on aesthetic principles.

Unfortunately there are people who hide behind the label of landscape architect. They aren't whole-hearted landscape architects, they're landscape architects because that's the pigeon-hole they've been put into. Plenty of people say that I'm not a landscape architect and cling to their own definitions of the profession. But beginning with the day that you realise that it's what you do that will take you where you want to go, irrespective of what pigeon-hole you've been put in, people can call you a director or

Le jardin noir (Black Garden), the first garden of Bernard Lassus, which he realised in 1967 in connection with a flamboyant dining room.

an antique dealer or anything. I don't care what I'm called. Why should I ask myself whether I'm an artist or a landscape architect? I have been engaged in a certain kind of work for quite some time and have already seen my first results. In the United States, not in France it should be noted, there are people who are convinced that I have contributed completely new aspects to landscape design – so much the better. I have friends in Germany who I work with, and we believe that we have developed new ideas for landscape design. One thing I'm certain of is that the profession of landscape architecture will be transformed completely in the next few years.

In what way will the profession change in your opinion?

One aspect which will play a major role in the future is social symbolism. The aesthetic question will not be able to free itself from social responsibility. This is something that a lot of landscape architects still haven't grasped. My involvement

Le jardin des buissons optiques
(Garden of Optical Bushes),
Niort, 1993.

Bernard Lassus

with landscape architecture has something to do with social interest, that's why I have involved myself with the people who inhabit the landscapes I design to such an extent. This is the only context in which the idea of *espace propre* makes any sense. A Land Artist, such as the American artist James Turrell, is unable to develop *espace propre* because he's caught up in his system, everybody else, being outside the system is, therefore, a spectator.

As far as the future is concerned, we will have to fundamentally change our conception of landscape – the world's ecological crisis gives us no other choice. We are forced to be inventive because the original landscape has been damaged. But it's completely wrong to want to

knows his trade and always tries to perfect what he does. I don't improve my work, what I do is try to realise ideas without knowing at the beginning what form this will take.

My purpose is not to teach my students things which they then reproduce afterwards, but for them to learn things which enable them to be inventive later on. This doesn't mean that we can ignore details: 21 centimetres, the step at the right place, so the woman who is pushing a pram doesn't fall over … this is, of course, also part of my work. But this has nothing to do with functionalism. I don't see this as a functional problem, but as something which addresses the question of a precise linking of what is real and what is imaginary.

The plan of the *Parc de la Corderie Royale* in Rochefort-sur-Mer shows the elongated building complex of the restored Corderie Royale, built in 1666 as the place where rigging was made for the navy of Louis XIV. It was from Rochefort that most of the French naturalists, merchants and warships began their voyages to the New World. Lassus made cuts through the dense vegetation along the river bank in order to reestablish the visual link between the Corderie and the river. In realising his design *Le jardin des retours*, which was awarded first prize in the 1982 competition, he created new references to the historical significance of the site.

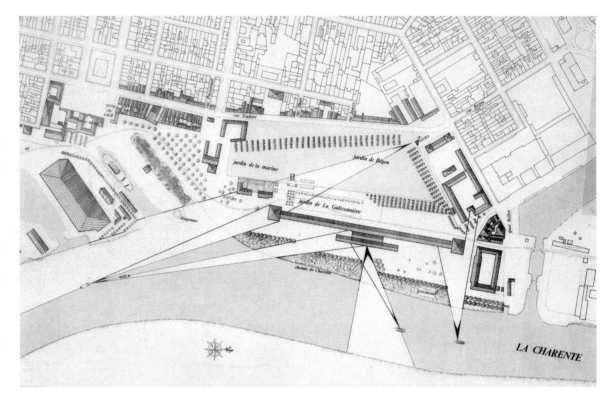

try and restore nature in the sense of naturalisation. That's not possible! We need to be inventive! Water must be clean in future, and we must be inventive. There's no way you can simply restore the landscape of the seventeenth or eighteenth centuries. This is something which I tried to make clear in my design for the *Tuileries Gardens*.

I develop my ideas in designs and the projects I realise and set off lengthy debates on the importance of theory and practice. Both are important: realisation of a project and the underlying theoretical ideas. If we don't move forward in the area of theory, there will be no progress. I reject the claim that we are craftsmen. In fact, we're the opposite of craftsmen because we do things which we aren't actually able to do. A craftsman

The uncomfortable question which is often asked is how theory can be made understandable to the beholder. The reproach which is often levelled at Ian Hamilton Finlay is that he sometimes demands too much intellectually of those who view his work.

He addresses a different audience as he has remained in the area of art to a greater extent than I have. What he does is to develop his garden and show works at galleries and exhibitions; what I do is concern myself with motorway rest areas and exits. My field of work is everyday life. I'm not interested in arranging an exhibition which doesn't have any reference to everyday life. Perhaps this is what makes my theory more accessible.

The English art critic, Professor Stephen Bann, who has been a friend of yours for many years, often sees your work as being connected with Land Art. What is Land Art for you?

Although there are Land Artists who have done interesting experiments, the question to be asked is this: What is the effect of such work on the

Lassus had the *Aire des grée-ments (Rigging Area)* erected on the foundation walls of a blockhouse from the Second World War; this area displays replicas of the masts and ropes which were once made in the Corderie.

landscape? People such as James Turrell and Robert Smithson have made interventions in the landscape, but this is not something which can be compared with my approach. I consider an artist such as Hamish Fulton to be far more interesting as, to my mind, his studies go much further than those of, for example, Richard Long. Chris Drury is also someone who has realised interesting projects. I'm interested in the work of these people because they have the same point of departure as I do and because I must, as a landscape architect, draw on many different sources.

For the *Rigging Area* in the *Parc de la Corderie Royale* in Rochefort I had, for example, to arrange for the reproduction of flags, the flags of the British and Dutch navies and of the Spanish fleet of the seventeenth and eighteenth centuries. They're finished now. Searching the archives to find out exactly what they looked like was a lot of work. Although we found out plenty about their formal design, we were able to discover next to nothing about their colours. We had to go to London to establish what the exact colour scheme of the British flags was; not even the British embassy knew what the colours were. This is attention to detail which is vital and it takes a lot of time. And, at the same time, I was working with a class at Rochefort's technical high school which had mastered the art of gold-thread embroidery. I had them embroider all the flags. It takes six months to embroider one flag, and we wanted to have all the eighteenth century flags embroidered in gold thread, just as they were in the eighteenth century. I spent several months working in the maritime museum, and we found the plans of all 21 ships with which Pierre Loti, a naval officer and a writer, sailed. The result of all this is that I will be able to do a work on his ships. We also found the drawings for "Radeau de la Méduse". In the Louvre there is a painting by Théodore Géricault, which dates from 1817 and depicts the dramatic sinking of the Méduse frigate off the west coast

of Africa in 1816. The captain of the Méduse was tried in Rochefort. Of course, many people will ask whether this is the work of an artist, a curator, an archaeologist or a landscape architect. For me it's something which has to be done. I'm not interested in the label that I'm given.

Do you number among the Romantics in landscape design?

The term Romantic is very popular in Germany and it's definitely important. Am I a Romantic? No, I don't think so. I uphold the idea of a sensitive approach to landscape, but this doesn't have anything to do with Romanticism. What concerns me is a certain way of making use of sensitivity. This is something which has always been one of the most important aspects of my work: how can I restore sensitivity to daily life? I don't think that Romanticism is the right term for this. My concern is to restore sensitivity to towns and industrial areas, to schools and

The *Parc de la Corderie Royale* contains concrete-moulded replicas of the *tontines*, the baskets which were used to transport exotic plants on long voyages. The conical lid of the baskets protected the delicate plants from the salty air.

architecture. The approach to this motif can take many different forms. I'm more worried about academicism than Romanticism.

Your conception of "minimal intervention" is one of the most important theoretical components of current landscape design. What does minimal intervention mean?

"Minimal intervention" doesn't mean not wanting to do anything, but using *espace propre* carefully. When in 1965 I used a red tulip to carry out the important experiment *Un air rosé*, this made clear what minimal intervention is. If you hold a strip of white paper in the goblet formed by the petals of a tulip, you will see that the air colours. This is the principle of minimal intervention: the place is not altered physically in any way and, nevertheless, you change the landscape. I carried out this experiment at the same time that Smithson realised his Land Art projects. All I needed to make the invisible visible was a strip of white paper.

S. 118/119 ▷
A wide ramp behind the old town wall, lined with tulip trees, leads to the park *Jardin de La Galissonière*, which is planted with palm trees. In 1711 Roland-Michel de la Galissonière brought back from his travels in America the first seeds of the large-flowered magnolia, which today is known as "galissoniensis". La Galissonière also introduced the tulip tree of Virginia to Europe in 1732.

Bernard Lassus

Biography and Selected Works

Bernard Lassus was born in Chamalières (Puy-de-Dôme) in 1929.
He began studying painting under Fernand Léger in 1949.
Studies at the Ecole Nationale Supérieure des Beaux-Arts.
Bernard Lassus lives and works in Paris.

Except where noted, locations are in France

Practice of Landscape Architecture and teaching activities (selection):

1961	Founded the Centre de Recherche d'Ambiance
Since 1967	Professor at the Ecole Nationale Supérieure des Beaux-Arts in Paris
1985	Visiting professor at the Kassel Polytechnic, Germany
1976–1986	Founded and headed the Atelier Charles Rivière Dufresny at the Ecole Nationale Supérieure du Paysage de Versailles
	At present professor at the Ecole d'Architecture de Paris-La Villette
1995–1999	Adjunct professor at the University of Pennsylvania, Department of Landscape Architecture, Philadelphia, U.S.A.

Selected art and landscape projects which have been realised:

1960	Kinetic art and environments
1965	Ambiance 6, *Un air rosé*
1967	*Le jardin noir*
1971–1978	Design of façades in Ville Nouvelle d'Evry
1975	*Jardin de l'anterieur* in Ile d'Abeau
1980–1981	*Passarelle d'Istres*, bridge in Bouches-du-Rhône
1981–1987	Design of façades and improvement of residential area in Uckange/Alsace
1982–1997	*Parc de la Corderie Royale* and *Jardin des retours* in Rochefort-sur-Mer; winner of a Ministry of Culture award in 1993
1989–1990	Redesign of rest area of Nîmes-Caissargues on the A 54
1989–1992	Boulevard Périphérique Sud in Nîmes
1990–1991	Participated in the Green Belt project in Frankfurt on Main, Germany
1990–1994	*Square de la ZAC Dorian* in Paris
1990–1996	*Jardin de la ZAC Dorian* in Paris
1991–1994	Landscape design for the A 837 Saintes-Rochefort motorway
1992–1995	*Les jardins de la paix* in Verdun
1993	*Les jardins des buissons optiques* in Niort
1994–1995	Landscape design for the Angers-Tours A 85 motorway
Since 1955	Numerous international exhibitions of art, town planning and garden art

Member of a number of commissions of experts as well as numerous studies and international competitions including:

1970	Studies on workers' gardens
1982	Competition *Parc de la Corderie Royale de Rochefort-sur-Mer* (1st prize)
1982	*Parc de la Villette* competition in Paris (short-listed)
1990	International competition for redesign of the Tuileries in Paris
1990–1991	Member of the international commission of experts of the International Building Exhibition, Berlin, Germany
1990–1992	Invited to take part in the international competition *Landschafts-park Duisburg-Nord*, Germany (short-listed)

Selected Bibliography

Lassus, B. *The Landscape Approach of Bernard Lassus.* London, 1983
Bann, S. "From Captain Cook to Neil Armstrong: Colonial Exploration and the Structure of Landscape." In *Projecting the Landscape*, edited by J.C. Eade. Canberra, 1987
Lassus, B. *Villes-Paysages, Couleurs en Lorraine.* 1990
Lassus, B. "Zwischen Schichtung und Tiefe." In *Vision offener Grünräume*, edited by T. Koenigs. Frankfurt/New York, 1991
Lassus, B. *Le Jardin des Tuileries de Bernard Lassus.* London, 1991
Lassus, B. *Hypothèse pour une Troisième Nature.* London, 1992
Lassus, B./Leyrit, C. *Autoroute et Paysage.* Paris, 1994

Numerous publications in international journals including:
Lassus, B. "The Landscape Approach of Bernard Lassus: Part II." In *Journal of Garden History*. London, 1995

Acknowledgements

Kindly provided by the landscape architect:
Arnaud Baumann: 109
Gérald Buthaud: 113 m./bottom
Bernard Lassus: 105, 114, 115, 117 r., 118/119
as well as:
from Sutherland Lyall, Künstliche Landschaften, Basel/Berlin/Boston 1991: 118/119

The Syntax of Landscape –
Peter Latz

Blue Footbridge in *Landschaftspark Duisburg-Nord*, 1995.

A park which has presented a lasting challenge to the bourgeois ideal of tranquil garden art was developed on the site of a former coal dock on the banks of the river Saar at Saarbrücken between 1985 and 1989. The *Hafeninsel (Harbour Island)*, created under the direction of landscape architect Peter Latz, divided his professional colleagues into two camps: one side speaking enthusiastically of a long-overdue contribution to the debate on a contemporary form of garden art which had finally shed the old clichés; the other protesting vociferously against what it claimed to be junk aesthetics, speaking of an unprecedented "chaos of materials, forms and figured elements".[1] Challenging the practices of a profession which tends towards opportunism, Peter Latz had dared to adopt a clear position. He is one of the best-known contemporary representatives of innovative European landscape architecture. He rejects ideas which seek to portray nature in terms of the bygone Arcadian ideal. Instead he points out the value of everyday nature, claiming it has much to offer our day-to-day life – more than cultivated sterility which forever has to fulfil functional criteria.

[1] Cf. Lührs, H. "Der Bürger-(meister)park Hafeninsel Saarbrücken." In *Bauwelt*, no. 39 (1990): 1973 ff.

121

The site of the former Saarbrücken coal dock, which covers an area of over 9 hectares close to the city centre, was filled in following destruction of the dock in the Second World War. Along with the remains of the former loading installations, it had almost entirely disappeared under a covering of rubble. It was not until a motorway bridge was planned across the Saar, using the *Hafeninsel* as the abutment of the northern end of the bridge, that attention was again turned to what by then was a very overgrown site. Instead of giving the area some superficial face-lifting – something which had been the standard procedure in such cases – the planning team chose an approach of minimal intervention. To explain what he wanted to do, Peter Latz wrote at the time, "a new syntax was to be developed for the centre of the city which would reknit the fragmented urban structure, would link its diverse aspects and, instead of covering up memories, would seek to reveal what the rubble concealed; the result was the syntactic design of an area of open urban space."[2] From the multitude of fragmented structural levels Latz selected the industrial remains and three further components: the urban transport network combined with visual axes, the existing flora of the derelict site and a number of public gardens. The aim of the "syntactic design" was to restore and preserve the genius loci, an aim which his unusual experiments have come very close to achieving. Today, the visitor to the site encounters widely differing set pieces from the past and the present, archetypal garden-art images and art installations which are subtly interwoven to form a dense fabric.

Whereas most artists tend to see patterns as being of lesser importance than *gestalt*,

[2] Latz, P. In *Garten und Landschaft*, no. 11 (1987): 42.

Detail of execution plan of the "syntactic" design of the *Hafeninsel Saarbrücken*, 1985–1989.

 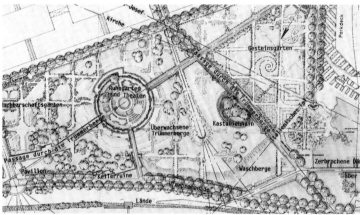

The docks and *Hafeninsel (Harbour Island)* in Saarbrücken seen in an oblique aerial photograph taken in 1946.

[3] Cf. Eco, Umberto. *The Open Work*. London, 1989.

patterns and grids play a decisive role for Peter Latz, providing a framework for independent action on the part of the individual user. The expressive force of the work does not lie in the meticulous realisation of an artistic design, but in the work of many designers realised within a framework which is as rational as possible. For example, the grid-structured western part of the park offers the possibility of individual use and design. In his planning for the *Hafeninsel* project Peter Latz had to accept the risk of open planning as the collective design process can take on unforeseen forms. Any work which is *open* in the way that Umberto Eco[3] defines the concept depends on the risk of the unpredictable and is to be understood as a dynamic creation. It does not follow any intransigent ideal, choosing instead to convey freedom and the capacity for change. The *Hafeninsel* is, in this sense, an *open* work of garden art.

Many of the principles and strategies used to approach destruction and decay, which were tried out on the *Hafeninsel* for the first time, such as recycling of material, are being put to impressive use to develop "the park of the 21st century", the *Landschaftspark Duisburg-Nord*, which is currently the largest project of the office of Latz + Partners. The landscape of what was once an iron and steel plant in Duisburg-Meiderich, where between 1900 and 1985 37 million tonnes of pig iron were produced, is characterised by innumerable old industrial buildings and structures, which very quickly became completely overgrown with wild and, in some cases, very rare vegetation. Peter Latz and his planning team have been working on this project since 1990 along with Latz's wife, landscape architect Anneliese Latz. The crucial question facing the

Hafeninsel Saarbrücken. The artificial ruin of the *Water Wall* in red brick.

Hafeninsel Saarbrücken. The sunken garden of rest in the mound of rubble in the western part of the park is in the tradition of historical garden art.

The rock gardens in the western part of *Hafeninsel Saarbrücken* evoke the sites of archaeological excavations. Their formal design was achieved by sorting the rubble.

Peter Latz

team was whether the remains of the industrial mass production plant – vast buildings and sheds, gigantic ore dumps, chimneys, blast furnaces, railway tracks, bridges, cranes and so on – could really serve as the basis for a park.

The approach adopted for the *Duisburg North landscape park* does not attempt to cover up discontinuities and fragments, but seeks a new interpretation of existing structures and elements. Four layers – the *water park* consisting of canals and reservoirs, the *main promenades*, the areas of use and the *Bahnpark (Rail Park)* with the elevated promenades – were to continue to exist independently and only be connected visually, functionally, spiritually or symbolically at certain points by special links such as ramps, steps, terraces and gardens. Thus, again, a syntactic design has been used in order to allow maximum future flexibility. As this planning approach is not compatible with the familiar practice of a finished overall design plan, Peter Latz and his team almost renunciated finalising the master plan.

The Duisburg-Meiderich iron and steel works, where Thyssen produced 37 million tonnes of pig iron between 1900 and 1985, has been left as it was at the time it was closed – 200 hectares of waste land for a postindustrial park.

The master plan of the *Duisburg North landscape park*, the result of the superimposition of levels of planning and structural elements. It shows the decision not to represent an alleged "totality" of the landscape, which consists of traces, fractures, harmonious and fragmented elements.

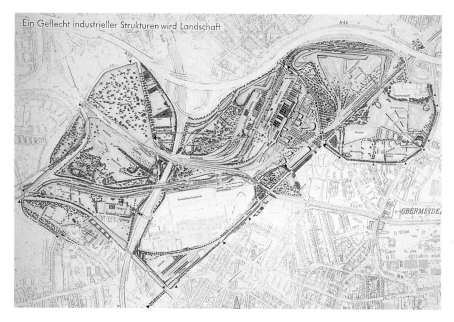

Professor Latz, what made you want to become a landscape architect?

My father was an architect and, in view of the conditions that existed during the post-war years, my first ambition was to have a large farm. The only problem was that I didn't have a farm. So at a very early age I started to grow vegetables for the family in my parents' garden. I planted an orchard of several hundred trees at the age of fifteen and also started to grow strawberries so that I'd have something I could sell quickly. In the end, I was able to keep my parents and their many relatives supplied with fresh fruit and vegetables for a few years. I used the money I got from selling the orchard to finance my studies. This explains my interest in fruit-growing and the fruit-tree motif still appears in my projects today. Building has always been important to me on account of my father's profession. I worked in landscape architecture at a very

Peter Latz converted an existing building in Kassel into an ecological house in collaboration with architect Thomas Herzog. The Latz family lived in this house for a time.

early age and acquired a lot of important skills and knowledge. By the time I started grammar school, I was already absolutely certain that I would become a landscape architect. What drew me to this profession was the prospect of being able to work creatively like an architect, only using much more plant material.

That sounds like an ideal link between architectural aspects on the one hand and archetypal garden art on the other. Did your studies live up to your expectations?

I learnt a lot during my studies at the Technische Universität München-Weihenstephan, and I began to participate in competitions very early on. I completed my studies in 1964 at the end of the minimum study period; after that I learnt the basics of urban planning in a supplementary course of studies at the Technische Hochschule in Aachen. The focus at the time was on issues of urban renewal. I was principally con-

cerned with an urban renewal project in Wattenscheid, in the heart of the Ruhr industrial district. This was also the time that I took up my first teaching position abroad, teaching urban planning and methodology at the Academy of Architecture in Maastricht. After that I taught at the Academy of Architecture in Amsterdam. I went into independent practice relatively quickly, in 1968 in fact. My time in Aachen came to an end when I was offered a chair in landscape architecture at Kassel. At that time I was working on a regional planning project in the Saarland, the *Saar-Hunsrück nature park*. This was a project which incorporated very many analytical components; it was at that time that I decided to involve myself much more in detailed planning again. Instead of working on a scale of 1:50,000, I wanted to get back to the scale of 1:1. Fortunately, this was something I was able to do in the workshops of what was then the Academy of Art in Kassel. I had a studio there and became very involved in alternative technologies, in terms of my own profession of course. The main issues ranged from roof gardens and the correct approach to water to questions of self-sufficiency. What particularly interested me was whether it was possible to put my theoretical knowledge into actual practice. This changeover to questions of detail certainly did me good.

It was at that time that I worked with other professions in an "Alternative Technologies" group, something which undoubtedly had an influence on me. For example, I still today work with Thomas Herzog, one of the architects from the group. At that time there were strong moves to provoke changes in architecture, moves which landscape architects were also involved in initiating. That was exciting. Our joint goal of working either actively or passively with the use of solar energy served as a stepping-stone to small, long-term research projects. Important results were worked out and tested in *my first house*, which Thomas Herzog and I built in Kassel. When I built my *second house*, here in Ampertshausen, I was able to profit from what I had learnt the first time around. Here I also assimilated my early experiences: reconstruction after the war and the first house that my father built. This was something I enjoyed very much and it taught me a lot about temporary processes. Suddenly it was no longer a question of understanding objects just as they are, but in terms of their potential. Experiencing this in relation to garden, landscape and architecture was very important.

My professorship at the Technische Universität München-Weihenstephan marked another

Peter Latz

Latz Office and home, ecological architecture in Ampertshausen near Freising.

125

Peter Latz

decisive turning-point. At the time I was involved in a long-term *housing project in Wattenscheid* and a project of the *Universität Marburg-Lahn-berge*, which was on a much larger scale. It gradually became apparent that today such projects are not so much concerned with across-the-board interventions but with selecting important places or areas to work on specifically. In comparison, it may well be possible to leave other, large areas to develop in their own way.

For an outsider it would seem that you have achieved a lot in a short space of time. Where do you get all your energy from?
Ever since childhood I've been accustomed to doing a lot of things myself, so this is not anything very unusual for me. Of course, necessity plays a role when you have no resources or capital and have only your own efforts to rely on. I experienced this both as a student and as someone trying to build a practice of his own. Need-

clear interventions are necessary and, if there's no other choice, this can involve the use of brutally hard materials such as iron and stone. It's often a question of exploring where the limits of your own ideas are, trying things out and, ultimately, realising them. The repertoire also includes seemingly conservative elements such as the box hedge. Being a landscape architect means continuously scanning the entire repertoire of our landscape and garden culture and being able to draw on its resources at any time to find the optimum solution for the task in hand. In the process, seemingly contradictory situations and sharp contrasts can emerge. There are projects which, for example, include a pretty, self-contained garden while nearby rubble is piling up, industrial architecture decaying, a steel structure rusting. However, these features always depend on the unique nature of the place in question.
When I begin working on a given task, I adopt an approach which is as rational and as struc-

Blue Footbridge and blast furnaces. *Duisburg North landscape park*, 1995.

less to say, I didn't always work according to the principles of economics and often experimented with ideas which were not really fully mature.

How do you define your role as a landscape architect today and what do you consider the main challenge facing landscape architecture today?
As my projects demonstrate, there's more than one answer to this question. It depends on the given situation and the way it's interpreted, so that it can be used in a new way or have a different function. As a rule, landscape architecture is concerned with change or with protection. Either you use elements which, as far as possible, appear natural in the given context or already exist there. Sometimes tiny details are decisive such as the perennials and geophytes in the box hedge, which spread almost imperceptibly and become permanent visitors in the vegetable garden. There are times when very

tural as possible. A definitive design rarely exists to begin with. This doesn't come until much later stages after the patterns are in place and the rational criteria have been fulfilled. First of all, it's a question of establishing rational systems, of a kind of ideology for the project in question, a kind of philosophy – although philosophy in its original sense is actually completely the wrong word in this context.
For *Duisburg North landscape park* I began by writing stories. Stories about a falcon circling a mountain. And it gradually became clear to me what I would do with the blast furnaces. The impression of the objects, their figurative meaning is actually of very little interest to me. To put it another way, the semantic aspect is not so important. Nor am I in any way interested in practical aspects, in feasibility to begin with. When I start, the only thing which matters is knowing how many elements and objects are available to me and what possibilities of linking

Cowperplatz in the *Duisburg North landscape park*.

them exist. I'm interested in the syntax of the levels, the degree of regularity with which one or a number of things are repeated. The rules can vary a great deal and can be used at different levels. The pencil is not the means by which to seek forms, nor is water-colour or a felt-tip pen. Rather it's a question of discovering a principle for the given place which it is also possible to experiment with. Of course, such experiments can go wrong, but once you have got the experiment working and it takes you further, you continue it as far as possible.

What does design mean for you in this context?

It's essentially a question what force the existing objects already have, what density of information they already possess and what density of information first has to be introduced into the project. Perhaps there are several different ways of understanding the design process: in the case of tasks and projects I'm not at all familiar with, I form layers of information and then combine them. For other kinds of projects, I quickly make a sketch on a piece of paper, a serviette or whatever is handy. Whenever I have new ideas, I alter the sketch, sometimes up to the point where the result no longer bears any resemblance to the original idea. If necessary, I continue this strategy until a sufficiently complex information structure emerges – of course this has to be a structure that's still manageable. As long as a project is growing, certain aspects of development or layers of meaning are not yet visible. This may mean that these layers of information first have to be made visible by temporary installations. It takes a while until the hedge of roses matures sufficiently to provide the desired show of blooms, whereas a centranthus planted between the roses produces a similar effect much more quickly.

What is your relationship to traditional garden art?

I said before that it's possible to use the entire repertoire of garden art, ranging from the medieval bank of grass to the interventions of the fifties. Of course, I neither believe that we can copy the Villa Lante nor that we should attempt to do so. But it's possible to learn a great deal from the villa gardens of the Renaissance. For me the *Duisburg North landscape park* has a lot to do with Bomarzo. This is not related to a particular object; anyway, I very quickly saw Bomarzo in Duisburg. Other projects have more in common with the serene seclusion of the Villa Lante or reflect the aloofness and anti-geometry of the palace gardens of Caprarola. Occasionally, one comes across the remains of a Baroque garden in the form of water or a single axis, revealing the potential in terms of perspective which the landscape unfolds. And, for me, many kinds of historical machinery also form part of the repertoire. Historical methods of building, rebuilding of urban and landscape structures using rational means of intervention, building of canals, locks, irrigation systems, sheds and greenhouses – these

are all elements which make it possible to recognise and interpret different kinds of space. I see some of my projects as being particularly good examples of this: the studies on the "Gleisdreieck" rail junction in Berlin or the *Bahnpark (Rail Park)* in Duisburg.

The spatial comprehension of landscape plays a vital role here. I consider the use of methods of landscape analysis to be very important, methods which make it possible to trace landscape back to very varied basic conditions. Landscape theory is also something which I've devoted a lot of time to. What matters to me is to show that landscape can only be comprehended by means of preformulated techniques. The acquired art of crossing a snowfield is, to my mind, one of these techniques. Landscape is only comprehended from those places which seem natural to the viewer. So the way that the landscape is staged determines the way it is subsequently perceived.

Many people find it difficult to reconcile your projects for the *Hafeninsel* in Saarbrücken and the *Duisburg North landscape park* with traditional concepts of garden art. On the other hand, there are ever increasing calls for a new garden art. What is you position here?

I have never felt that I wanted to do something new or that what I was doing was new. What I did want to do was to develop something which was appropriate to the place in question. Admittedly, I used 'filters' which were different from the ones normally used in landscape architecture. A consequence of my experiences during the post-war years is that I don't have any problems with rubble. I knew that it was both possible and necessary to use it to build fantastic houses. I found quarries extremely attractive at a very early age; I enjoyed exploring them when I was only ten years old. I have never understood why such exciting places are deemed to be blotches on the landscape. Perhaps this is the reason why I had no other choice than to look at things differently. I was certainly not aware that so many different kinds of perception existed here. Of course, I was aware that what I had done differed from a traditional park, but the violent, in some cases aggressive reactions on the part of colleagues was something I hadn't anticipated.

So this was not a conscious provocation or breach of the conventions of perception?

It was a consciously different application of conventions. Basically, what I was seeking was the genius loci. This is certainly nothing new. Perhaps I wanted to give clear expression to a new, abstract idea. I have been interested in the architecture of Mies van der Rohe for many years, particularly with regard to the question of reduction and redundancy of information. I have always been fascinated by simple, additive systems in the landscape, and these are systems which can be found everywhere. So to me it was quite natural to use the Gauß-Krüger grid to subdivide the park on the *Hafeninsel* in Saarbrücken, as this rational system was already on the ground plan. I could have invented another grid, but there wouldn't have been any point.

What I find particularly interesting is that you number two projects on sites which have been devastated among your most fascinating works.
Of course I also seek out the beautiful parts of the landscape and enjoy them. But that's not the point. The point is: where is the imagination most challenged, in a state of harmony or in a state of disharmony? Disharmony pos-

That sounds a little like the fascination of the awe-inspiring, like affinity for the beauty of ruins. These do rather seem like the views of a Romantic.
On the occasion of a lecture which I recently gave in Dresden, I called for the protection of destruction from destruction. The seemingly chance results of human interference, which are generally judged to be negative, also have immensely exciting, positive aspects and are, on closer inspection, ultimately even a contribution to nature conservation. These sites offer potential for the development of things which are completely different. It's no coincidence

sibly produces a different statement, a different harmony, a different reconciliation. If you come from a region of low hills like the Saarland, unusual phenomena such as quarries naturally appear much more dynamic and exciting. A bunker from the Second World War which has been dynamited also possesses such qualities, and you know that things are possible there, unlike in many other places which are still today taboo. These places of devastation offer much greater freedom of action, not only to landscape architects but, above all, to the user. That's why many people feel drawn to such places.

that I began my career as a landscape architect in the Ruhr district. This certainly didn't have anything to do with Romanticism. I don't happen to be of the opinion that Classicism, Romanticism and other cultural movements are alternative functions, but believe that they can exist synchronously. So it's not always possible to strictly separate the rational and the romantic. Of course, it's possible, at least for a second, to interpret every flower, every stone romantically. I can build a wooden building according to rational principles, and then, suddenly, the sun shines through one corner of the glass roof,

Wall in the *private garden of the Latz family* in Amperts-hausen.

Peter Latz

creating an incredibly romantic image generated by chance. And, by the same logic, I can also create images which are deliberately Romantic, but which can look so banal on a foggy day that I don't even notice them. I know that sounds very bourgeois but, to my mind, there is a multitude of predetermined, rehearsed modes of thinking, feeling and experiencing. When I go to the coast, I basically know weeks in advance what experiences I can have there. As I already said, the semantic effects don't interest me at all. For me it's far more important to find a structure in which large numbers such semantic manifestations can alternate with each other and initiative each other of. Changing seasons, weather and events are to allow ever-changing modes of expression to manifest themselves.

In *Stadt-Parks*, which was published in 1993, you write: "The time for a new understanding of nature has come." How do you define your own understanding of nature and which are the features of your projects where this becomes visible?
The ways of understanding nature are, generally speaking, as diverse as the ways that any forms of culture are understood. Today, it is very apparent what we understand by cultural landscape. This so-called cultural landscape is in reality a brutally functional landscape which for a long time has been exploited for agriculture and forestry. I try to discuss this general understanding of nature in lectures and articles, an undertaking which is undoubtedly seen as a provocation. This isn't only a question of my own work. Although I don't always succeed, I try to make a fairly clear-cut distinction between landscape and nature; the reason being that they don't actually have anything to do with each other. Landscape is a cultural concept which, in a modified form, is cherished by a society. Nature is a law unto itself, a myth.
Basically, we are all stuck in nature, something which becomes clear to all of us as soon as we experience physical pain. I believe that all objects I create, particularly when they're made of iron, steel or stone, enter into a dialogue with nature. When I grow flowers for cutting and plant vegetable beds, this has, to my mind, more to do with a cultural technique and nothing to do with nature, irrespective of how close to nature this might seem. It is particularly in this context that very many people like to speak of nature. In view of this ambivalence of the concepts we have to be careful about the way we use them.
What I find most fascinating are systems which, on the one hand, have to meet extremely high technical standards and, on the other hand, develop virtually ideal ecological qualities. The components of these systems are so closely linked that the ecological aspect disappears if the technology goes and the technology disappears if the ecology no longer works. We need to understand that this is the way that much of the world we live in works. What nature conservationists fought against thirty years ago as being

an extreme form of environmental destruction is today protected by law.
What I have just described as a synchronous process is, as a rule, understood as a dialectical relationship. However, I find the synchronous aspect of far greater interest. Of course I love to look at the meadow of flowers around my house in May, but I think that it's our duty to experiment with nature and landscape, even if only in our mind's eye. The result of putting these experiments into actual practice can be a wealth of discoveries and, in consequence, established values are suddenly displaced. I can imagine a garden bed which is entirely made up of a substrate of rusty screws. Of course, I can also imagine a sixty-centimetre bed of compost, where radishes, lettuce and pumpkins thrive. These are a gardener's approaches. It is, however, possible to become quite fascinated by an existing technical landscape and to recognise it as a typical segment of landscape. This may be of absolutely no interest twenty years on, but right now it's very exciting. We have always believed there's nothing left to discover in the world, except perhaps in the virgin forests of Indochina, Indonesia and Brazil. We even went to the moon to look for something new,

Dusts, minerals, coal, coke, scrap-metal, ashes and pellets are tested in the area of the *Hamborn Stadtgarten* to investigate their suitability for use in garden soils. Very unusual plant societies already exist on contaminated ground in the *Duisburg North landscape park*.

yet there are fascinating and accessible areas to be discovered right in the middle of our cities. We just have to look a little more closely.

Elsewhere in the book I just mentioned you write: "It is time to combine the developments in the arts from the past two decades to form a forward-looking idea."
As far as its intellectual and theoretical state of development is concerned, our profession is, to put it favourably, two decades behind art and architecture. Perhaps the amount of catching up we have to do is even greater. We need to introduce into landscape architecture the ways that art perceives and represents the environment, its experimental strategies, not just in one or two projects but on a large scale. Simply defaming anyone who departs from the rules which were established by Lenné and von Sckell around two hundred years ago is not the answer. It's not possible to pretend that the developments which have taken place since then don't exist. In the history of garden art there are very many alternative approaches which have been disregarded. Incidentally, a closer look sometimes reveals that no more than a pretence of following the tradition of Lenné and von Sckell

The massive Möller bunkers of reinforced concrete, where huge quantities of different kinds of ore and other materials used to be stored, are today a popular climbing garden in the *Duisburg North landscape park*. The cross at the summit marks "Monte Thyssino", named after the Thyssen steel firm.

has been made. These are the reasons for the provocative demands I formulated during my work on the *Frankfurt Green Belt*.

Another provocative demand is, "I want to create a park without any trees and bushes." This means we must try to step back from the clichés, and from this distance we should consider what kinds of potential are really available to us. Take, as an example, the absurd attempt to cover slag-heaps with vegetation. A lot of effort is put into correcting gradients and planting greenery on slopes to stop any erosion whatsoever. The slag-heaps are given landscape treatment, they are sculpted, angled and terraced into rounded hillocks or steep flanks to make sure that nothing whatsoever can change. The sole natural principle of such accumulations of material is a proper erosion process, which produces entirely new formations. The only interesting thing would be provocation and encouragement of erosion and then to use the ensuing fantastic structures to depict the environment. Instead, effort is entirely directed towards preventing this. The same procedure is being used to recultivate the disused brown-coal mines in Germany's new states. The recultivation process always aims to achieve an aesthetic technical image, which is thenusually deadly boring, and, on top of that, a great amount of time and effort is then spent on preserving this state of affairs. Erosion can certainly be a terrible thing in other contexts, but here it seems to me to be of great importance.

Take the example of the *Piazza Metallica* in the *Duisburg North landscape park*. This square of massive iron plates derives its interest from two physical processes. One is the formation of hardened metal, which was once covered by a layer of slag and could only be exposed with difficulty, the other is the process of erosion. The Piazza is related to a technology and a time where, instead of water, molten iron with a temperature of thirteen hundred degrees centigrade was poured over the plates. This created fluvial systems which are very similar to a glacier's cutting edge, in other words primordial formations which were created by the force of molten elements. As a symbol of nature I find this infinitely more interesting than a few forlorn birches!

Even so, could you describe in what way landscape architecture is at least two decades behind art? What inspiration can art provide? I am assuming that the straightforward imitation of artistic models is out of the question.

Precisely. The relatively banal formal assumption of Modernist elements in the architecturally designed gardens of the fifties was a passing phenomenon. With a very few exceptions, a genuine intellectual dialogue with Modernism in the garden was lacking. Most of the attempts were no more than superficial efforts. For instance, there have never been any really convincing examples of pop culture in the garden. And, basically, there are also no examples of

using other Postmodern trends. Very few realistic approaches to Postmodern garden art exist. Hardly anyone has given any serious consideration to the ideas of structuralism although structuralist principles are particularly suitable vehicles for generating landscape structures. Perhaps Holland is an exception here. There are very few viable aesthetic concepts attempting to show economical principles of thought. I'm not referring to garden-like modes of production and their specific organisational form, but to an entirely different dimension of representation. All of this leaves no mark on a profession which continues to take its cues from people such as Fürst Pückler-Muskau and unwaveringly carries on the traditions of the last century. Meanwhile new experiments are being carried out in other fields, and once again we are looking the other way.

Generally, our profession is happy to play design games or delve into the past. Perhaps this can be explained by the mechanisms of our media world. Most landscape architects don't have the courage to make use of the languages of our

contemporary culture. Of course, problems of acceptance play a significant role here, problems which I'm all too familiar with. But contemporary art and architecture also face these problems. They are something we have to learn to confront.

Have you ever consciously made use of the language of art in any of your projects?

Yes, with a variety of results. In garden art there are objects and situations which require the addition of a genuine work of art. In other cases the project stands by itself and does not need any additional object. The range between these two situations is fairly large. For the *Hafeninsel* project I would have liked artistic interpretations of certain situations, but this was not possible for financial reasons. At other times, for example in the case of the *Piazza Metallica*, I was happy that we only needed our own languages and methods to achieve an excellent result.

The object-relatedness of art is practical for our profession. Process Art is more than just practical,

Special steel plates, measuring 2.20 by 2.20 metres and weighing nearly 8 tonnes each, once served to line the casting-pits in the foundry. Latz used them to build the Piazza Metallica. "As a symbol of nature I find this infinitely more interesting than a few forlorn birches!" (Peter Latz)

it's ideal because it exists independently, it doesn't change the other object, which can grow undisturbed. The art of light is a good example, as a work will possibly be interpreted in light which is entirely different from what was anticipated. There are plenty of artists, Richard Serra for example, who develop their own surrounding space.

Collaboration with artists worked very well in the case of our projects and, ultimately, it was never entirely clear where the dividing line between art and landscape lay. The open space design at *Marburg University* is a good example and so is the design of the square at the *Landeszentralbank (Central Regional Bank)* in Kassel. Here we combined the art objects with our design ideas for the open space. I'm not talking about Baroque niches filled by some object or other. Today, landscape forms the setting for the art installation, and the project is seen as a whole although this was not intended initially. Actually in some projects one develops quite a laconic structure, and art gains particular

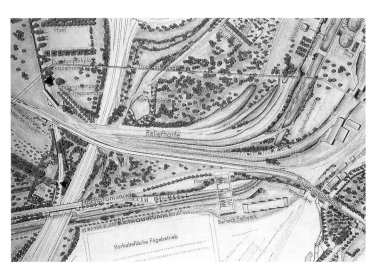

"The movements occasioned by the pattern of the tracks have the complexity of ballet." (Peter Latz)
Section of the *Bahnpark* plan.

significance in them. In other projects, in contrast, the design as developed by landscape architecture is so extensive and comprehensive that there may be no room at all for other artistic statements.

It is striking that you gave a "Land Art" interpretation to part of the topography of the *Duisburg North landscape park*. Why do you make use of a term which clearly belongs to art?
The "Gleisharfe" ("The Rail Harp") is an intermeshing of railway tracks where every second track leads downwards and the ones in between lead upwards – a fantastic, technological object. My affinity for the sensitive railway technology of dividing and recombining strands of tracks led me to discover the *Railway Park* in Duisburg very quickly. The movements occasioned by the pattern of the tracks have the complexity of ballet. The engineers who designed this set of tracks over a period of sixty to seventy years certainly had technology in mind and not art. If they had been told at the time that what they

were doing was art, they would probably have reacted very negatively and it might even have cost them their job. The history of technology has very often produced fascinating structures. These should be given recognition and supported in their force of expression. That's why I used the term Land Art even though no artist was involved. What mattered to me more was the association. Such qualities are inherent in very many objects. One of the ambivalent questions of our culture is whether such creations of technology, and I include the slagheaps in this category, should be protected as cultural monuments.

The extensive development programme of the Emscherpark International Building Exhibition includes an increasing number of art events. What are your views on this strategy?
I am firmly convinced that garden art exists. Whether certain projects I have done are classified as garden art is something I can't really say, but I hope that they are. Despite the large proportion of functional aspects, I feel that there are certain parts of my work which should not be judged in terms of their utility value as they convey other qualities. However, in our day-to-day work we have to come to terms with quite substantial constraints: there are large periods of time to be bridged, the information relating to the given task is never sufficient. The International Building Exhibition has integrated art as a natural means of making certain relationships visible quickly. Irrespective of whether it is a question of landscape art or objects, I think that they will continue to be essential integral parts of the programme. When I am seeking specific interpretations of places, space and situations, the whole variety of different cultural languages has to be used. Art is one of these languages. In the history of architecture there has always been a search for objective criteria of construction technology, the heritage of civilisation, the heritage of art, theological meaning and so on. Although our civilisation always treats these components separately, I feel that the distinction between art, architecture and landscape architecture possibly does not really make much sense.

Special saws were used to cut openings in some of the sinter bunkers. The openings afford views of the gardens or make it possible to walk from one bunker to the next.

Fern garden in the *Duisburg North landscape park*, 1995.

Peter Latz

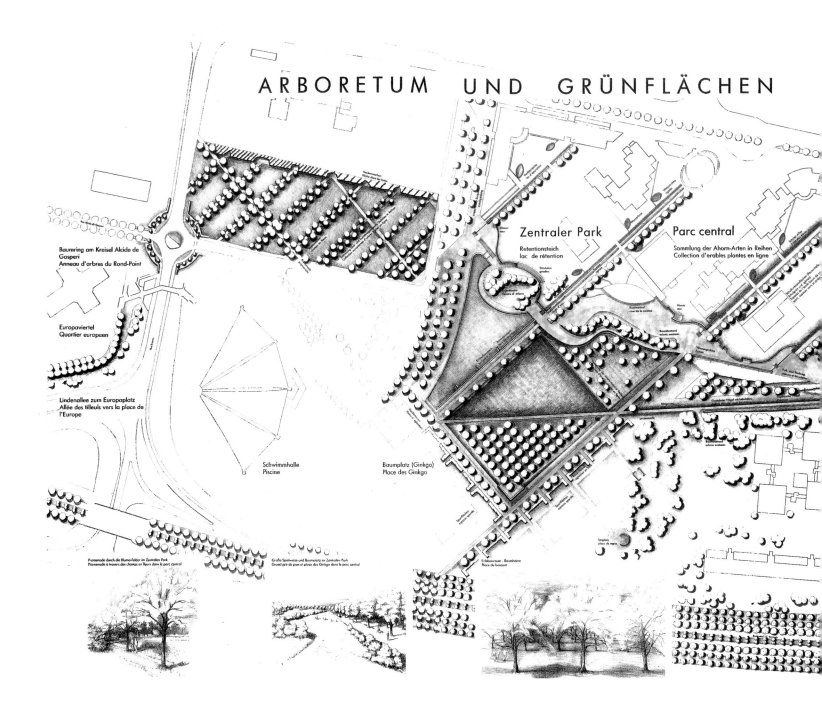

ARBORETUM UND GRÜNFLÄCHEN

Zentraler Park

Retentionsteich
lac de rétention

Parc central

Sammlung der Ahorn-Arten in Reihen
Collection d'erables plantes en ligne

Baumring am Kreisel Alcide de
Gasperi
Anneau d'arbres du Rond-Point

Europaviertel
Quartier europeen

Lindenallee zum Europaplatz
Allée des tilleuls vers la place de
l'Europe

Schwimmhalle
Piscine

Baumplatz (Ginkgo)
Place des Ginkgo

Promenade durch die Blumenfelder im Zentralen Park
Promenade à travers des champs en fleurs dans le parc central

Große Spielwiese und Baumplatz im Zentralen Park
Grand pré de gson ot place des Ginkgo dans le parc central

Erlebnisroute - Baumhaine
Place de bosquet

Römerwegpark   Parc de la voie romaine

Sammlung: Europäische Eichen
Collection de chênes

PAP Reimerwe

Eichensammlung entlang des Weges im Römerwegpark
Collection de chênes du Parc du chêne romain

Blick auf den Boulevard
Vue sur le boulevard

Master plan for *Arboretum and Green Areas on the Plateau de Kirchberg, Luxembourg,* part of the project Luxembourg 1995 European City.

Peter Latz

Biography and Selected Works

Peter Latz was born in Darmstadt in 1939. He and his wife, Anneliese Latz, who is a landscape architect, live and work in Kranzberg near Freising in the Munich area.

He graduated from the Technische Universität München-Weihenstephan in landscape architecture in 1964 and subsequently did postgraduate studies in landscape architecture at the Institute of Urban and Regional Planning at the Technische Hochschule in Aachen, completing his studies in 1968. Since then he has worked as a landscape architect and urban planner in independent practice.

Except where noted, locations are in Germany

Work for landscape design offices and teaching activities:

1965–1968	Office of Professor Kühn-Meurer in Aachen (urban planning)
1968	Founded his own landscape design practice together with Dipl. Hort. Anneliese Latz in Aachen and Saarbrücken and became a founding partner in an urban planning, landscape and systems planning office in Aachen
1974	Moved his office to Kassel, various partnerships; since then research work and projects on new technologies between landscape architecture and architecture
Since 1989	Latz und Partner, landscape design and planning practice in Kranzberg, with Anneliese Latz, project office in Duisburg
1968–1973	Lecturer at the Academy of Architecture in Maastricht and the Academy of Architecture in Amsterdam, Netherlands
1973–1978	Chair of landscape architecture, Gesamthochschule Kassel
Since 1983	Chair of landscape architecture and planning, Technische Universität München-Weihenstephan

Selected realised projects:

1968/1969	Urban renewal Dillingen/Saar, with C. Schmitz and O. Neuloh
1970/1971	Open space planning for the head office of DSD, Saarlouis-Röderberg (won award for integration of an industrial site into landscape)
1973–1978	Research programme on landscape function planning and master planning for the Saar-Hunsrück national park, with G. Kaule, P. v. Pattay, M. Sitthard, E. Schneider
1976–1985	Open space planning for the Universität Marburg-Lahnberge, landscaping, wall covering with vines and rooftop planting for the buildings of the central clinic, institutes and refectory
1978–1981	General planning and landscaping, Technische Hochschule Darmstadt-Lichtwiese
1979–1983	Latz passive solar house in Kassel with Th. Herzog and R. Baumann (award for exemplary glass house extensions)
1979–1989	Hafeninsel municipal park, Saarbrücken, awarded the 1989 prize of the Federation of German Landscape Architects (BDLA)
1983–1986	"Grüne Häuser" and "Grüne Straße", Federal Horticultural Exhibition Berlin 1985, in collaboration with O. Steidle, Th. Herzog, E. Schneider-Wessling and others, architects Landscaping for the buildings of Universität 2, Ulm, in collaboration with O. Steidle, architect
Since 1988	Energy and rain-water schemes, wall covering with vines and rooftop planting, consultancy for Munich-Freimann industrial estate
1990/1991	Development planning for the "Grüngürtel" of Frankfurt on Main, with P. Lieser and M. Hegger
Since 1991	"Landschaftspark Duisburg-Nord", part of the IBA Emscher Park
Since 1991	Luxembourg, European City: urban planning, landscape and artistic development of the European urban district of Kirchberg, with J. Jourdan, C. König and Chr. Bauer, architects

Numerous international competitions, exhibitions and lectures, member of a number of commissions of experts

Selected Bibliography

Koenigs, Tom, editor. *Vision offener Grünräume*. Frankfurt am Main/New York, 1991

Wernersche Verlagsgesellschaft, editor. *Die Gartenkunst*, no. 1 (1991)

Uitgeverij Toth, editor. *Modern Park Design. Recent Trends*. Amsterdam, 1993

Koenigs, Tom, editor. *Stadt-Parks*. Frankfurt am Main, 1993

Burckardt, Lucius. "La memoria, come renderla visibile?" In *Eden*, no. 2 (1993), Milan

Lancaster, Michael. *The New European Landscape*. London, 1994

Numerous publications in German and international architecture, landscape architecture and urban planning journals

Acknowledgements

Kindly provided by the landscape architect:
Office Latz + Partner: 122, 124, 125 bottom, 126, 129, 130, 131 r.
Michael Latz: 125 top/m.
Monika Nikolic: 123 top
Christa Panick: 121, 127, 133
Claus Reisinger: 123 m.
as well as:
Rita Weilacher: 131 top

"Severity alone can be very dogmatic." (Dieter Kienast) Severely clipped box hedges in the *private garden of E.* on Uetliberg in Zurich, 1993.

Cultivating Discontinuity –
Dieter Kienast

To most landscape architects the issue of renewal in garden art occurs merely as a formal problem. They cling to historical models, reproduce artistic patterns, develop conspicuous design graphics or get caught up in superficial, formalistic approaches to design, constantly in search of a style to make into their own, readily recognisable trademark.

The Swiss landscape architect Dieter Kienast, born in 1945, views such trends as symptomatic of an acute lack of theory. Kienast sees the renewal of garden culture as primarily being a problem of content. The overriding aim of the work that he does in his Zurich office – along with his wife, Erika Kienast, who is an art historian, and Günther Vogt, who, like Kienast, is a landscape architect – is to make garden architecture an expression of the spirit of the age, the garden as a place of meaning, intended to heighten awareness and awaken the senses. This requires not only a study of the history of our culture, but also receptiveness to the diverse cultural manifestations of our age in cinema, video, philosophy, literature, music, advertising and contemporary art – a range which extends from Peter Greenaway to Sol LeWitt. Whereas many fear that they will lose their way in the labyrinthine structure of society today, Dieter Kienast recognizes that it is precisely this complexity which offers an exciting opportunity for experimental thought and action. Dieter Kienast's preference for works of Minimal Art, works which seek objectivity, is unmistakable. The declaration of the American Minimalist Robert Morris in support of formal simplicity could easily have been taken from one of the many treatises by the Zurich landscape architect:

1 Morris, Robert "Notes on Sculpture". In Battock, Gregory, editor. *Minimal art. A critical anthology*. New York, 1968: p. 228

"Simplicity of shape does not necessarily equate with simplicity of experience. Unitary forms do not reduce relationships. They order them. If the predominant, hieratic nature of the unitary form functions as a constant, all those particularising relations of scale, proportion etc., are not thereby cancelled. Rather they are bound more cohesively and indivisibly together."[1]

Just as the aloof projects of the artistic avant-garde of the sixties were an expression of opposition to the lack of imagination in art, Dieter Kienast opposes the disappearance of meaning in garden culture and fights to preserve the authenticity of the place. He uses only very few elements and only uses them where they further interpretation of the situation and reflect the nature of the place. Using seemingly natural means to conceal what is artificial, such as a showy biotope on the roof of an underground garage, falls into that class of wrongly-placed superficial images which the provocative planner categorically rejects.

Can this organism, which we call garden, developing as slowly as it does, have any claim to contemporary relevance without being degraded into an object which reflects no more than a passing fashion? The countless designs and the many projects the Zurich team has realised in Germany and Switzerland are certainly anything but a short-lived barrage of forms and colours, on the contrary: the work reveals a clarity of design which incorporates the commonplace as a matter of course and, with its powerful simplicity, gives even diversity its distinctive appeal. Complexity of content and formal simplicity are combined to provide a design which, true to the principles of transparency and ambivalence, affirms heterogeneity, not only allowing discontinuity, but cultivating it.

The design entered in the competition to enlarge the *Günthersburg Park* in Frankfurt am Main is an excellent example of what "cultivating of discontinuity" means in actual practice. The relocation of the municipal nurseries at the end of the eighties gave rise to the possibility of enlarging the old *Günthersburg Park*, a much over-used landscape park dating from the last century, to create an area twice the size of the existing park and develop it into a link between the inner city and Frankfurt's future green belt. Whereas the historical part entirely rejected the city, acting like a green oasis in the urban chaos, the new part of the park wants to live with the city and all its contradictions and dispenses with any kind of structural separation from the adjoining built-up areas. The new part of the park assimilates existing elements and structures and develops them into a new design language of contemporary individuality. Picturesque groups of trees in the historical part crystallise into clear tree structures, some linear, some two-dimensional. These form heterogeneous peripheral areas or mysterious park woodland, accentuated by precisely formulated clearings. Winding paths in the new part become linear lines of motion, underlining the spatial experience, instead of defining space themselves. Topiaries, reminiscent of fabulous creatures, populate the entrance area to the park and are a reference to earlier garden art traditions. A large, open expanse of grass lies at the centre of the new park, the focal point of the clearly designed framework, waiting for the city's inhabitants to fill it with life.

Despite the clear linking of the historical park with its new counterpart, the discontinuity remains tangible. The fracture is most visibly bridged by what used to be an entirely functional gardener's pathway, which today is covered by arches of roses. It forms the prelude to the romantically ironic puzzle picture at the end of the path: the modern gardener's house by the water-lily pond is overgrown with ivy and is transformed into the new Günthersburg, which once existed in the park as a tiny moated

Günthersburg Park in Frankfurt on Main. The entry which won the 1991 competition links the nineteenth-century landscape park to the south with the new part of the park without covering up the discontinuity between old and new.

Dieter Kienast

[2] from the Competition brief submitted in the 1991 competition.

castle of the Knights of Bornheim and gave the park its name. The new Günthersburg is no longer an introverted fortification, but allows a view of the everyday, changing reality of the city of Frankfurt. "The park relates history and stories. It can be experienced at different levels. It is a playground and, at the same time, a place of garden culture. It lives, ages and changes with itself and the people who use it."[2]

Günthersburg Park in Frankfurt on Main, perspectives
top left: pond and "Burghaus"
top right: sand clearing
bottom left: park wood with shrubbery
bottom right: bamboo entrance

Mr. Kienast, you learnt your trade at an early age in the gardening business of your parents.

We had to help our parents when we were children, but at that time I wasn't the slightest bit interested in gardens. When, at some time or other, I was told I was to train as a gardener, I was fairly indifferent. All I was interested in at the time was climbing. The daily work in the nursery was nothing more than an unavoidable interlude between weekends, when I could go climbing again. I think this is typical of me: I either do something body and soul or not at all. When I was about twenty, I realised that I needed to have a professional qualification and so I began working for the garden architects, Albert Zulauf and Fred Eicher. It was there that I basically learnt everything you need to know to run an architect's practice. Fred Eicher is one of the old guard of Swiss garden architecture. He taught me basic principles, for example how important it is to reduce the means used for each work to a few essential aspects. Eicher always said that what really mattered was to put the trees in the right place, this was something he excelled at. After a while I was convinced that I could do things very well and all that I now needed was some kind of certificate of my abilities. In Switzerland it was standard practice to work for an established garden architect for some years and then to start out on your own. But I wanted a degree and so – with my wife and a child – I started studying at the Polytechnic in Kassel at the age of twenty-four.

In Kassel it became clear to me that, in fact, I knew very little. The course of studies was still in its infancy, and students had a lot of freedom and had to organise themselves. This was very good for me. As I had nobody pushing me, I did a lot. Our projects were always the result of a great deal of struggle as the problems facing us first of all had to be intensively debated. The main debate in Kassel was about a social approach and how to achieve this in terms of planning. After I'd completed undergraduate studies, I realised that I lacked a number of important theoretical aspects, for example the fundamental principles of design and the history of art as well as the fundamental principles of botany. Therefore I decided to concentrate on one particular area. I chose plant sociology as Professor Karl-Heinrich Hülbusch was very active in this field and succeeded in awakening my enthusiasm for the subject. As I am naturally a chaotic sort of person, the strictly logical structure of this field helped me to discipline myself. During the holidays I had to earn money to support my family – by then there were four of us. I worked for Fred Eicher again for a while and, later on, for Peter Stöckli, who had worked for Albert Zulauf before starting up on his own.

I realised my first projects during this period. I found the combination of theoretical background knowledge from the university and the

specialized, almost traditional experience I had gained from actual practice to be a great help. I have always enjoyed both parts of my work: the designing aspect and the theoretical aspect.

After I had graduated, I still had the feeling that I didn't know enough; I was awarded a scholarship and studied for my doctorate under Professor Hülbusch and Professor Tüxen, the doyens of plant sociology. My topic was spontaneous inner-city plant societies in Kassel. I wanted to demonstrate that the approach of plant sociology was something which could be incorporated into planning. However, in the course of my studies it became apparent that demonstrating planning uses took up a lot of time, and so I was forced to confine myself to a natural science focus and only touch on practical applications.

You say that your systematic approach to planning developed during your studies. What sources does your creativity in the field of design draw on?

Basically, I'm a self-taught designer. I learnt hardly anything about design from Professor Grzimek; Professor Latz primarily taught the underlying principles of planning theory. So I began by reproducing what I had seen when I worked for Fred Eicher. His work clearly stood apart from all the work that I was familiar with at that time.

Your particular liking of the works of the Minimalist Carl Andre seems to indicate that you were particularly interested in the art scene of the late sixties.

I would say I was aware of it unconsciously, but that it still made an impression on me. For example, I recall George Trakas' contribution to documenta 6[1]. It consisted of two bridges, one of steel and one of wood, which had been blown up at their point of intersection. It made a great impression on me, but at the time I didn't in any way associate it with my work, as I was very much engrossed in plant sociology. If you'd asked me then what my plans for the future were, I'd have seen myself in research rather than working as a designer.

The plant sociologist has clearly not remained in his field. Why is this?

The prospect of only being able to discuss a special area of plant sociology with a total of about ten international experts didn't seem very exciting. I returned to Zurich, became a partner in Peter Stöckli's office and was engaged in work of very different kinds over a two-year period; designing, mapping in the field of plant sociology and so on.

It wasn't long before I realised that I was unable to develop in either the area of design or in plant sociology and, eventually, I decided to concentrate exclusively on working as a designer. Ambition certainly also played a role, and in 1980 I was appointed professor of garden

Dieter Kienast

architecture at the Federal Polytechnic in Rapperswil. This marked the beginning of an intensive debate on questions of design in conjunction with my colleagues, Jürg Altherr and Peter Erni. Jürg Altherr is a sculptor and also studied garden architecture. Peter Erni is an architect by profession. He has taught art history and has an astounding knowledge of theory, which, however, he had in the past never been able to make interdisciplinary use of. I tried to combine these different disciplines in student projects. This was sometimes very confusing for the students, but it taught them that there are always

encountered in any other work. Their application of the deductive principle, concentration on a few elements, becoming more powerful in consequence, made a lasting impression on me. Cramer's work was certainly the more forceful and followed an approach which was more innovative and programmatic. Fred Eicher's works don't contain any discontinuity and are always cautious. His plans from the fifties reveal that he once studied under Hermann Mattern at Kassel. I still today consider some of Eicher's works to be the best to have come out of the last twenty to thirty years. Here, I'm thinking, for

Brühl Park in Wettingen, 1982/1983, is one of the first major projects which Dieter Kienast realised. The design is modelled on the conception of the public park at the beginning of the twentieth century. Its nature is determined by the simplicity and force of the few design elements, which defy any naturalistic expression.

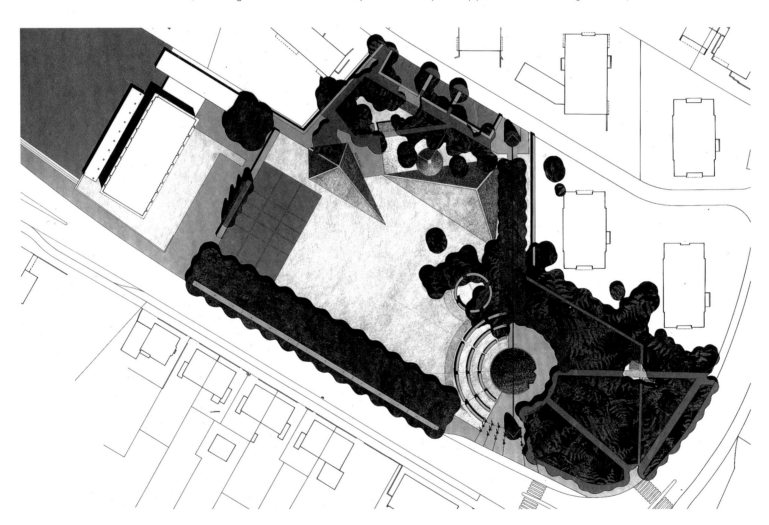

different ideas and approaches when discussing a project. This is why I have always felt interdisciplinary cooperation is vital.

Are the Swiss garden architects Ernst Cramer and Fred Eicher still role models, are they still relevant to your work today?
The things which were relevant in the early eighties are not the same as those which are relevant in 1995, but, despite this, the works of Ernst Cramer still inspire me today. As for the agreeable simplicity of the work of Fred Eicher, this is a quality which I have virtually never

example, of the Eichbühl cemetery in Zurich. As they were also fellow-countrymen, I often tried to imitate them in the early years.
I consider Bernard Lassus to be a very significant figure in present-day landscape design. His works are certainly not without contradictions, nevertheless they are some of the most exciting ones I know today. The purpose of Lassus' works is not only development of existing theories, but also an attempt to bring practicality and poetry into their realisation. There came a point when the works of Ernst Cramer and Fred Eicher no longer provided any inspiration in this

respect as the formal aspect plays the more important role in their work. But what I see as being essential is precisely the successful combination of content and form.

I have always attached a great deal of importance to theory as it's not possible to carry out an important aspect of landscape design on an emotional level. The lack of theory which is deplored by everyone is, to my mind, indeed a serious issue. I'm not talking about something like a lack of planning theory, but a general understanding of culture, in other words knowledge of garden history, the history of art, social theory and so on. Theory belongs to the intellectual part of our work. Of course, if it's only a question of creating pretty little shapes, I don't need any theory.

The relationship to historical garden art is of special significance to many landscape architects. How important is this relationship for you?

I didn't start to concern myself with garden art intensively until I had to when I started lecturing in the eighties. I had to work my way right through the history of garden art; in the course of my studies, I realised that many historical conceptions were not outdated, but still have relevance for us today. Or perhaps it's just that we continue to concern ourselves with these

outdated conceptions? There's not, however, any one epoch in the history of garden art that I find particularly interesting.

How has the way you see yourself altered over the years?

Shortly after I started studying, I had the feeling that I fully understood landscape design. Then in 1973 I won a national competition in Switzerland, and that was devastating for me. For the first time I had the impression that I really was the best. At that time the only criterion I used to judge works was whether I liked them or not. However, the older you get, the more self-critical you become and such uncritical views become relative. My critical ability increased as a result of working with students and colleagues. And it was only then that I did my first reasonably intelligent designs.

Which projects would you include in this category?

I still consider *Brühl Park* in Wettingen to be one of my better projects, not least on account of its simple means of design. The park does have a few small mistakes as it was one of my first larger projects. For example, I'm still not entirely satisfied with the children's play area as it doesn't work very well. And then there's the narrow strip of ground linking two streets which

The circular pool and paddling area, framed by a small wood in the background and clipped hedges in the foreground, lies at the point of intersection of the townhall axis and the park axis, which spans *Brühl Park* at its widest point.

Geometrically shaped sledging hills underline the artificial nature of the design of *Brühl Park* in Wettingen and enter into a dialogue with the "Lägernrücken", the mountain chain in the background.

Dieter Kienast

Redesigning the park of the *Waldhaus psychiatric clinic* in Chur, 1994. Behind the central building two large, concrete mirrored pools pull light into the courtyard and transform the former side entrance into a main entrance.

border the park on either side. This strip follows the course of a main path and even crosses the circular water-pool. For a while I felt it to be immensely important in order to reveal the full breadth of the park. In retrospect I'm rather puzzled by this need as it only conveys the appearance of logic. I no longer have the feeling that there are certain things which it is vital to point out.

Reduction to very simple, almost archaic fundamental principles of design was, incidentally, the consequence of having to make sensible use of a limited budget. This constraint has the fortunate side-effect that one has to be disciplined. A few of the younger members of the profession had, to my mind, the misfortune of having too much money at their disposal. The

Behind your gardens and landscape images there is, I assume, a definite vision of the future quality of the environment we live in.

That's correct. However, designing outside space is initially a relatively simple task. Difficulties only arise when an attempt is made to create a special place. I don't see this as being a question of a certain style or prescribed use of certain materials and plants. For me it's a question of an architect exploring his own possibilities. These emerge from the accumulation of the individual cultural sediment. Of course, the site and the nature of the task also play an essential role. The combination of these factors produces what I always see as a surprising diversity of answers. In my opinion, it's

projects which came into being were in some cases awful. In view of the circumstances I just mentioned, the planning of *Brühl Park* resulted in a design of striking individuality. The earth pyramids bring Pückler and Cramer to mind. This link was not intended and nearly led to a new formal design with a lot of hills. But, in the end, I left it as it was as I felt that the park could only take a very small number of simple elements. The hills were intended as a contrast to the flat surroundings and the mountain ridge of the Lägern.

How would you describe the way you see yourself as a landscape architect today?

That's a tricky question. Recently an architect asked me what my "message" was. My reply was: "Do good things."

more of a coincidence if two works are developed on the basis of similar conceptions. Sometimes the question of how I see myself does come up. At such moments I ask myself whether I can simply do what I want without this depending on certain moral concepts.

In what way do you consider garden art to be relevant to society today, to the culture of our time?

The question as to the state of garden art today or what contemporary garden art means doesn't interest me. I don't think it's the job of the designer to answer these questions. Discussion of this kind doesn't get me anywhere. What good does distinguishing between what is garden art and what is not do me? The philosopher Hans-Georg Gadamer has a good defini-

In the garden-courtyard of the acute psychiatric wing, which is enclosed on three sides, the ground-surfaces consist of strips of narrow concrete slabs and expanses of gravel. Small trees, a long, sweeping bench and a narrow, elevated pool of rust-coloured steel plates form the spatial structure.

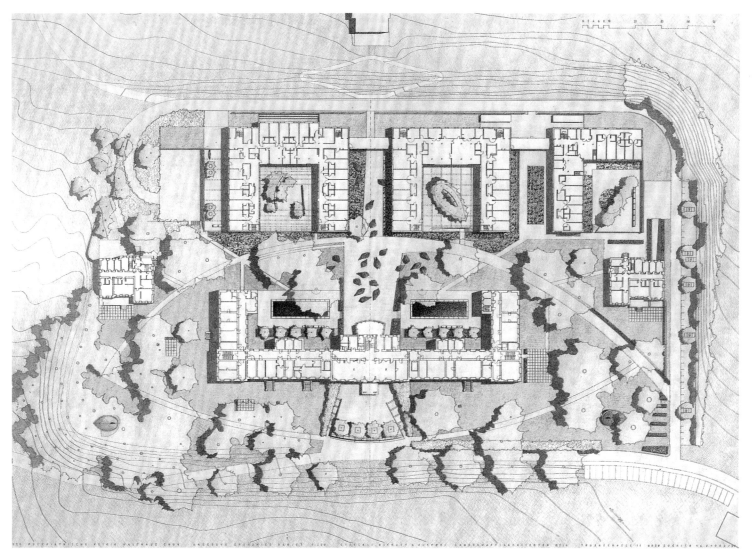

Two small pavilions, identical in form and style, are located in different situations in the old park. Leaf-shaped metal roofs with plywood on the underside are supported by a structure of steel ribs. The concrete floors repeat the form of the roof twice and alter the perspective of the two surfaces.

Layout of the *Waldhaus clinic*. The new design is confined to no more than a few subdued and interestingly varied elements both in the area of the large central building and in the courtyards of the three clinics: trees, water, surfaces. The small trees deliberately contrast with the mature trees in the old part of the park, but the new design also creates a spatial link with the old park.

Dieter Kienast

tion of this; he says that anything which is secular has nothing to do with art. If we propose to follow this definition, there is no garden art.

Perhaps we should follow the example of Leberecht Migge, who neatly avoided the problem and spoke of garden culture. I feel incapable of judging individual works in terms of whether they qualify as art or don't qualify as art. Let's leave this debate up to theorists like Lucius Burckhardt, who are much better qualified to judge this question. Otherwise, I see the danger that people will only be working with a view to going down in the annals of garden art.

You once said that the profession didn't have any examples to follow. So the obvious question is what you take as your example.

I don't follow any example. The fact is that our social, political and religious situation hangs in the balance and there's very little we can do about it. The longer this precarious situation continues, the greater our tendency to cling to particular principles or role-models. I find this state of flux particularly exciting as it offers the possibility of moving unencumbered and experimenting. Particularly when we're working on small projects, we often try out new ideas, materials and forms, although we may later on

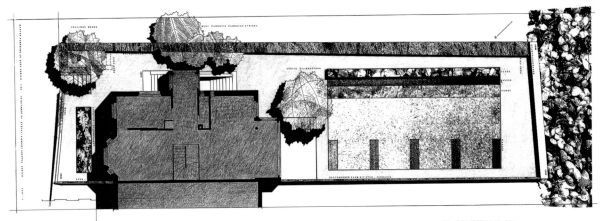

A new adobe wall in front of a backdrop of yew and 20-metre-high beech trees forms the southern boundary of the *private garden of the K. family*. Rectilinear pools have been let into the lawn. Realised in 1995.

The shape of the small *private garden of the K. family* in Zurich, realised in 1995, is emphasized by a 40-metre-long, slightly wedge-shaped beech hedge along the east side of the property. The old fence opposite is covered in vine.

Yet, despite what you've just said, many of your projects don't exactly bear out the proposition that landscape design is nothing more than a straightforward, secular matter.

What I just said about landscape design being basically something very simple was certainly not pretentiousness, it just happens to be true. Despite all the different approaches, solutions and conceptions to be found in our work, I don't rule out the existence of some projects which are terribly simple. Sometimes, it really is only a matter of the right tree in the right place, the right path and perhaps a bench. Linking these elements with each other is sometimes difficult and sometimes very easy. Afterwards, the finished result always tells us whether the intervention works or not. This is a question of atmosphere and mood, and of poetry. I don't want to use the word beauty in this context as it is always associated with the emotive concept of natural beauty, and this is always taken to be prettiness. The outside space, the garden can be pretty, but it doesn't have to be. I also like places which aren't beautiful in the widely-accepted view; what is ugly can also be beautiful, can possess a beauty which doesn't have a soothing effect, but startles. Capturing the particular character of an individual place, preserving its authenticity is something I consider to be tricky. That's why I always judge our work in terms of whether it truly reflects the character of the place and its atmosphere. This often has nothing to do with either formal means or content.

never use them again. If I do have a typical approach, it can be described as a process of continual experiment.

But your publications and lectures always refer to an extensive collection of empirical principles to be used in working with outside space.[2] This seems to indicate a firm idea of what landscape architecture is supposed to do.

You see, postmodernism was, for example, often misunderstood as a programme which allowed one to do anything. Of course, every-

[2] cf. Kienast, Dieter. "Ohne Leitbild." In *Garten + Landschaft* 11/86: p. 34

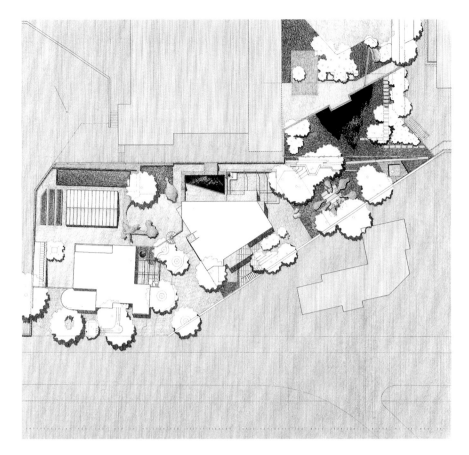

Layout plan of the *private garden of the Kienast family* in Zurich. It shows how structures and vegetation blend to form a collage.

Fabulous creatures, several metres high, cut out of horn-beams populate the *private garden of the Kienast family*, changing the perspective from an adult's to that of child and, at the same time, evoking topiaries, elements typical of historical garden art.

A high fence marks the boundary of the *private garden of the Kienast family*; how-ever, it is not an insurmount-able screen, but a transparent curtain.

147

Dieter Kienast

thing is possible, but only within a limited area. I think it was Henry Ford who said that a car could be any colour as long as it was black. We certainly do have clear conceptual ideas for our work, but application of these conceptions and principles changes all the time and produces widely differing results, not just in formal terms. The astonishing thing is that most of our principles are generally accepted as they are far from being unusual. To give you an example, every landscape architect tries to convey the special character of the place. One problem is that the collection of principles you mentioned contains statements which I would no longer make today as some of them are so generally applicable that they find universal acceptance. Yet, despite this agreement beforehand, the resulting projects would all be quite different

from the garden. The result was an ambivalent image, composed of the soil as the foundation of the garden and the wall as a typical urban element. The wall makes the invisible visible, as the soil, which is usually hidden below the garden wall, frames the garden in its typical colour. I consider this simple measure to be an ecological contribution in more ways than one.

Our *own garden*, which we see as a kind of playground for all kinds of experiments, contains large topiaries. Everyone who visits us always asks what they are supposed to mean, and my answer is, "I don't know, what do you think they're supposed to mean?"

Ambiguity, both in the conception of our works and in their subsequent perceptibility, is important to us. We believe the complex relationships of dependence in the world make it so difficult to understand it as a whole that we can no longer afford to only think in one direction if we want to achieve our goal of doing something for a lot of people. I learnt from Bernard Lassus that there are very different levels for us to read. Perhaps this is the part of our principles which not everyone readily subscribes to.

You realise your projects in collaboration with your wife, Erika Kienast, and the landscape architect Günther Vogt. How does this team work?

Collaboration takes place on a variety of different levels. I do discuss individual projects with my wife, and she brings to my attention any oddities she notices and considers to be problematic. But the indirect comments are far more important for our work together.

I have been working with Günther Vogt for about eight years. We understand each other spontaneously without needing a lot of words. We also have discussions and disputes with each other, pencil in hand. Words are, as a rule, followed by actions, in the form of drawings. This is often my job, but as far as possible we always develop the underlying conception jointly. Our projects aren't created by each of us working on his own.

A blue ceramic square is to be found at the lowest point of the garden in the middle of the uncultivated part. An interplay of chaos and order.

from each other. So when you ask me about our viewpoint, it's important to realise that having an unequivocal position of one's own has given way to ambivalence, simultaneity and ambiguity.

Can you explain the specific effects the principles you have mentioned have on a project?

In *Zurich*, for example, we are working on a small *private garden*. The garden is located in the middle of the city and a railway tunnel runs under the site. We asked ourselves what the special character of the place was and took the theme of earth as a raw material which is always manipulated. The garden space had to be enclosed and so we built a wall using soil

Your wife is an art historian. This would suggest that art plays an important role in your work together. What kind of art is particularly significant in your work?

My preference is for Minimal Art and the music concepts derived from it. Quite a number of my finds are from this movement. What I find so interesting about these works is, of course, the aspect of reduction, restriction to only very few elements, the clear and logical conception. However, as we don't only work with dead materials such as concrete, steel and glass, but also with plants in a different context, there is no danger of us adopting Minimal Art literally. That's why I much prefer Minimalists such as Carl Andre and Donald Judd to Land Artists. I already mentioned that the need to be logical

"OGNI PENSIERO VOLA" – "Every thought flies."

The words in blue concrete letters form the boundary of a simple pavilion in a *private garden* in South Germany. They are taken from a sixteenth-century inscription by Vicino Orsini in the garden of Bomarzo. Whereas these words open the jaws of hell in Bomarzo, in Kienast's garden they frame the picturesque view across the garden on the slope and the town at the foot of the mountain. Kienast's translation is: "The thoughts are free."

Dieter Kienast

is very helpful to me. I have enough chaotic tendencies of my own.

So reducing things to what is essential is also a way of exercising self-discipline?

Undoubtedly a certain idea of order also plays a role. We don't need to create chaos, it comes about of its own accord. So it's more a question of whether I can or should create order. We oppose chaos, which, to some extent, nature provides us with, by creating order as a viable system. This requires discipline, including self-discipline. Of course, the dual principle of order and chaos exists in our own thinking and actions and has to be guided. I can't think and draw at the same time, but have to do each alternately. This reciprocal relationship definitely shapes the form of open space. But reduction also has a social background: the enrichment of space occurs of its own accord, whereas we have to ensure the creation of a viable context. If the dish is full from the beginning, it can't be filled up any further or the additional mass will pose a problem. That's why we have to confine ourselves to completing part of the picture only.

Renovation of *Augustusplatz in Leipzig*, model photo. Two curves formed by avenues of lime-trees stretching from the opera to the Gewandhaus give the square its distinct space.

For poetry to unfold what elements form part of a design for outside space in addition to reticent severity?

Severity alone can be very dogmatic. For example, the design for the *Augustusplatz* in Leipzig communicates a certain severity at first sight. It is the skilful use of light which brings the poetic element into play. At night the square provides a fascinating experience of light by means of two-tone ground lights. It's not the space but the ground which is lit up. I can imagine that immersing oneself in a sea of subdued, coloured light would be something very impressive. In *Güntherburg Park* in Frankfurt a modern building gives the situation poetry by presenting itself as a medieval castle. To my mind, there are different kinds of poetry. The poetry in *Günthersburg Park* has Romantic overtones.

In what way does poetry with Romantic overtones differ from Romanticism pure?

Pure Romanticism is characterised by a revelling in feelings which precludes any kind of objective reflection. It's only when you look again that you see that the supposed medieval

castle is basically a simple box surrounded by a wall one hundred and thirty metres in length and six metres high. This is a discontinuity of the Romantic image as the language of architecture comes from a different context.

Do you have a tendency towards Romanticism?

Of course.

You are one of the few people to say so openly; most people associate Romanticism with concepts like petit bourgeois, nationalistic, trivial.

We have different souls in us, and the Romantic side of mine is very pronounced. I like to go climbing and enjoy the grandeur of the Alps. Isn't that Romanticism at its best? I don't mind being called a Romantic as there's also the other side of me which calls my Romantic side into question. I enjoy going into the mountains, and after three days I find myself longing for the stink of exhaust fumes. I was climbing in the Mont Blanc area not long ago and just as the trip got particularly difficult, I had an incredible longing to be back in the hustle and bustle, eating a Big Mac, sitting somewhere warm and comfortable, watching TV.

Our garden also contains elements of Romantic enchantment. But you also suddenly come across a ceramic square, which gives expression to something entirely different. I live in this duality of Romanticism on the one hand and the relationship to everyday reality and rationalism on the other. At any rate, I feel that what is Romantic will increase in importance again in the future.

When I think back to the 1994 International Horticultural Exhibition in Stuttgart, Romanticism had its place there, but it was not the same kind of Romanticism that we stand for. What I miss in the Romanticism of horticultural shows is, quite simply, the elucidatory aspect, perhaps I'd even go so far as to say an intellectual approach. The ephemeral and superficial formal language which is presented at horticultural shows is just as repugnant to me as the popular and widespread phenomenon of so-called contemporary landscape design. There's always discontinuity in the Romanticism in our projects: before the point is reached where the emotional takes over completely, elements are introduced which call for reflexion.

Is it true, as was once written about you, that you create gardens for intellectuals?

No, that's utter nonsense. We are not interested in doing something because it's different and exciting and attracts a lot of attention; our concern is people. Particularly people who live in urban areas have a right to experience a tree when they go out of the house – just think of "Herr K." by Bertolt Brecht. I think we have to learn to come to terms with these seemingly problematic, allegedly unmodern elements and aspects. Romanticism is part of this, as is a dis-

SCHNITT A-A' 1:50

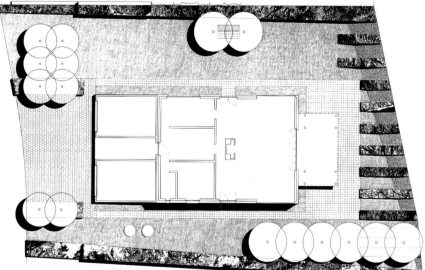

Garden of a mathematician,
1993, sections and perspectives.

Layout of the *garden of a
mathematician.*

Dieter Kienast

cerning use of plants, something which has been wickedly neglected. We've been happy creating gardens and parks which very much resemble the treeless designs of architects for far too long. We thought we were being horribly progressive. The desire to be a bit eccentric also played too great a part. It's not my purpose to do something which is especially different. If people nevertheless like our designs this both pleases and surprises me.

We built a very small *Garden for a Mathematician*. I felt that the plans and the garden itself were very beautiful and very disciplined. The poetry in this garden results from, at the most, the arrangements of the plants, which we placed in geometrical lines. In the end, the mathematician liked it very much, but to begin with we always have great difficulties in getting people to accept our designs. The basic structure of our sites is relatively rigid and is clearly dominant in the early stages. It's not until later, when the vegetation develops, that a certain balance is established. Vegetation plays a vital role in our designs.

In addition to vegetation, words as an inscription or sculptural element are also important in some of your projects. This would seem to suggest that you also draw your inspiration from other trends in art; I'm thinking, for example, of the works of Ian Hamilton Finlay.

That's certainly true, Ian Hamilton Finlay is undoubtedly one of my favourites. I find his one-word poems quite fascinating. In architecture too we notice that information is increasingly being absorbed through language; people are more able to relate to the written word than to the language of architecture. Things which we would have difficulty in accomplishing in the garden using other means can readily be achieved with words, for example by using ambiguity. Words can be read, they can make us think, and we can use words to create a certain mood, something which is an extremely important aspect of our work. The criticism which is sometimes made of Ian Hamilton Finlay is that his work can only be understood by intellectuals. But, in my opinion, this kind of intervention is one which can also be read by someone who doesn't have extensive analytical abilities. Our proposal for the entrance area to a strip of park at *EXPO 2000* in Hanover is Laurie Anderson's sentence "Paradise is just where you are" in five-metre-high letters. It doesn't require any intellectual flights of fancy to decode this sentence.

The catalogue of your first exhibition is entitled "Zwischen Arkadien und Restfläche". What do you associate with the concept of Arcadia?

I equate Arcadia with the longing always to be somewhere else. I'm sure this longing to escape from all our problems exists in all of us. Our garden designs contain both aspects: the Arca-

dian and everyday life. The discontinuity is immanent. Without this discontinuity we would be in danger of sinking into banality.

So you're not interested in achieving harmony at all costs?

No, we cultivate discontinuity. Discontinuity also occurs in my own life and this is what provides stimulation. This can be strenuous sometimes, but it leads to the discovery of new horizons of experience and widening of sensory fields. Outside space must be a place perceptible by the senses. These experiences are only possible at the fractures between the poles. In other words, designing is always a process of oscillation between opposites.

When developing your projects, you're not afraid to collaborate with people from associated disciplines such as architecture, engineering and sculpture; in fact you regard this as a natural step which produces innovative results for all concerned.

That's right. For example, during the ten years I taught at Rapperswil, I never once worked with landscape architects, but always with artists such as Jürg Altherr and Esther Gisler. I also realised projects with both of them later on. Recently we've been working less with artists and more with architects. I very much appreciate this collaboration, which is not to say that we always have to synchronize our work with that of other disciplines. Sometimes we're quite thankful not to be the first to work on the site. When we're not, certain basic structures are already in place and some of the fundamental problems don't need to be overcome.

The artist is always to be envied for the great freedom he has in contrast with the landscape architect.

This freedom is something we also have, I'm sure of that. I have noticed that when students of architecture first come into contact with landscape architecture it bothers them a lot that there is no prescribed programme for them to complete. This seems to indicate that we have a great deal of freedom in comparison with other disciplines.

How do you fulfil the many and diverse sociological, ecological and functional demands placed on the outside space?

I never say that we have to take everything into consideration at the same time and all the time. The ecological approach can usually even be realised in very small projects without being dominant. Ecology is anyway no longer an independent aspect for us, as it now forms part of every project as a matter of course. In consequence, we don't make a lot of fuss about the ecological qualities of our projects. For example, we are using decreasing amounts of technologically processed materials and pay attention to the problem of surface water and

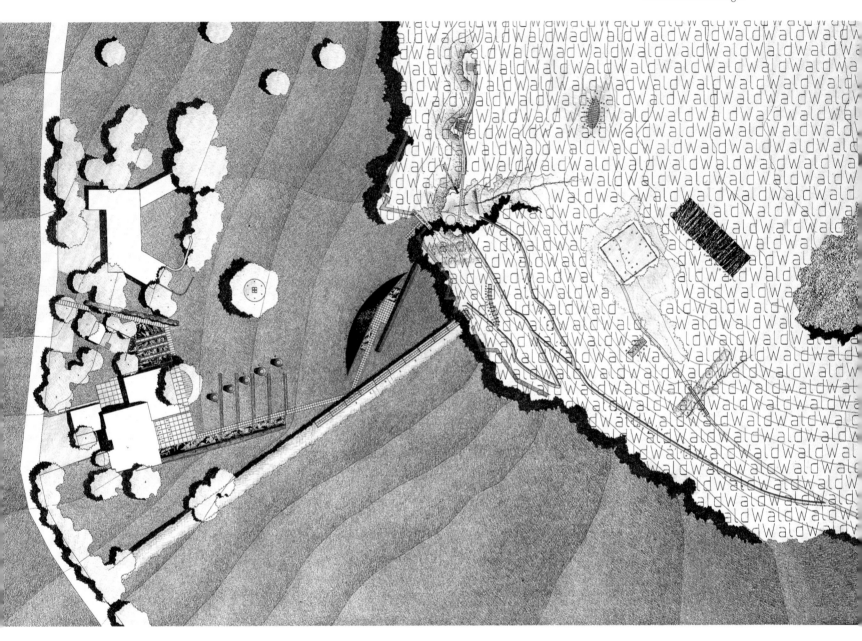

153

Dieter Kienast

so on. Although it has something to do with ecology, this is not the main issue.

I consider purely functional thinking to be far more problematic. Take the kind of town planning which was practised in the former GDR as an example. The expedient approach and the attempt to always and everywhere provide an optimum reaction to functional requirements and the demands of space resulted in the disappearance of the relationship between the urban elements, of the quality and sensory nature of urban space. The open spaces which were created were mediocre. Of course, the same problems also existed to a lesser extent in major settlement projects in the West. Expediency may not be allowed to become the be all and end all. Nor may ecology become the be all and end all.

And what about artistic freedom? Can it be the be all and end all?

No. However, if the alternative to artistic freedom is taken to be involving users, it's important to be aware that, after twenty years, the results of participation are so modest that this is an approach which it would be better to abandon sooner rather than later. It has emerged that the possibilities of having any influence are so limited that projects which were developed with public participation do not substantially differ from projects based entirely on designs by architects. Admittedly, there's the saying which states that everybody should be given the opportunity of self-expression, no matter what form this takes, but, to my mind, this doesn't apply to public space. Perhaps the call for more creative work is to be understood as an indication that we should rely less on majority decisions and pay more attention to independent work. All too often planners hide behind the majority decisions of the users. In Switzerland we know that the majority is not always right. So we don't pay lip-service to people who don't bear responsibility, but nor is unlimited freedom the antipode.

In both the United States and Europe Martha Schwartz's daring designs and her demand for freedom have set off much discussion on the role of art and landscape design.

Martha Schwartz claims that she is an artist. I think the reason she does so is that she doesn't want to be attacked, either by planners or ecologists. People who confine themselves to purely aesthetic works often appear to be fighting something of a rearguard action. Perhaps they make it a bit too easy for themselves. But their work does have something of a refreshing, liberating quality. However, it's my opinion that we work in public space and what we plan shapes part of people's everyday life. There's a difference between working in a gallery, in the Nevada desert or a private garden and working in a public park. Here we have a responsibility, which we can't simply avoid by

references to freedom of the artist or having to accommodate wishes of the general public. What matters much more is to keep looking at what one is doing in terms of its quality and validity, to develop mental alertness and to find new answers to Adorno's old question: How can a specific purpose be translated into space, using what forms and what material? Seen in this way, architectural imagination would be the ability to articulate space through its purposes, to let them become space, to build forms to fulfil purposes.

"Et in Arcadia ego" – "I too was in Arcadia". These words form the railing of a vantage point at the edge of the woods which surveys the surrounding countryside. *Private garden of E.* on Uetliberg in Zurich, 1993.

Dieter Kienast

Biography and Selected Works

Dieter Kienast was born in Zurich in 1945. He and his wife, Erika Kienast-Lüder, live and work in Zurich.
Schooling and apprenticeship in gardening in Zurich.
He studied landscape planning at Gesamthochschule Kassel.
In 1978 he was awarded a doctorate for his thesis on plant sociology.

Except where noted, locations are in Switzerland

Practice of Landscape Architecture and teaching activities:

1979–1994	Founding partner of Stöckli, Kienast & Koeppel, landscape architects in Zurich, Bern and Wettingen
1980–1991	Professor of garden architecture at Interkantonales Technikum in Rapperswil
1981–1985	Technical director at the botanical gardens in Brügglingen/Basle
Since 1985	Lecturer in landscape design at Eidgenössische Technische Hochschule Zürich
Since 1992	Professor at Institut für Landschaft und Garten, Technische Hochschule Karlsruhe
Since 1995	Founding partner of Kienast Vogt Partner, landscape architects, Zurich and Bern, with Erika Kienast-Lüder and Günther Vogt.

Selected realised projects:

1982	Brühl Park in Wettingen
1987/1993	Municipal Park in St. Gallen
1988/1994	Open space planning for Inselspital Lory-Spital, PKT 2 etc., Bern with U. Strasser, A. Roost, architects, Bern
1989	Medici garden in Erlenbach with U. Marbach and A. Rüegg, architects, Zurich
1990	Rütihof cemetery, Baden with J.+ B. Fosco-Oppenheim and K. Vogt, architects, Scherz
1991	*Ecole cantonale de langue française*, Bern with Häflinger, Grunder, von Allmen, architects, Bern
1992	Vogelbach residential development, Riehen with M. Alder, architect, Basle
1994	Waldhaus psychiatric clinic, Chur with F. Chiaverio and F. Censi, architects, Grono
1994	Urban and landscape renewal of Neustädter Feld, Magdeburg, Germany with Herzog & de Meuron, architects, Basle
1995	Hotel Zürichberg, Zurich with M. Buchhalter and Ch. Suni, architects, Zurich

Numerous private gardens

Numerous competitions including:

1990	Bärenplatz and Waisenhausplatz Bern (1st prize)
	Park for Moabiter Werder in Berlin, Germany (1st prize)
1991	Günthersburg Park in Frankfurt on Main, Germany (1st prize)
1992	Witikon cemetery in Zurich (1st prize)
	Cemetery in Chur (1st prize)
1993	Park for the spa town of Bad Münder, Germany (1st prize)
1994	Urban Design Landscaping Competition Dreissigacker Meiningen, Germany with Schnebli, Ammann, Ruchat, architects, Zurich (1st prize)
	Centre for Art and Media Technology in Karlsruhe, Germany (1st prize)
1992–1995	Exhibition *Zwischen Arkadien und Restfläche*, in Lucerne, Karlsruhe, Germany, Freising-Weihenstephan, Germany, and Zurich

Selected Bibliography

Kienast, D. "Die Sehnsucht nach dem Paradies." In *Hochparterre* 2/7 (1990)
Edition Architekturgalerie Luzern, editor. *Zwischen Arkadien und Restfläche*. Lucerne, 1992 (catalogue)
Kienast, D. "Die Natur der Sache – Stadtlandschaften." In *Stadtparks*, edited by T. Koenigs. Frankfurt am Main, 1993
Kienast, D./Vogt, G. "Die Form, der Inhalt und die Zeit." In *Topos*, no. 2 (1993)
Kienast, D. "Zwischen Poesie und Geschwätzigkeit." In *Garten und Landschaft*, no. 1 (1994)
Kienast, D. "Zur Dichte der Stadt." In *Topos*, no. 7 (1994)
Kienast, D. "Der Garten als geistige Landschaft." In *Topos*, no. 11 (1995)

Acknowledgements

All illustrations were kindly provided by the landscape architect.
Büro Kienast: 150
Wolfram Müller/Institut für Landschaft und Garten, Universität Karlsruhe: 141
Christian Vogt: 137, 143, 144, 145 bottom, 147 bottom, 148, 149, 155

"Topiary abstractions. I love them." Sven-Ingvar Andersson

The Antidote to Virtual Reality – Sven-Ingvar Andersson

Danish landscape architecture has derived its inspiration from the visual arts since the thirties. "How this happens is not quite certain, but it is reasonable to presume that successful collaboration between architects and landscape architects, which is still unusual in other countries, aided the landscape architects in establishing contact with the visual arts. This understanding of the visual arts nurtured a desire to achieve artistic qualities at the same level as in the visual arts."[1]

The unassuming grandseigneur of contemporary Scandinavian landscape architecture believes that garden art is one of the visual arts and that, in contrast to the stagnation occurring in many European countries, Danish garden art is developing a wide range of activities. Its particular charm lies in the successful blending of an artistic approach to design and a profound feeling for the nature of the Danish cultural and natural landscape: its spatial composition, the changing seasons of life and the genius loci. Formal austerity, clarity of lines, sparing, specific use of plants and building materials and, last not

[1] Andersson, Sven-Ingvar. Quoted from "Havekunst in Danmark." In *Arkitektur DK*, no. 4 (1990): p. 174

but least, a well-developed sense of creating effective space are the characteristic features of Danish garden art.

Sven-Ingvar Andersson follows on in the tradition of Danish landscape architecture, its most prominent representatives include Gudmund Nyeland Brandt (1878–1945) and Carl Theodor Sørensen (1893–1979). Andersson was Sørensen's assistant at the chair of landscape architecture at the Royal Danish Academy of Fine Arts from 1959 to 1963. The influence of the professor on his assistant and successor at the Academy is unmistakable. Decades before the distinctive landscape interventions by the Land Art movement in America, C. Th. Sørensen developed and realised projects which in their formal simplicity and spatial force still stand up to any comparison with the works of Earth Art. Sørensen preferred to use archetypal geometries such as the spiral, the circle and the square and also discovered the appeal of oval forms, forms which are unmistakably part of Sven-Ingvar Andersson's repertoire. Andersson's works do not depend on elaborate, superficial effects, but gradually reveal their remarkable qualities to the visitor in a direct experience of real space. The diversity of plants and building materials in the garden and park is perceptibly reduced in favour of spatial

clarity and concentration on the subtle qualities inherent in the materials used. Sensitive shaping of the terrain and a virtuoso use of the hedge as an element which defines space often suffice to achieve conceptions of outside space which are intriguing but also flexible in the way they can be used.

Marna's have, the hedge garden of "Marna", Andersson's country cottage in Södra Sandby, which lies to the north-east of Malmø, has served the garden artist as a place of experiments for many years.[2] It is here that Andersson's understanding of himself as a garden artist is particularly well-illustrated by an intensive dialogue with the principles of historical garden art. The origins of his garden lie in his early dream of a sequence of clearly defined, green spaces, open to the sky, intended to allow a flexibility of use. At Easter 1965, Andersson planted 600 small hawthorns over an area of approximately 1,000 square metres to form an irregular hedge pattern, which related to vistas, boundaries of the garden and future open spaces. In order to overcome the differences of as much as 3 metres in the level of the ground, the hedges were cut to a uniform level of 1 metre above the highest point in the garden, creating "hedge walls" with a height of four metres in some parts of the garden. The result

[2] cf. Andersson, Sven-Ingvar. "Häckar och höns – min torparträdgård." In *Landscap* no. 8 (1976): p. 180

Carl Theodor Sørensen intended his design proposal for the *Musical Garden in Vitus Bering Park* in Horsens to be an expression of his conviction that garden art fulfils a purely aesthetic function. His architecturally structured design for outside space, shown here as a watercolour from 1954, was not realised at the time.

is an attractive spatial structure composed of accessible and usable areas of different sizes, enclosed and open parts, walls and tunnels. When the design required removal of a number of hedge shrubs, they were planted individually in the largest spatial unit of the garden among low privet hedges, sweet-smelling clumps of lavender and pink, white and blue perennials. In the beginning they were allowed to develop naturally. Today the large, bird-like clipped hedge figures give the *Hönsgård*, the *Chicken-Run*, as Andersson calls it, its character. He deliberately makes use of the contrast between the clipped hedge as controlled form and the unclipped hedge as natural form. This spatial context of a sensitively designed artistic garden setting is able to accommodate a diversity of family activities, ranging from a barbecue area to a flower garden. Details alter to reflect the changing seasons and the needs of the family, but the composition remains open to new uses and interpretations, while the clear hedge

structure gives the garden its spatial definition. "Whether I shall have the chance," Andersson writes, "of enjoying this hawthorn garden in my old age I do not know, but the hawthorn plants are thriving, and in spring the branches scatter their white blossoms on the ground below like new-fallen snow, only to be weighed down in autumn by masses of dark-red berries and the birds that thrive on them."[3]

3 ibid., p. 184

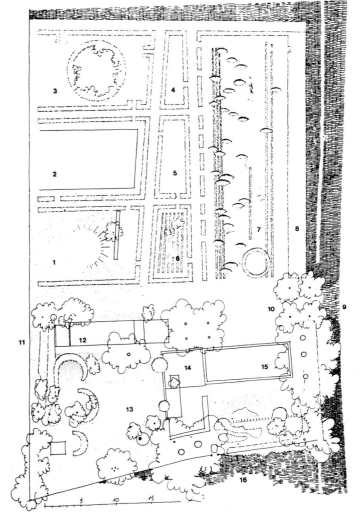

Marna's have in Södra Sandby: a private garden and the place where Sven-Ingvar Andersson engages in his personal experiments in garden art. The plan of the garden reveals the interplay of the geometric design of architecture and free landscape design.

Sven-Ingvar Andersson

Professor Andersson, is the love of nature which Scandinavians are said to have a cliché or reality?

I feel that the love of nature is definitely more typical of Scandinavia than, for example, of Germany. The relationship to nature has shaped national identities for over one hundred years. This is more pronounced in Finland and Norway than in Denmark, where the link is less strong because the natural environment is less distinctive here. It is easier to identify with a powerful environment, particularly when it comes to defining national identity. Many Danish poets and artists have made an intensive study of the characteristic features of Danish landscape, the gentle topography and the close relationship to water, to the coast, which has a magic attraction for people.

You grew up on a farm and so you have known nature from early childhood. How would you define your relationship to nature today?

Alhambra. Drawing by Sven-Ingvar Andersson

That's hard to say. Growing up on a farm doesn't necessarily mean that you are really aware of what nature is. There wasn't actually any need to think about nature. When I was a child, I experienced what it is like to be surrounded by nature. This was very much helped by the fact that my mother felt it was important for me to experience nature. She often spoke about a beautiful sky, a magnificent sunset or the glorious colours of autumn leaves. She was very interested in beauty and my father, who ran the farm, had a well-developed aesthetic sense. These qualities influenced me and I developed a love of drawing at a very early age. My teacher advised me to become a painter or a sculptor, but I lacked the necessary courage. My mother was a very good gardener and I learnt a lot from her. I have never experienced the conflict between garden design and ecology as it was quite clear to me that a good gardener always includes ecological factors in his work, no matter how elaborate the design is. Le Nôtre was not only a gifted artist, he was also an extremely intelligent ecologist.

I've had difficulties with all the discussion on nature and being natural ever since I started working as a landscape architect. I've experienced times when leading landscape architects have rejected the garden, its planning and design. The only thing which was deemed to be valuable and interesting was nature and nothing but nature. If nature itself was not available, it had to be imitated. This is a strategy which has always run contrary to my convictions and my feelings. I see the task of a landscape architect as being to create a quality environment for people who spend most of their lives in settlements and towns. To my mind, emphasizing naturalness come what may seems like avoiding the responsibilities which a landscape architect has. There was a time when Copenhagen was not interested in parks and gardens but only in the question of how to achieve the greatest degree of naturalness and conservation of nature. The city was supposed to function as a city during the week and provide the feeling of being in the open country at the weekend. This is an attitude I reject. What I want is urban planning which underlines the character of the city while also integrating landscape elements in the form of gardens. For me nature in cities is synonymous with the garden. Of course our idea of nature also has something to do with the way we perceive and understand landscape. Denmark consists almost entirely of cultural landscape in which the boundaries of forests play an important role. A Danish forestry act, passed in 1805, laid down that the entire country was to be used for either forestry or agriculture. The reason for this act was the shortage of firewood which prevailed at the time. Wherever there were a few isolated trees these were to become the nucleus of a forrest. The land owner was required to fence it off and was prohibited by law from allowing livestock to graze there. This was the only way to ensure that forrests could mature without disturbance. The ensuing demarcations of permitted use still define the spatial structure of the land today.

You were born in Sweden and work in Denmark today. What do you consider to be the fundamental cultural differences between these Scandinavian countries?

Let me say that I was born in a part of Sweden where the landscape is very "Danish". In this respect southern Sweden and Denmark are very similar. Only about 10 per cent of Denmark is woodland. The woods are small and form islands in farmland. In contrast, Sweden is basically a forest landscape interspersed with clearings. It has, in other words, an entirely different spatial structure, which in turn has traditionally had a greater influence on art than in Denmark.

Where does your specific interest in landscape architecture come from?

I wasn't aware of any interest in landscape to begin with. I was interested in gardens and art.

Sven-Ingvar Andersson

Hawthorn birds, four metres high, "roam" gracefully through *Marna's have*.

For Andersson the clipped figures in *Marna's have* represent aggressive forms with a gentle outer skin, reminiscent of softly rolling hills.

The geometric structure of the clipped hedges in *Marna's have* is interspersed with patches of deep-violet allium flowers.

Sven-Ingvar Andersson

I spent my childhood in surroundings which were very aesthetic. When I finished high school at the age of 18, I was sure that I would become a landscape architect although, at the time, I had no idea that landscape architecture existed as a profession. My teacher asked me about my plans for the future, and when I told him about what I wanted to do, he told me that this was a way of earning a living. This was something I'd never considered! I started my work with ambitions of a mainly artistic nature and soon realised that I could combine my interest in gardens with my interest in art. Yet, despite this, I never wanted to emphasize the "art" aspect of garden art. I never saw the garden as just a place where plants exist, but as something much more. Early on, I dreamed of a garden which is a sequence of clearly defined spaces with walls and hedges, steps and courtyards which are accessible and can be experienced. When I went to England a few years later, I saw my ideas reflected in some of the gardens I visited there, Hidcote for example.

In what way do you consider garden art to differ from landscape planning and landscape architecture?

In terms of approach there is actually no difference, but I worked with all three separately as distinguishing them made teaching easier. For me landscape planning is not only a question of larger scale, but also means developing strategies and social awareness and, of course, requires a profound knowledge of ecology. Landscape architecture is primarily concerned with the use of landscape in the urban context. What always matters here is finding solutions to functional problems such as the positioning of paths, using space and so on. Of course social aspects and quality of experience also play an important role. Whereas a landscape planner is one of a number of experts who has a special task, a landscape architect is in overall charge and must be capable of making independent decisions.

Garden art is not primarily concerned with functional problems but has the purpose of conveying mental, aesthetic experiences. Garden art should, like sculpture or painting, be a means of artistic expression. Personal commitment and the force of subjective expressive power are crucial. I don't believe that landscape architects should only concentrate on artistic aspects; I also consider it to be vitally important that they become aware of the responsibility they have towards garden art.

In your 1990 publication *Havekunsten i Danmark* you wrote that since the thirties landscape architecture has mainly drawn its inspiration from art.

I believe that there's always been a relationship between the different forms of art. Garden art is one of the visual arts for me. This is not to say that it should try and imitate other arts. But that's exactly what is happening at present.

People are trying to work artistically at all costs, they are trying to do installations or produce Minimalism or other movements. I think this is all wrong. While we need to emulate art by setting the same standards for what we do and be in contact with art, I think it's far more important to be in contact with life. Art always enters into a dialogue with life anyway. If garden artists find their way to art through another art form, they have lost something. If we try to be as clever as the artist, it will take us much longer to find our own form of expression.

So are you saying that art should spark off a process instead of providing a model for copycats?

Precisely. In Denmark we have the tradition established by G. N. Brandt and C. Th. Sørensen available to us. Sørensen certainly never worked as an artist, but he was nevertheless receptive to contemporary art forms. He spoke neither of the kind of inspiration which he derived from the arts nor of individual artists. But his designs clearly reveal the references and sources which inspired his exceptional work. He was obviously greatly influenced by concrete art, futuristic influences are also recognizable. Art helped him to define his aims, but he never imitated art. Sørensen had very little contact with other professionals outside Denmark. People he knew well were Pietro Porcinai of Italy and Hans Warnau, who is Dutch. Hans Warnau is a Minimalist and Purist and was, incidentally, the teacher of the young Dutch landscape architect, Adriaan Geuze. Warnau's Minimalist thinking is reflected in the way he lives. When I visited him two years ago, all he had in his living-room was a few chairs, a carpet and a tiny painting on the wall. I consider Hans Warnau to be a fascinating personality.

The stark simplicity of your projects would seem to indicate that you are also fascinated by Minimalism.

Possibly, but my restrained formal language also has something to do with the use of plants. If you really want to achieve a dialogue between plants and space, it's vital to bear in mind that the plant is a living thing. It needs simplicity of space. This aspect of Sørensen's work was not understood. People saw his drawings and judged him as a very dour person who only designed stiff forms. In fact, he knew very well that the vitality of vegetation means that only simple, formal placing of plants is necessary for all the qualities desired in the garden to unfold. When Sonja Poll and I restored the Sørensen's *Geometric Garden* in Herning a few years ago, I had to make sure that I ignored calls for more attractive decoration and retained the simplicity of form. Basically, Sørensen's aim was to create wide, open areas, to be able to see the sky. Which doesn't exclude the possibility of using and experiencing the park in other ways.

In 1981 it was decided to realise Sørensen's 1954 design for the *Musical Garden* in Horsens in the grounds of the Art Museum of Herning as a large, accessible hedge sculpture of hedges between 6 and 8 metres high. Realisation of the *Geometric Garden* began in 1983. Parterres in typical Sørensen style are to be created inside some of the hedge enclosures. The large oval has a diameter of 51 metres at its widest point. Plan by Sonja Poll, landscape architect.

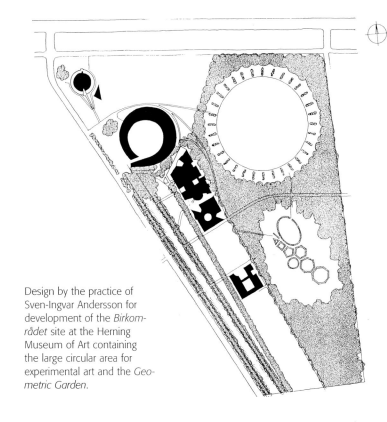

Design by the practice of Sven-Ingvar Andersson for development of the *Birkom-rådet* site at the Herning Museum of Art containing the large circular area for experimental art and the *Geometric Garden*.

What is your relationship to contemporary forms of art? Can you tell me which are your sources of inspiration in art?

In this respect, I'm an omnivore and make use of everything. I think that artists such as Christo and Richard Serra have provided landscape architecture with important stimuli. But I can't say exactly where my inspiration essentially comes from. An artist might be able to speak about a particular interest in dance, but actually there aren't any set boundaries between the disciplines. I do my best to work like Shakespeare. I try to bring out different levels in my projects. I want to make them easy to read, and I want to offer people something they can understand directly, something which perhaps even inspires them. These qualities go beyond artistic and aesthetic considerations. A garden should be such that it can be experienced over and over again, just as it's possible to see a Shakespeare play or look at a good painting more than once and discover new aspects each time. For me it's particularly important to be open to many different kinds of influences and approaches. What has always mattered to me in all the very different projects I've done is to find out about the nature of the task in the individual case and the way I can approach it. I don't have specific ideas in mind which I want to realise at all costs.

Take, for example, my project at the *Harbour of Helsingborg*. I wanted people to be aware of the water in the harbour, but the harbour walls are too high for people to see the water. So in one of the walls I integrated a large ring-shaped pipe out of which water shoots radially at three points, a clear visual and acoustic experience of water. It was not my intention to create a work

of art, but that's the way people interpret it. They use the ring like a work of art. Tourists take photos of it, getting the whole family to pose beneath the arc of water.

Does it bother you when individual elements of your projects are understood as isolated works of art? Would you rather that people saw the site as a whole?

Most people usually don't know why they like some things and not others. If you take a photo of your family standing in front of a sculpture, presumably you like the setting and feel at ease there. What basically matters is defining space with sufficient precision for people to be able to use it. If you're lucky, people will use the space in a way quite different from what you originally intended.

For example, for *La Défense* in Paris we planned a strip of white marble solely for the purpose of providing pedestrians with an aesthetic experience. I didn't have any particular use in mind. Today a lot of people walk along it, and, as it's

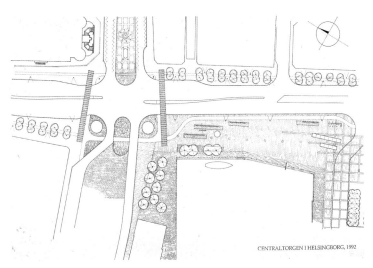

CENTRALTORGEN I HELSINGBORG, 1992

on a slight incline, skateboarders place empty cans along its length, turning it into a slalom-course. This is an aspect I find very interesting. If you design something which has an identity and an expressive force, it will get used.

Artists frequently say that garden art is not really an independent art form. What are your views on this?

I came into contact with a lot of art experts and artists during the time I studied art history at the University of Lund, and I've been friends with many of them for thirty to forty years now. In the last ten years I've observed a development which is bringing many artists back into greater contact with garden art. Architecture and garden art are taught at the Art Academy, which goes back to 1754. Architecture, sculpture and painting have equal status and enjoy the same rights at the Academy. Needless to say, this has a beneficial effect on the image of architecture and landscape architecture. Con-

Andersson redesigned the *Havnetorget*, the central area of the inner harbour of Helsingborg, in 1992/1993. The main challenge was to find a way of realising the design while taking into account the requirements of traffic in the area of the major road junction.

163

"Blåbærkagerne" ("Blueberry Cake") is the name Andersson gives to the two sculptural fountains, eight metres in diameter, in the area of the junction at *Havnetorget*. The artist Betty Engholm encased the fountain in blue ceramic.

To remind visitors and local residents of the proximity of the water, a ring-shaped well-sculpture sprays three jets of water across the harbour basin in a wide arc. *Havnetorget*, Helsingborg.

Between 1984 and 1986 the office of Sven-Ingvar Andersson developed a plan for the outside space at *Tête Défense* in Paris in collaboration with architect Otto von Spreckelsen. In contrast to Andersson's original concept, this area is today very geometric and open. Drawing from July 1985.

In 1992 the sculptor Jørgen Haugen Sørensen was commissioned to create a sculpture for *Sankt Hans Torv*, a small square in Copenhagen. The entire square was redesigned in 1993 in collaboration with Sven-Ingvar Andersson. The essential design elements in addition to the sculpture are a slight shaping of the terrain, light-coloured strips of granite set in the paving-stones and the installation of a fountain.

cerning the relationship between art, garden art and landscape architecture in our time, it's important to realise that present-day art has turned away from aesthetic considerations to a certain extent and often assumes the role of an oppositional force. This is something which architecture, landscape architecture and garden art are not able to do. At least, it doesn't make any sense to design ugly gardens just in order to demonstrate that ugliness is part of our society. There is really an essential difference between some progressive art forms and landscape architecture. That's why landscape architects find direct inspiration from art so problematic. For example, Martha Schwartz is far more interested in making ironic comments than creating art in the environment. I feel that this approach is too limited.

Some of your projects were realised in collaboration with artists.

I haven't realised very many projects in collaboration with artists, but I would say that, as a rule,

the project as he had already worked with me on other projects to his satisfaction. It then turned out that Sørensen had already done a stone sculpture; however, it hadn't been directly created with my design of the square in mind. I initially had a lot of problems with his work, but gradually I began to understand what he wanted to do and liked the idea. The Arts Council wanted the sculpture to have a reference to water as one of the sponsors was only willing to give money on the condition that a water-sculpture was created. Sørensen wanted to pass water-pipes through his sculpture, but I managed to convince him that he shouldn't treat it like an apple riddled with maggot-holes. I sought another solution. There wasn't sufficient room available for a pool and, anyway, I didn't want a pool as it would have to be emptied in winter and would look unattractive. Instead, I had a shallow trough let into the site and installed a number of water-jets, which sprayed water onto the sculpture at different levels. This seemed appropriate as the title of the work is *Huset de*

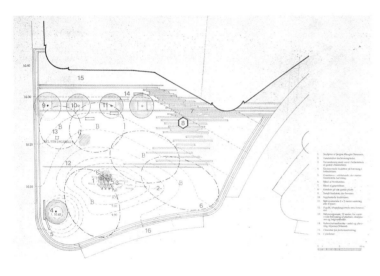

this was not very different from working with architects. For example, in Vienna I once had the job of finding the right setting for a sculpture by Henry Moore. Although Moore hadn't specifically adapted his work to the design scheme it turned out that we both had the same views on where it should be placed. Henry Moore was very happy with the solution, and I had the feeling that we spoke the same language to some extent.
I had a similar experience when I worked with Jørgen Haugen Sørensen, who is a sculptor. The National Arts Council had commissioned him to do a sculpture for the *Sankt Hans Torv* in Copenhagen a few years earlier. It had been realised that sculptures are often not seen to their best advantage in public space and decided that this was to be avoided here, and, in consequence, the Council stipulated that funding would only be made available provided that the sculptor collaborated with a landscape architect. Sørensen asked me to join him on

regner, House of Rain. I also felt that the sculpture should be placed on two elongated blocks of granite, not only for spatial considerations but also as a place where passers-by would be able to sit. Sørensen agreed, and it turned out that the three ideas worked very well in combination.
The remainder of the square was to be designed with minimal means. What counted for me was to show the sculpture to its best advantage and preserve the square as a place which could be used. We extended the paving-stones as far as possible and took long, narrow flagstones and a pavilion, which is used as a kiosk, to create the necessary links and spatial counterpoints. Small, deliberately placed elements underlined the character of the square. There was already a lime-tree on the square at a slightly higher elevation, and I wanted to preserve the tree. So we put in a gentle hill to balance the differences in height. This hill enters into a pleasing dialogue with the trough, but to

"Huset der regner" ("House of Rain") is the name Jørgen Haugen Sørensen has given his sculpture at *Sankt Hans Torv* in Copenhagen.

Sven-Ingvar Andersson

begin with nobody really understood its purpose. It was there because of the given conditions. Two granite blocks were added in order to support the hill on the street side, and today they are welcomed as places to sit. I find it stimulating to develop given situations further.

The individual elements on the more or less neutral area appear like pieces on a board, giving the site a coherent, almost casual ambiance.

It was very difficult to achieve simplicity and make the objects appear natural. I'm often asked what I have actually changed at the site. The task facing us at the *Park of Ronneby* was quite different and was one which we greatly enjoyed. But even there, although we created

Powerful jets spray water directly onto the surface of the sculpture, particularly in summer an invitation to enjoy water. *Sankt Hans Torv* in Copenhagen.

large expanses of water there, people kept asking, "Ronneby is a wonderful park, but what was it that you built there?"

Another aspect of your designs is the use of oval forms, which frequently occur not only in your own work but also in the designs of Carl Theodor Sørensen. What are the origins of using the oval form?

There's more than one answer to this question. The Danish tradition has always taken up forms which are part of the repertoire of historical garden art. In contrast to the Dutch view, namely that only orthogonal forms are acceptable, we are interested in precise forms which are not necessarily contained in geometry textbooks. Take the new areas of water in the *Park of Ronneby* as an example. It contains precise

forms which did not come about by means of geometry alone.

Another answer comes from pragmatism, from logical analysis of functions. The oval is a very pragmatic form, it's an area which is easy to go round. It avoids the typical problems of corners. The third answer has something to do with plants. If you want to plant a grove of trees or a rose-bed, the oval is an ideal form. The way that trees grow is not angular, they develop as round forms. Perhaps there's another answer to the question: this answer relates to the beauty. The tension contained in the oval is something I find very appealing. I mentioned earlier on that Carl Theodor Sørensen was greatly interested in futurism. The particular experience of the space between ovals is significant here. In the *allotment colony of Nærum*, one moves very elegantly between the oval boundaries of the individual plots. It could almost be described as choreography. It's extremely important to be aware of typical sequences of human movement, both are necessary: dynamic and static space.

We've already talked about Carl Theodor Sørensen. What kind of relationship did you have to your teacher?

I was a pupil of Sørensen and didn't know it to begin with. Later on, I had a very close relationship to him and was his assistant during his last four years at the Academy. I learnt a great deal from him, above all that I had to believe in myself. Our relationship was, despite the differences in our ages, characterised by mutual respect. Sørensen was used to people who either didn't listen properly to what he was saying or believed every word he said. There was a period of a few years when I had the feeling that I was no more than Sørensen's echo, but gradually I began to realise that I had had ideas of my own before I met Sørensen. Of course he was an authority for me and rejection of authority is part of the Danish mentality. It wasn't until later that I saw that students need authority in order to develop and learn how to defend themselves. A teacher not only has to understand the subject he's teaching, he also has to be a good listener. It's important for us to be able to give expression to our own ideas. We have to learn how to say "I". Sørensen imparted his own experience to me in a way which was very clear.

Your work is often compared with Zen gardens in Japan. What meaning do these gardens have for you?

This brings out the omnivore in me again. The Japanese gardens played a very influential role in the development of Western garden art. Still, I have my problems with the highly-specialised, élitist and passive aspects of the concept. Many years ago I described it in the following way: the Japanese garden is a set, but the Western garden is a stage. Admittedly, both are based on an artistic design, but the Western garden is conceived as space for action.

A difference in heights which had to be overcome gave rise to the dialogue between two blocks of granite. *Sankt Hans Torv* in Copenhagen.

Andersson still today considers the *Project for the Expo 1967* in Montreal to be one his best designs. Elliptical walls of concrete, two metres high, filled with earth and covered in greenery like huge banks of grass, formed a labyrinthine sculpture garden for the Scandinavian Pavilion designed by the architect Erik Herløw.

Sven-Ingvar Andersson

Why has Scandinavian garden art so stubbornly resisted fashionable influences from outside over the decades? Today the functional, austere style of Scandinavian design is once again in demand; yet this is a style which has existed for a long time. How do you explain this stability?

A large degree of scepticism is part of the Danish mentality, and Sørensen's friend, Steen Eiler Rasmussen, the architect and journalist, credited the Danish people with common sense. I feel that Danes also have a sense of pragmatism. Instead of always waiting for something new to appear, people in Denmark choose to seek ways of improving existing solutions. For example, the chair I'm sitting on was designed by Arne Jacobsen forty years ago, and its design still receives awards today. It's a very simple and practical chair and it's a chair I like to sit on, the materials which were used to make it are simple, it can be stacked and

Why has Danish design become so attractive again on the international market over the last few years?

An international interest in Modernism has developed over the past few years. It has become important to establish what Modernism actually was and the effects that it had on landscape architecture and garden art. Anne Whiston Spirn[1] has dealt with the socio-aesthetic qualities of Danish Modernism, and Dorothée Imbert's book discusses French Modernism in garden art,[2] a phenomenon which was very interesting, but was soon forgotten as being very élitist and specialised. She established that Modernism did not survive in landscape architecture and that landscape architects returned to a traditional style. Contemporary French garden design is generally considered to be the best in Europe. The fact that so much attention has been paid to American landscape architecture over the past two decades has something to do with the

[1] Professor of landscape architecture at the University of Pennsylvania in Philadelphia, USA

[2] Imbert, Dorothée. *The modernist garden in France.* London, 1993

Ronneby is a sanatorium in southern Sweden and has existed since 1705. Andersson's practice was commissioned to convert and extend the 85-hectare park in 1983. New lakes were created in 1987; their shorelines are very clearly yet not geometrically shaped.

so on. It's traditional and, at the same time, it's ideally suited to everyday use. Everyday use also plays an important part in the design of a garden. People want comfort and the Danish way of life sets great store by comfort.

This consistency also has something to do with Denmark's relationship to Germany. Denmark is a small country and has always felt somewhat threatened by its closest neighbour. This explains why major developments which originated in Germany have always been regarded with suspicion. Danes have never seen any reason to enter into seemingly hopeless competition with their powerful neighbour in the form of monumental or spectacular manifestations. The comfortable way was always more important and more promising.

fact that it was possible to realise projects in the United States which were very elaborate and costly. While economic factors do play a role, it's also true that the ambition to realise such bombastic projects is alien to the Danish mentality. What Sørensen cared about were simple things, not elaborate ones. He and his colleagues wanted to combine social qualities with aesthetic qualities. This is something which is important to me.

There is a renewed interest in Romanticism in landscape architecture. Particularly Scandinavian landscape is often described as being in the Romantic tradition.

You'll never find a Dane who is willing to admit that he's a Romantic. Romanticism is equated with petit bourgeois in Denmark. Which is not to say that Danes aren't Romantics. Everyone

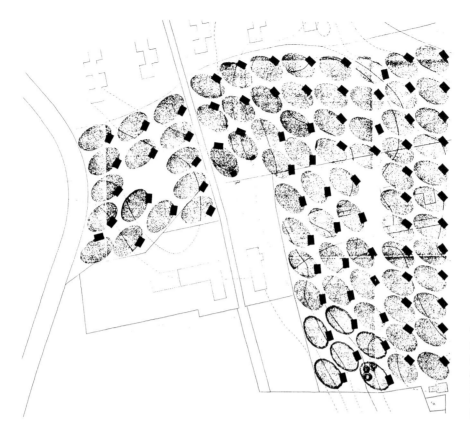

The oval, a favourite form in the designs of Carl Theodor Sørensen, still today gives the *Allotment Colony of Nærum* its unmistakable character. Drawing by Carl Theodor Sørensen.

Carl Theodor Sørensen, *Allotment Colony of Nærum.*

Sven-Ingvar Andersson

has a Romantic side. It's important to understand what is meant by the term. Basically, it is about sensitivity and appealing to all our senses, something which I consider to be a crucial aspect of landscape architecture. Physical and mental sensitivity should not be separated. Danish architecture has always paid special attention to the conscious design of surfaces. Hard-edge forms are rare; although the influence of Mies van der Rohe was felt in Denmark, his style never succeeded in developing its full austere potential here.

In Denmark I have a reputation for having introduced poetry to garden art. This is a reputation I am quite happy with. Sensitivity is the distinguishing feature of poetry, and this applies to landscape architecture and garden art as well. This aspect, always important, has become even more significant today in view of the fact that daily life is increasingly ruled by substitute contacts in the form of television and the computer. The images they produce have virtually become more important than reality. To put it in a nutshell: garden art and landscape architecture rely on sensitivity to convey experiences which are authentic. Garden art and landscape architecture are the antidote to virtual reality.

In the "Garden of Fragrance" in *Ronneby* park Andersson had 150 slender concrete columns built to serve as supports for a pergola. The contrast between the delicate concrete supports and the gnarled cross-beams of the pergola creates a subtle tension which is underlined by flowering creepers.

Sven-Ingvar Andersson

Biography and Selected Works

Sven-Ingvar Andersson was born in Södra Sandby in southern Sweden in 1927.
He lives and works in Copenhagen.
He graduated in landscape architecture at the University of Alnarp, Sweden in 1954 and also studied art history and botany at the University of Lund.

Except where noted, locations are in Denmark

Practice in Landscape Architecture and principal teaching activities:

1959–63	Office of his own in Helsingborg, Sweden
1959–63	Assistant to Carl Theodor Sørensen at the Chair of Landscape Architecture at the Royal Danish Academy of Fine Arts in Copenhagen
1963–94	Professor at the Chair of Landscape Architecture at the Royal Danish Academy of Fine Arts in Copenhagen
1992	Visiting professor at the University of Pennsylvania, USA
Since 1963	Office of landscape architecture in Copenhagen. Staff in 1995: Henrik Pøhlsgaard, Lise Schou, Jacob Fischer

Member of numerous professional associations in Denmark and abroad, including the Academic Council of National Art

Selection of realised projects:

1958	Arkiv för Dekorativ Konst in Lund, Sweden
1961	Town Hall in Höganäs, water-and-fire installation
1963	Vilanden students' hall of residence in Lund, Sweden
1964	*Marna's have*, Andersson's own garden in Södra Sandby, Sweden
1967	Project as part of Expo 1967 in Montréal, Canada
1968	Klarskovgård, training centre of Denmark's Sparekasseforening
1969	Sophienholm
1970	*Eremitageparken* housing development in Lundtofte Ådalsparken in Kokkedal
1971–78	Karlsplatz-Resselpark, park and urban redevelopment in Vienna, Austria
1965–85	*Frederiksdal* in Helsingborg, Sweden
1982	Trinitatis church square in Copenhagen
1984–86	*Tête Défense* in Paris, France
1986	Danish school of tailoring and knitting, Herning
1987	Garden of Ronneby Sanatorium, Sweden
1990	*Hosebinderlauget* in Herning
1992	*Sankt Hans Torv* in Copenhagen Uraniborg, island of Ven, Sweden
1992–93	Museum square in Amsterdam, Netherlands
1993	*Havnetorget*, Helsingborg harbour, Sweden
	Campus of the University of Lund, Sweden
1994	*Gustav Adolph's Torg* in Malmö, Sweden

Numerous competitions, including:

1971	Karlsplatz in Vienna, Austria
1982	Parc de la Villette international competition, Paris (short-listed)

Selected Bibliography

Andersson, S.-I./Christiansen, H. H./Hammer, B. *Parker og haver i København og omegn.* Copenhagen, 1979

Andersson, S.-I./Bramsnæs, A./Olsen, I. A. *Parkpolitik: boligområderne, byerne og det åbne land.* Copenhagen, 1984

Andersson, S.-I./Lund, A. *Havekunst i Danmark/ Landscape Art in Denmark.* Copenhagen, 1990

Andersson, S.-I./Høyer, S. *C. Th. Sørensen – en havekunstner.* Copenhagen, 1993

Høyer, S./Lund, A./Møldrup, S. *Festskrift Tilegnet Sven-Ingvar Andersson, September 1994.* Copenhagen 1994

Most of the articles by and on Andersson after 1967 were published in the Danish journal *Landskap/Landskab* (formerly *Havekunst*). Prior to 1967 S.-I. Andersson's articles mainly appeared in the magazine *Hem i Sverige*.

Acknowledgements

Kindly provided by the landscape architect:
Sven-Ingvar Andersson: 157, 161, 164, 166, 168, 171
Annemarie Lund: 165 r.
Carl Theodor Sørensen: 169
as well as:
Gunnar Martinsson/Institut für Landschaft und Garten, Universität Karlsruhe: 160

The Mad Dance of Entropy and Evolution –
Herman Prigann

Zeichen der Wandlung (Signs of Change) in Hamm, 1994. Herman Prigann built a metamorphous object using material from a demolished factory.

In the sixties it became evident that our civilisation was facing an ecological crisis of disastrous proportions. Since that time a number of committed artists has turned away from art in the business-as-usual sense and began to tackle environmental issues in their work. Among the best known artists active in this field are undoubtedly the American husband and wife team of Helen Mayer Harrison and Newton Harrison. For many years the focus of their work has been on areas of ecological crisis all over the world. One of the sharpest protagonists of this movement in Europe is Herman Prigann, born in 1942, who is seen as unconventional migrant between all the disciplines which are in any way connected with landscape and the environment. After studying painting and urban planning in the sixties, Herman Prigann has been active on behalf of drug addicts, has organised happenings and installations critical of society, has directed radio plays, has realised sculptures in the open space, has painted, written and, since the late eighties, attracted attention particularly on account of his intensive theoretical and artistic dialogue with disrupted landscapes. Far from shunning contact with politicians, scientists, planners, engineers and other involved parties, he has preferred to enter into a constructive dialogue with them, regardless of the fact that experts have repeatedly called into question his competence and his authority.

The theoretical core of his present work is "Terra Nova", an ambitious, interdisciplinary programme which aims to achieve the aesthetic and ecological recycling of disrupted parts of the landscape. Terra Nova was born out of the realisation that society largely represses the responsibility which it has for the present state of the natural environment. Prigann is concerned with nothing less than a redefinition of our understanding of nature and landscape and the development of an aesthetic awareness of "beauty" in nature which accepts traces of destruction as bearing witness to cultural acts. Without limiting himself to superficial, cosmetic treatment, the artist not only aims to achieve the restoration and recultivation of destroyed environments. He also wants to give the people directly affected the prospect of new jobs and of an environment which is worth living in.

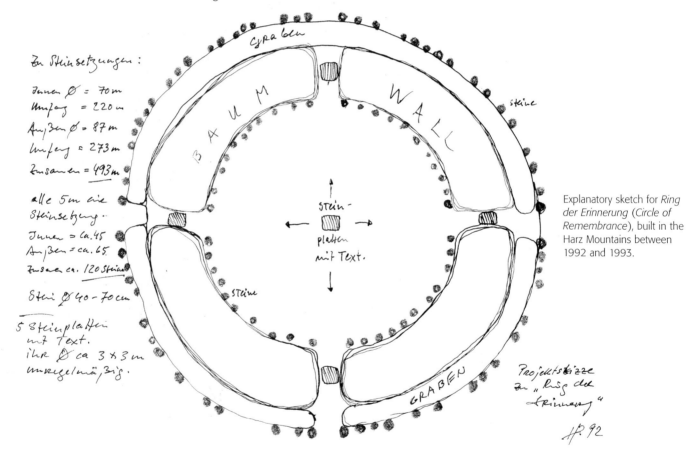

Explanatory sketch for *Ring der Erinnerung* (*Circle of Remembrance*), built in the Harz Mountains between 1992 and 1993.

Whereas American Land Art of the sixties largely avoided any direct contact with society, Prigann believes that the time has finally come to reinstate art, in keeping with the vision of Joseph Beuys, in its fundamental role in social discourse. Prigann is not a withdrawn aesthete. He includes people in his work directly and spontaneously, he has the ability to get all parties involved to enter into frank discussion and, where necessary, he contributes his profound knowledge of interactions in nature and landscape to achieve enthusiastic support for his vision. Since 1990 Terra Nova has not been just a forum for interdisciplinary discussion but also the driving force of experimental projects in the environment. It will be possible to gauge its success only in a number of years from now.

It would not do justice to Herman Prigann's creative ability to judge it only on the basis of his few permanent works in the landscape; his conception of art is wide and his means of expression are many and diverse. The 'sculptural sites' and metamorphous objects, as he likes to call his works in public space, are usually only the visible part of a complex creative process involving large numbers of people in a wide variety of ways. This process, public debate, discussions with engineers, scientists, politicians, planners and the dialogue with those who are directly affected, is an essential yet invisible part of his work.

On the occasion of "Art and Nature – Nature and Ecology", an international symposium which took place at Wernigerode in the Harz Mountains in 1993, Herman Prigann exposed the Terra Nova programme for the first time to a round of experts for critical discussion. The participating scholars and artists had the opportunity to widely discuss the programme's theoretical basis. At the same time, they were able to gain an impression of Prigann's sculptural work during a visit to a site on the former border between the two Germanies near the town of Sorge, a place located only a few kilometres from the symposium's venue. As in all of the artist's works, the formal design of *Ring der Erinnerung* (*Circle of Remembrance*) is very simple and the work uses only very few archetypal elements. A wall of dead trees from the vicinity forms

Ring der Erinnerung of dead tree trunks and erratics evokes an ancient ritual place of assembly. A few posts which formed part of the former border fence have been left standing.

the boundary of a large circular area with an internal diameter of 70 metres. The wall is 4 to 5 metres high and interrupted by four entrances, which face each of the four points of the compass. Large stone slabs, inscribed with "flora", "fauna", "aqua" and "aer", mark the entrances; a stone slab bearing the inscription "terra" lies in the middle of the circle. The course of the former border runs through the circle, marked by nine fence-posts from the border installations which have since been dismantled.

The circle's meaning is obvious: it forms an archetypal symbol of unity, spanning the scar which the border has left. The use of dead wood is a reminder of the fact that our trees and woods are dying. But the concept of the sculpture's gradual decay while becoming overgrown with dogroses is a positive sign: decay and growth, entropy and evolution are processes of life inseparably intertwined. The circular space also evokes the image of a ritual place of assembly, and perhaps there are those who will discover these deliberate associations in a chance encounter with this site. However, it cannot be ruled out that the circular site located in a remote part of the woods may ultimately be

Ring der Erinnerung transcends the scar of the former border between the two Germanies.

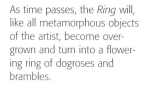

seen as no more than a romantically played-down escape into the realm of non-reality. Herman Prigann is well aware that art can never change the mind directly, but can only provide the spark which initiates such change. The fact remains that even while it was still in the process of being realised, the *Circle of Remembrance* led to public debate on ecology, art, politics and history.

As time passes, the *Ring* will, like all metamorphous objects of the artist, become overgrown and turn into a flowering ring of dogroses and brambles.

Herman Prigann

Mr. Prigann, you studied painting and urban planning in Hamburg from 1963 to 1968. Surely this is not standard training for an artist?

No, it's not. In the early sixties I was one of those young students at the Academy of Arts in Hamburg who were obsessed by the vision of a new city. Things we were perfectly serious about at the time are in such stark contrast to what I stand for today that I feel I should mention it. The city we envisaged then was to exist under an imaginary dome, a kind of energy field which was supposed to prevent the influence of weather and turn the city into an unchanging, stable climate zone. Underground rail services would have been superfluous as it was intended to create moving pavements. I remember one of the details which occupied us at the time: how will it be possible to regulate the system so that everyone can jump off at his own speed when he gets to the boutique of his choice? Of course there was an atomic

Duftender Meiler (*Fragrant Kiln*) in Vienna, 1985. For six weeks the smell of smouldering wood hung in the air in the city centre.

power station underneath the entire city. In addition to painting and doing installations, it was at this time that I began to stage a large number of public happenings with the left-wing political movement of the sixties. No matter whether it was a question of the emergency laws, Vietnam or the tabloid journalism of Springer – I was always very involved in happenings and brought in a lot of people. The contrast to city-planning utopianism could not have been more marked. In my work as an artist I have always concerned myself with very different kinds of media and social criticism, not for the sake of criticism but always from the point of view of developing an alternative. To give an example, in 1972 I did a radio play with the Release Music Orchestra in which I showed environmental problems on another level. The play was entitled *Brain Pollution* and was a satirical view of environmental pollution, society, consumer madness and so forth.

In the five years before I left Germany in 1974, I had helped to build a programme to help

drug-addicts. I saw my work with "Release", an organisation which aimed to combat the use of hard drugs, as being a social sculpture in terms of the way that I understand art. Release came to an end because of politically influential forces which wanted to have an organisation subject to public control – something which Release clearly was not. I got together with friends from Vienna in Switzerland in 1974. Their number included an engineer who had a vision of a new type of airship. Together we spent three years in southern France on the site of what had been a bauxite mine. Our intention was to test the structures of a rigid airship which would one day fly using helium. It was here in the bauxite mines that I first encountered land which had been devastated. Engineering work had changed the landscape back into, as it were, virgin soil. For the first time I realised how exciting the interplay between cultural landscape, in this case the forests of Provence, and the succession process is.

After southern France, I eventually went to Vienna in order to concentrate more on painting again. I visited the Vienna Woods, where I was confronted with beech-woods in the process of dying. This catastrophe led me to ask myself what I could do as an artist to contribute to raising people's consciousness. I would never go so far as to say that art changes consciousness, but an artist can definitely develop a canon of forms which reflects our problems and encourages people to take a different look at the world. During my time in Vienna, I developed the idea *Der Wald, ein Zyklus* (*The forest, a cycle*). It formed the basis for a book with the same name – a reflexion on the history of the tree and the forest in the cultures of the world. I created the concept of "metamorphous objects – sculptural sites" at that time; the first metamorphous object I built was a large charcoal kiln right in front of Vienna's city hall. The kiln stood there for six weeks in January and February. I called it *Duftender Meiler* (*Fragrant Kiln*), which was, of course, a provocation for urban noses. At the time, the press wrote that the urban nose is no longer capable of noticing the stink of cars, but people experienced a smell associated with nature as stinking.

Hanging Tree, my first work which was meant as a serious warning, was installed in the summer: a fifty-year old larch, its roots uppermost, was suspended from a steel frame like a pendulum. It is still standing on the Danube opposite the UN city. The same year I erected a large pyramid on the Danube island; the edges of the faces measured 15 metres and the whole pyramid was made of the trunks of dead beeches, which I set fire to at night: the *Brennende Pyramide* (*Burning Pyramid*). I also did things with fire at the art and literature event "Steirischer Herbst" in Graz and at the Federal Horticultural Exhibition in Berlin. The point of the fire was to introduce nature into an urban context. For me, fire is the aesthetic moment which most brilliantly demonstrates metamorphosis.

It wasn't until the end of the eighties when I left

Herman Prigann

Hanging Tree, 1985, an early symbol warning that the Vienna Woods were in the process of dying.

The artist is fascinated by the peaks of debris, wide expanses of sand and extensive rain-water lakes of the Niederlausitz area where brown coal was once mined. Prigann does not see the bizarre holes which have been left as ugly wounds but as part of the cultural landscape of the region.

Herman Prigann

◁ p. 178–179:
Gelbe Rampe (*Yellow Ramp*) towers like an archaic calendar structure behind the cornfield on the edge of the former area of opencast mining.

Austria and went to live in Spain that I began to develop the first ideas and sketches for the "Terra Nova" idea. My main interest was an aspect of my dialogue as an artist with the artificial landscape: what kind of space is this landscape? What kind of landscape in its quality as space is interesting from the point of view of art? I came to the conclusion that this kind of landscape was neither the English Landscape Garden nor the relatively intact cultural landscape. Nor am I willing to, as it were, refurnish the landscape in an aesthetic way. As long as I can remember, I've been excited by the idea of working in wooded areas where the trees are dead, in military training ground, in old quarries, in devastated areas. When I first visited the brown coalfields in Niederlausitz and saw the giant sandpits there, it was like a revelation for me.

What is it about these devastated landscapes which you find so fascinating?

We have devastated landscapes with our industrial culture, and we will have to go on destroying them in order to obtain raw materials. I don't mean this to be understood as moral criticism; I have to accept that I benefit from the technology of our civilisation, that I live in it and use it to maintain my standard of living. So we have to see devastated areas as being part of our cultural landscape. As an artist I find myself at a decisive turning-point: the traditional nature of art has always been to make things more beautiful, and this is something I have to call into question in view of the environmental problems we face. I have to decide whether to remain in the tradition of art and treat landscape as a beautiful background which I enter into dialogue with by means of my art, or to abandon this traditional approach and start to create a reserve in which the artistic design relates to the space as a whole.
I find devastated landscapes just as exciting as an empty canvas. Everything is possible with the small difference that these landscapes prove themselves to be active partners! Nature is already at work: the process of succession is taking its course, the process of recapturing by means of metamorphosis, the evolution interacting with entropy. Their dance in the landscape is a process which holds unbelievable fascination for me. What makes it so exciting is that, as an artist, I am confronted with these two fundamental laws of nature, with entropy and evolution. Incidentally, I see both laws as being related not only to ecology but also to culture. I see the world as it is today in terms of a ubiquitous cultural ecological movement. The way I see culture and nature is that they are subject to the same laws. Evolution and entropy are not, to my mind, a pair of opposites but intertwined processes.
When I apply my vision and my ideas to a disrupted landscape, I see a partner which is already at work. Mine is not a tabula rasa approach, rather my idea of restructuring and reformulating disrupted landscape enters into an immediate dialogue with succession and

other processes which are already happening. An opencast brown-coal mine isn't a sandpit and a quarry isn't a pile of rubble. Nature has already made its mark and this is a fact we have to come to terms with. Here the traditional notion of sculpture in landscape is developing into something else. Landscape itself is becoming a sculpture made up of many different layers.
In the vast dimensions of this space, art is only possible by means of geoglyphics. These signs are fully recognisable only from an aerial perspective; as accessible structures they can convey a special spatial experience. I understand geoglyphics as being a reference to the Neolithic tradition, in which particular mound formations of ritual significance were created. Today, we could interpret the geoglyphics as being symbols of aesthetic perception. The overburden landscapes are zero landscapes with regard to form, but as biotopes they are interspersed with a large number of succession areas, evidence of the regenerative process which is already taking place. To my mind, harmonising these two aspects means providing the landscape with a form which will eventually be an attractive environment, with niches for the ensemble of flora and fauna to unfold.

Adopting an artistic approach to disrupted landscapes is an approach which has already been developed by Land Art. Robert Smithson's Spiral Jetty is a case in point. What do you see as being the fundamental differences between the two approaches?

At the time that Smithson was working, it would never have occurred to me to work in the brown-coal mining areas. I'd probably have gone to the Moroccan desert and, like him, I'd have done installations in this empty landscape. Artists like Smithson were working at a time when it was still important to say, "I am here, I was here, and I will always have been here." However, unlike some art critics, I wouldn't go so far as to describe Land Art as an imperial gesture.
All that I have just described is the logical development of the approaches adopted by Land Art. Land Art made aesthetic statements, created large signs in the tradition of early civilisations. What I am primarily interested in today is reflecting a change in environmental awareness and greater environmental concern in the face of the environmental catastrophes which threaten us. These self-made catastrophes are not a negative utopia. How are they to be approached? In fact what Land Art has done is to exclude the individual, the being who gives life to landscape. In other words, it was basically an art form which distanced itself from the problems which faced society.
If I were to suggest to the Rheinbraun mining company today that it use the displaced earth masses only in order to define large geoglyphic signs, I would be continuing the Land Art tradition in the same way that the architectural installations of Hannsjörg Voth continue the tra-

dition of Michael Heizer. That's not enough for me. If I were to adopt this approach, I would be guilty of ignoring the human factor as a cause of cultural landscape. My understanding of nature differs from the conventional Western definition insofar as I am absolutely certain that we are not in some vague way part of what we call nature, but are part of it absolutely. Thus, my definition of art does not see art and nature as being opposites, but I understand art as being an integral part of the social life of man. Art is not an extra, it's not the icing on the cake, it's not background, embellishment or anything similar, but an integral part of our cultural history. As an artist, it is in this context that I have to understand the landscape I work in as being the environment I live in and do something for me and my fellow human beings. People should be given the chance to participate in this newly defined landscape.

lections of Neolithic times. This may sound somewhat far-fetched, but it has nothing to do with an esoteric attitude. Why is the fascination of ancient places of worship so great for some people that they can't get them out of their minds? To these people, every stone speaks and the site is consecrated in the sense of a kind of personal memory. This fascination took hold of me when I was only a boy. I grew up in Westphalia, and when I was nine I went looking for old stone graves. Where does this feeling come from?

I believe that we only know very little about the evolution of our consciousness. It's a fact that we are causally related to the people who lived at that time through reproduction. If we imagine that we are part of a continuous chain of development of human existence, we step into dimensions which are beyond the scope of scientific study and verification.

Gelbe Rampe on completion of the second building phase. Mixed technique on card, 1993, 9 x 13 cm

Does one have to be an artist for doing this? What's behind the label?

That's a good question. I see myself as an artist who has always found the classic range of possibilities of realising art too restricting. Art has to mean that I submit myself to the world as a phenomenon to be perceived, submit myself to my fellow men and my inner self in a permanent journey of discovery which lasts a lifetime, ever-receptive to surprises and ever-ready to abandon everything which, only a minute previously, I believed that I had seen. To me, art is an inner attitude of constant willingness to keep collecting things until a kind of quantum leap occurs and once again calls into question everything I had thought. This is the creative moment.

When I look at my life, everything spirals around a central point. There is something which is completely part of me. I'm talking about recol-

These early experiences of landscape and nature have influenced my work fundamentally. But this influence was not in my consciousness during the many years I lived in cities. It wasn't until I was able to break out of the traditional concept of art and its limitations which I had assimilated and internalised that I succeeded in challenging the problematic conventional concept of nature and the belief in technological progress and all its attendant consequences. This is only possible if art is not understood as embellishment according to aesthetic rules.

I recall that Beuys came to the same conclusion; he said that art should once again play a concrete role in social discourse, not just pose affirmative questions or engage in sarcastic social criticism. Rather, it needs to become a verifiable alternative. In other words, art has a specific job to do in society and isn't "L' art pour l' art." The purpose of "L' art pour l' art" was to

Herman Prigann

demonstrate the notion of liberty, but this is something which now belongs to the past.

It is my opinion that the entire purpose of art is to be innovative. The artist shouldn't confine himself to one particular medium, but should act like a seismograph for the problems which surround him and his fellow men. Concrete art needs to place itself in the context of other disciplines. We have to redefine the medieval and Renaissance concepts of art for the age we live in: the artist as someone who can think in global terms without having to be a specialist in every individual field. The artist needs to be someone who is knowledgeable enough to discuss the complex of disrupted landscapes with biologists, ecologists, landscape planners and engineers. Such artists are a rare breed as art schools still insist on producing geniuses. The genius is a Romantic notion from the last century, which has been done to death in ours.

How do scientists and the profit-orientated art business react to such an unconventional definition of art?

I have been able to develop extremely interesting and innovative dialogues with scientists from a variety of disciplines during the past few years, and this has formed the basis of mutual understanding. It has become clear to me that scientists are also interested in a greater degree of interaction.

Dialogue with the art business is much more problematic. People there want to know what I actually do: painting, sculpture, landscape art, how is it possible to reconcile all these different approaches? What I tell people in the art business is that they're mentally lazy; people who are genuinely interested in art don't take it amiss if an artist uses different media and means of expression recognisably in his style in order to put his work in a broader context of social reflexion. It's not a question of dabbling in a number of different areas but of having a clear style and a clear conception for each of these areas and a philosophy which seeks to answer the questions: "In what way is art a reflexion of nature? In what way is nature a reflexion of art?" The art business is trapped in the nineteenth century, and I'm working for the twenty-first century. People who are thirteen or fourteen years old see my painting, my objects and programmes and understand my approach. They have understood that it's their future that is at stake and, for this reason, they're very receptive to an artistic language which gives expression to this 'debasement' and oscillates between the concepts of art and nature.

It is striking that you categorically reject a Romantic approach to nature in your theoretical discussions.

Early Romanticism had a genuine radical aspect which sought social change. In the further course of its development Romanticism increasingly led to an esoteric blurring of the way that nature was perceived: suddenly there was talk of "brother tree" and "mother earth".

The risk of returning to this late Romantic view of nature is that we lose sight of the real problems. We are pragmatic in our dealings with things we call nature and environment. We have to be pragmatic in our dealings with them as otherwise the human race would not have the slightest chance in the evolutionary process. It doesn't help the trees if we first declare them to be our brothers and then fell them. This puts us back in the tradition of our ancestors who always made their sacrifices to the things which they destroyed.

But wasn't it the purely functional approach to landscape which has led to its disruption?

Seeing a tree as a brother isn't the only alternative to a pragmatic belief in progress which sees nature as nothing more than a resource. I believe it is a question of recognising that nature goes beyond the esoteric and is similar to us in many ways. A vital nerve makes all the

things around me tick and also makes me tick. It's actually possible to define this nerve in terms of physics: certain elements such as water and minerals are relevant in a wide variety of combinations all over the world. I am such a combination and so is the tree, and evolution and entropy charge through everything in their mad dance, which we call life. But, unlike all other combinations, we have an undreamt-of possibility: we are able to make decisions. And this is the point where we become the only beings in the world who can bear responsibility. I can't escape this responsibility by surrounding myself with teak furniture while I talk about "brother tree". Nor can I call for a return to untamed nature and the abandonment of civilisation, that is the epitome of utopianism, is blindness and a lack of self-knowledge. Belief in progress and progressive ideologies were conceived as linear, exaggerated ideas. The esoteric or Romantic variety is also a dead-end leading to nothing more than a different ideologisation of landscape and

The artist intends *Gelbe Rampe* to be covered in yellow broom and roses in a few years, a contrast to the blue of the lake which will come into being. Mixed technique on card, 1993, approx. 30 x 41 cm

The *Yellow Ramp* during the first building phase in summer 1993.

A calendar structure which marks the position of the sun at the solstices is located at the highest point of the ramp.

The front of the *Yellow Ramp* is made up of large concrete slabs, piled on top of each other. The slabs are the same ones used to make the mining access roads. Glaciers transported large boulders from Scandinavia to Niederlausitz during the ice ages. Prigann has used ice age erratics and modern slabs of concrete to stage a dialogue between the ages.

Herman Prigann

nature. This prevents any concrete dealings with ourselves, with man and with what we call nature and environment. Today it's surely a question of the marvellous idea of humanity, which has never been redeemed, transcending the interhuman aspect in order to become part of our global being.

What matters to me is to liberate the concept of art from linear thinking and, instead, to develop networked thinking which shows us that our thinking always comes up against the fourth dimension. In fact the idea in itself is the fourth dimension because we know that it will come into being. Oppenheimer and his research team were not capable of preventing the atom bomb because the idea was already there. Manipulation of genes can't be stopped because the idea is already there. It is the power of the idea which sets us apart from everything else. This is the burden of responsibility we bear.

Despite your rejection of Romanticism, your work does have poetic elements.

It is the material which is the poetic element. The material I use, be it in a painting or a sculpture, has a language, the reason being that the material has a name. As soon as I use ash, sand or earth in my work, I introduce poetic space. There's a difference between doing an installation in the landscape using large blocks of marble and one which combines steel girders and concrete from an old industrial factory to create a new patchwork. There is also a qualitative difference in terms of aesthetic perception. The marble one only tells us about marble, but the steel-and-concrete one not only tells us something about concrete but also about old industrial structures and so on. If you like, marble takes us back to Michelangelo. An erratic takes us back to the ice age.

Romanticism is a historical concept as far as I'm concerned. I consider poetic space to be a very clear and important term and one which only comes into play by means of materials which are steeped in history.

How does your approach differ specifically from the conventional recultivation programme which is scientifically underpinned and implemented using technology?

Opencast mines are being closed one after the other in the brown-coal mining area of Niederlausitz around Cottbus. The proposal for the landscape which is to be realised here is based on the assumption that this region needs what the planners have called "a wet skin". People are being given the impression that there will be large lakes here in a relatively short space of time and tourism will soon be flourishing along their shores. I seriously doubt this. For one thing, flooding of the pits won't be possible in a short space of time, but will take at least twenty to thirty years. What's more, the water of these lakes will have extremely poor pH counts and will be unable to support any life forms. A very interesting natural succession will develop spontaneously in the course of time and this

would disappear if the area were to be flooded. People who have not yet been born may be able to run a successful bar on the lake shore and hire out fishing equipment thirty years from now. But this isn't going to help the people who live in the brown-coal areas and are out of work now. That's why my approach to the problem is to subject the contaminated groundwater, which is gradually seeping into the ground, to a recycling process. Wind turbines on the edges of the pits could generate power to drive pumps and distribute the water over terrace-like sewage farms. The pH count of the water would improve relatively quickly and the plants would regenerate the soil. It would be possible to preserve large succession areas and the higher parts of the surrounding area could be reafforested. In other words, there would be a possibility of developing new agricultural areas and creating biomass in the form of nettles, miscanthus and hemp.

Anyone who knows anything about the uses of these plants will recognise their significance in the paper and furniture industries and for the production of chipboard. The paper industry can use the fibre to manufacture high-quality paper without using chlorine bleach. Miscanthus is ideally suited to making chipboard without adding formaldehyde. The chemical industry can use these plants to make medicaments, the ethereal oils of the nettle and hemp being particularly valuable. During the regeneration phase of the terrace landscape, which could by all means accommodate a lake in its lower sections, there would be productive work available for the people who live in the region. These are only some of the interdisciplinary aspects which an artist can integrate in the context of such a programme.

There's another important aspect to consider. The present plans only use the overburden from the mines to even out large stretches of land. In addition, there are to be perfectly straight rows of trees in conventional forestry style. The result will be a slightly undulating, flat savannah landscape, which people will experience as boring, particularly once woods develop and block the view. Instead of all this, an entirely different environment could be achieved by seeing the masses of earth as geoglyphics and shifting them in an entirely different way: designing a large area of open space. At the same time, it would be possible to integrate an ecologically valuable diversity of small landscape elements, elements for which existing planning makes no provision.

To me, this sounds suspiciously like the artificial reshaping of a landscape which is the result of the cultural process you already described.

What landscape architects and planners are doing with these landscapes now is an attempt to imitate natural landscape. But this isn't natural landscape, it's an artificial landscape and the product of engineering. So why shouldn't we have the courage to deliberately create a landscape which is artificial in terms of its

Ring der Erinnerung, Harz Mountains, between 1992 and 1993.

Ring der Erinnerung, gouache on card. 1992, 50 x 70 cm.

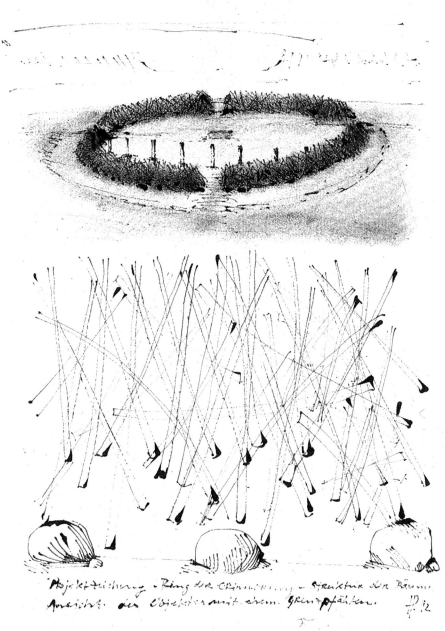

formal design, but integrates all ecological elements in a constructive way. My answer to the traditional recultivation model, which relies on trying to imitate nature and cover up traces, is an approach which doesn't seek to deny the landscape's history as a mining area and makes its mark on the landscape.

The *Gelbe Rampe* (*Yellow Ramp*), which is being built at the edge of the former Greifenhain mine near Pritzen is, to my mind, a model on a small scale. I can imagine a ramp on the other side which is ten times as large. The formal dialogue between the *Yellow Ramp*, which is twelve metres high and two hundred metres long, and a ramp thirty metres high and five hundred metres long would, I feel, be stimulating. This dialogue between artificial forms which proclaim their artificiality would be an expression of the reshaping of this devastated landscape. We shouldn't try to cover over these scars in the landscape.

You are building a structure at the highest point of the *Yellow Ramp* which evokes the calendar structures of ancient civilisations.

The idea is that of interplay between the time process in the former coalmines, which was controlled by technical means, and the natural process of time. The ramp is not only made of earth but also of huge concrete slabs which were used to provide temporary roads for the mining industry. The front part of the cone is constructed like a step pyramid. Seen from certain angles, it evokes the observatories built by ancient civilisations. I use contemporary materials to create a place which evokes a culture which manifested itself in this area in a wide variety of ways around fifteen thousand years ago. This region was relatively densely populated during the Mesolithic Age. That's why I have deliberately used these associations. On the other hand, the end of the ramp is the crossing point from exposed open space to enclosed inside space, which seen from outside again acts as a widely visible sign. This creates a context of meaning and poetic space.

Which were the main considerations for the design of the *Ring der Erinnerung* (*Circle of Remembrance)* at the former border between the two Germanies in the Harz Mountains?

Circular sites play an important role in the history of the Harz Mountains. Leaving aside popular belief and the defamatory Christian accounts of witches' dances, it has to be assumed that many sites in the Harz Mountains were very important assembly places for the Germanic tribes and were used for ritual purposes. The Harz was widely known, just as the "Externsteine" in the Teutoburger Wald were. The site is intended to evoke the old forms of culture which once existed in the Harz Mountains and the recent history of the area. The former border passes through the ring; I have left seven steel posts, which once formed part of the border, in place and integrated them into the site.

If you cross a border by means of a circle, this is obviously a significant symbol of a border being transcended. The four openings in the ring face the four points of the compass; a stone has been placed in each opening and inscribed with the words flora, fauna, aqua and aer respectively. The inscription "terra" has been chiselled by hand in the stone at the circle centre. These five concepts are a reference to the ecological nature of my work. The former border is in fact an area which is heavily contaminated with pesticides, but the mantle of plants is already in the process of regenerating itself. I had a few thousand dead spruces felled in the adjacent woods in order to build a kind of enormous hedge. The hedge has already developed into a valuable biotope for insects and rodents and is also a metamorphous object; it will rot in the course of time and become a mound of humus and then be transformed into a flourishing refuge. The contours of the site will be lost in the young wood of birches and spruces which will be growing there thirty years from now. Perhaps walkers will come across the wall or stones and ask themselves how old the site is. The Latin inscriptions will be overgrown with moss and have the appearance of being very old.

This would all seem to add up to a clearly romantic image …

Ab-so-lute-ly! I'm romantic through and through. By this, I don't mean Romanticism but poetic space. I'm perfectly aware that the old Romantics would give me a hug if they could hear this. In a project like this I see Romanticism as being concrete poetry and having nothing to do with Romanticsm as an ideological concept. Whether it's a question of painting, sculpture or landscape, what always concerns me is the resulting ambiences in which associations are evoked. If in the middle of these metamorphous processes someone has a romantic experience of the world, dwells on memories and so on at some time or other, that's fine by me.

What experiences have you had with the Terra Nova programme so far? What are the concrete problems and advantages, the possibilities and limitations of your approach?

After five years of working with this idea in the realm of society and politics two sides have emerged. There are those who make money out of their conventional recultivation methods and just don't want to know about my ideas. Others outside the process of making money, mainly scientists and some politicians, are very open to Terra Nova. I have the impression that the present political climate can be exploited with a view to putting Terra Nova to the test. Approximately ten years after its conception, it will then be possible to see the extent to which it has proved itself. Experts such as hydrologists and ecologists have confirmed the suitability of my ideas. What we need to do to implement the artistic idea is to convince all those involved that it is necessary to reinstate the coal-mining machinery for creating geoglyphics. The essential problem is the ecological situation, which however cannot be fully understood because no data to base experience on exist yet.

An artist probably first has to gain credibility in this field?

Although most people are very polite and listen, the way that their pupils flicker reveals what they basically think: "Typical of artists, they're even starting to talk about things they know nothing about." This puts me in the position of having to provide detailed explanations as to why I do have the necessary expertise. But at present it is more a question of achieving a political breakthrough. After all it is a political

these artistic installations form a structured ensemble which people can understand without any written or verbal explanations.

Are you in contact with artists pursuing ideas similar to your own or whose approach is compatible?

Yes. In the United States Mel Chin is working with an ecological research institute near Boston which mainly does research into the ways that plants can be used to decontaminate soil. His ideas have already been realised under the title *Revival Fields*. I think the work he's doing is good and I'd like to integrate it into what I'm doing. As far as the aesthetic side is concerned,

"This *Feuerlinie* (*Line of Fire*), its extreme transience is to be understood as a reference to the limitedness of our civilisation. Also as a reference to the warning fire of old times which was lit when danger threatened. – Fire can also be a bonfire, a reason for people to come together, symbolising the burning of the old and the dawn of something new."

decision whether the billions to be spent on recultivation measures are used to simply bevel the edges of what is left of the mines and wait for flooding to happen, or if the money is used to start experimental work and locate new branches of production in these landscape reserves in only five years time.

An independent association has already been set up to further the Terra Nova project. As part of EXPO 2000 it will, for example, be realising a scheme to achieve ecological conversion of a military training area. I also want to involve other artists in this project. This collaboration with colleagues will be an opportunity to formulate landscaping measures in a way that

people such as Alan Sonfist and Chris Drury are very interesting. It's very exciting to work with a few colleagues and develop a reserve, a kind of park where the different ensembles are shaped by the place, by the know-how and canon of forms of the individual artists, but in a broader sense, so that a totality is created. Many other artists working in this sector are concerned with sculpture in the traditional sense, even though they use living or dead natural material. Such projects are unsuited to the Terra Nova programme. Today, the assertion of the self throught an individual work of art appears inadequate when the actually intended reference is the realm of the landscape.

Herman Prigann's words at the time of the *Feuerlinie* happening in September 1991 as part of the Europa-Biennale I in the area near Cottbus where opencast mining of brown coal was once carried out.

Biography and Selected Works

Herman Prigann was born in Recklinghausen in 1942.
He lives and works in Portals Nous, Majorca.
From 1963 to 1968 he studied painting and urban planning in Hamburg.
He is a member of the German Studienstiftung.

Except where noted, locations are in Germany

Exhibitions, happenings, projects:

1966–1968   Exhibitions and happenings in Hamburg, Zurich/Switzerland, Göttingen, Wolfsburg

1969–1974   Foundation of "Release", collectives in the Federal Republic of Germany opposed to the use of hard drugs, actionist work with these groups

1980   Beginning of the series of happenings *Graffiti zum Thema Zukunft*, a collection of anonymous painting in collaboration with the Museum moderner Kunst, Vienna/Austria, exhibition of the *Akkurate Gesellschaft* cycle of pictures, Künstlerhaus, Vienna/Austria

1982   *Dorn im Auge* group exhibition, Hamburg

1983/1984   Planning of *Der Wald – ein Zyklus*, consisting of the *Feuertürme – Brandstätten* series of happenings, the *Metamorphe Objekte* and the book *Der Wald – ein Zyklus*

1985   Beginning of the *Feuertürme – Brandstätten* series of happenings with the *Meiler* and the *Pyramide* in Vienna/Austria, and the *Schwimmender Feuerkranz* in Berlin
Der Wald, documentary exhibition, Vienna/Austria
Hanging Tree from *Metamorphe Objekte*, Vienna/Austria

1986   *Adam im Feuer* happening for the *Steierischer Herbst* near Graz/Austria

1987   Group exhibition on the theme "water", Stuttgart and Hamburg
Realisation of the object *Das verlorene Ei* from *Metamorphe Objekte*, Schloß Buchberg/Kamptal – permanent exhibition of object drawings and texts
Waldung exhibition, with the installation *Die Falle*, Akademie der Künste, Berlin

1989   Continuation of the *Graffiti zum Thema Zukunft – Frieden* in Paris/France, Luxembourg, Federal Republic of Germany and German Democratic Republic, Poland and Moscow/Soviet Union

1991   *Torfturm* installation and participation in *Naturraum – Kunstraum* exhibition, Ostwall Museum, Dortmund, as part of the Federal Horticultural Exhibition

Feuerlinie installation/event during the Europa-Biennale I, International symposiums on Land Art, brown-coal opencast mining, Cottbus

1992   *Terra Nova* exhibition and installation, Galerie/Edition Bea Voigt, Munich

1992–1993   Realisation of *Ring der Erinnerung* near Sorge in the Harz Mountains in collaboration with the Sprengel Museum, Hanover

1993–1995   *Gelbe Rampe* from *Metamorphe Objekte – Skulpturale Orte* as part of the Europa-Biennale Niederlausitz II und III, Pritzen near Cottbus

1995   *Two Trunks—Four Stones* at Krakamarken Art Park, Denmark
Towers of Change at the *Art and Environment* symposium, Petange, Luxembourg

Selected Bibliography

Dorn im Auge. Hamburg, 1982 (catalogue)
Prigann, Herman. *Der Wald – ein Zyklus*. Vienna-Berlin, 1985
Kunstaktion im Park. Berlin, 1986 (catalogue)
Waldungen. Akademie der Künste. Berlin, 1986 (catalogue)
Prigann, H.. "Thesen zu 'Metamorphen Objekten." In *Kunstforum International*, vol. 93, Feb./Mar. 1988: p. 180/181
Art in Nature. Italy/Germany, 1990 (catalogue)
Naturraum – Kunstraum. Ostwall Museum, Dortmund, 1991 (catalogue)
Förderverein Kulturlandschaft Niederlausitz e.V., editor. *Kunstszene Tagebau – Dokumentation eines ungewöhnlichen Kunstereignisses*. Heidelberg, 1992
Prigann, H. *Ring der Erinnerung. Circle of Remembrance*. Berlin, 1993
Förderverein Kulturlandschaft Niederlausitz e.V., editor. *Europa-Biennale Niederlausitz II 1993*. Cottbus, 1994

Acknowledgements

Kindly provided by the artist:
Ulrike Damm: 176 bottom r.
Hermann Prigann: 173, 175 l., 176 l.
as well as:
Thomas Kläber: 176 top r., 177, 183
Maria Otte: 178/179, 187
Udo Weilacher: 184

Mind Structures – Hans Dieter Schaal

Imaginary entrance to *Moser-Leibfried Villa* at the International Horticultural Exhibition 1993.

Hans Dieter Schaal, born in Ulm in 1943, is an unobtrusive but keen observer of the relationship between man, architecture and landscape. The drawings, paintings, photo collages and striking architectonic environments of this architect, landscape architect, stage designer and artist allow new, often symbolically visionary insights into the fundamental positions and strategies of architecture and landscape architecture. The spontaneity and directness of his undogmatic analysis of the essential features of the formal and conceptual relationship between architectural space and landscape, between inside and outside give his work a liberating freshness. Schaal's intention is not to develop a new theory of garden art; the majority of his subtle designs and dream landscapes are primarily to be understood as intellectual experiments which lay no claims to possible realisation.

After studying art history and philosophy for a few years, Hans Dieter Schaal changed over to architecture, which he studied from 1965 to 1970. Soon after he had graduated, Schaal broke out of the rigid conventions of the business of designing buildings and embarked upon an intensive search for archetypal modules which form the basis of both the built and the natural environment. Schaal's typological research into the dialectic between architectural nature and natural architecture began in the late sixties and early seventies at a time when planning of public space was entangled in debate on ecological principles and had, on the whole, lost sight of the design and aesthetic standards of its own craft. From an art history point of view, Schaal's approaches are to be seen in connection with the movements in art in the United States and Europe which, since the end of the sixties, had been increasingly involved in seeking approaches to the themes of nature and environment. Whereas art still today has extreme difficulty in relating to garden art, it is precisely in this context that Hans Dieter Schaal has found his métier. In his book entitled *New Landscape Architecture*, published in 1994 and described by Sir Geoffrey Jellicoe, the doyen of English landscape architecture, as a "design source book", Hans Dieter Schaal demonstrates his belief that garden art is a most important area of artistic design in landscape architecture. His means of achieving this purpose are sketches, collages, photographs, plans, literary quotations and philosophical texts.

Yet no matter how innovative the interdisciplinary theoretical work between architecture, landscape architecture and art may be, it also has its price. Schaal is rarely granted recognition by any of the disciplines in which he works. When he and his team won the 1978 competition for the 1985 Federal Horticultural Exhibition in Berlin, the jury was not, despite the exceptional quality of the design, willing to recommend that it be realised. Instead, all sorts of pretexts were found for awarding a special prize; the reason being that the design's ruthless artificiality and critical reflection on the rapid destruction of the landscape were so contradictory to conventional taste in garden

Competition project for the *1985 Federal Horticultural Exhibition (Bundesgartenschau)* in Berlin. The core of the project was to be a built landscape diagram showing segments of a circle of different sizes, representing the percentage of the landscape in Germany which building development has used up. Special award, 1978.

ZENTRUM ALS FREIZEITPARADIES
ZENTRALE HALLE MIT GLASDACH, GETRAGEN DURCH MITTIGEN STAHLBETONBAUM
(AUFZÜGE ENTHALTEND) UND ASTWERK

AUF DEM BODEN: FELSEN
PALMEN
SANDSTRAND
MEER
SCHNEEBERGEN
EISFLÄCHEN
HÖHLENSAUNA
UNTERWASSERTHEATER

IN DEN ASTGABELN UND
ÄSTENDEN:
CAFES
KINOS
TREFFS
SPIELECKEN
KINDERGARTEN
AUSSTELLUNGSRÄUME

SYMBOLISCHE FORM DES
GLASDACHES - BLÜTE
BLÜTENMITTE:
AUSSICHTSCAFE

BERLINER LANDSCHAFTEN
LANDSCHAFTSCHARAKTER
VON
HAVEL
WANNSEE
SCHLACHTENSEE

KÜNSTLICHER ASPHALTFLUSS
ZUFAHRT ZUR TIEFGARAGE
VERKEHRSSCHILDER - WALD - INSEL

GÄRTEN
DER LÄNDER UND STÄDTE

SPORTZENTRUM

ROMANTISCHER - NATÜRLICHER PARK
URWALDCHARAKTER
WILDFLORA
SCHLING- UND KLETTERPFLANZEN
FARNE UND MOOSE

KÜNSTLICHE LANDSCHAFT
WASSERBAHNHOF
WASSERSTRASSE   MIT BEIDSEITIG HOCHGEKLAPPTEN FELDERREIHEN
MIT KÜNSTLICHER LANDSCHAFT
FELDER MIT: BETONTULPEN
ASPHALT
BÜCHERN
RADIOS
DACHZIEGELN
KUNSTSTOFFBLUMEN
GERÄTEN
ZÄUNEN
POSTKARTEN
ANTENNEN
KÜNSTLICHER KÜHEN
GEWEHREN

KÜNSTLICHER GARTEN
NACHBAU VON NATURTEILEN MIT MODERNEN
BAUMATERIALIEN
GEKACHELTES FELD MIT: FELSEN
BRANDUNGSTEILEN
WELLEN
VERSENKTEM
GEBIRGE
STÄHLERNER
BAUMALLEE
KUNSTSTOFF-
- TANNENBÄUMEN
GLASKASTEN

MODELLEN VON SEHENSWÜRDIGKEITEN
KÜNSTLICHEN BLUMENDÜFTEN
AUFGEROLLTEM RASEN
VERSICHERUNGSVORHANGSFASSADE
KAUFHAUSEINRICHTUNGEN
GRUNDFUNDAMENTEN DEUTSCHER EINFAMILIENHÄUSER
TYPISCHEN DEUTSCHEN VORGÄRTEN
- GARTENZWERGE, WINDMÜHLEN, SCHLÖSSER
MIT ERDE, SAND, MUSCHELN
TANNENNADELN, RAUCH
GEFRORENEM WASSERFALL
LUFTMATRATZENFELD
AUTOMATENALLEE
LABYRINTH AUS SPIEGELN-U. NEON
VERSENKTEN KISSENWOHNLANDSCHAFTEN
ALS KULISSE FÜR SPIELE Z.B.

URFORMEN
DES WOHNENS, BAUENS
UND DER LANDWIRTSCHAFT
TYPISCHE FRÜHE
DORFFORMEN: HAUFENDORF
STRASSENDORF
REGELMÄSSIGE ANLAGE
RUNDLING

LANDSCHAFTSDIAGRAMM
VON DEUTSCHLAND
PROZENTUALE VERTEILUNG VON
WIESEN FELDERN FORSTEN WÄLDERN WEINBAU
GARTEN WASSER
VERBAUTER LANDSCHAFT

URNENFRIEDHOF
EXPERIMENTE VON STEINMETZEN U. BILDHAUERN
RASENPYRAMIDE · URNENSENKPYRAMIDE

LANDSCHAFTS-SCHULE
TYPISCHE DEUTSCHE LANDSCHAFTEN
KÜSTE
HEIDE
MITTELGEBIRGE
HOCHGEBIRGE

BAUM-SCHULE
VERSCHIEBEN VON REGELMÄSSIGEN BAUMINSELN
INS WASSER
+ NEULANDGEWINNUNG

0 50 100 150 200 250 M

art at the time that it set off prolonged and intense public debate. Disillusionment and frustration are also perceptible in the way that the artist-philosopher, as he is sometimes called, describes his encounters with fellow artists who dismiss his creative approach to garden art and landscape design as a complete waste of time.

One of the few projects which Schaal has realised is the strictly symmetrical *urnfield at the cemetery* of Singen at Hohentwiel, which was realised between 1983 and 1986. The project was built on a slope, which had previously been the site of a hall of last blessing, now replaced by a new building at a different location. Only the original avenue of trees forming the entrance axis was preserved. Today access is from a side-entrance to the cemetery along the avenue of oaks directly to the building on a slightly higher level, which resembles a small Greek temple. Steps link the upper terrace and the interior of the temple with the lowest level of the site, the square "courtyard", which is spatially enclosed by a cloister. The niches for the urns are set into the surrounding walls. There is a round pool at the centre of the courtyard, fed by a small watercourse. On the bottom of the circular pool a model of a small ruined town appears, a metaphor of transience and decay at the end of life. The source of the watercourse, symbolising the course of life, lies in a stone vessel at the centre of the small temple. The steps which ascend to the upper terrace lead past the stone vessel in the temple and through a door into an open surrounding area, again with urn niches. Continuing along the central axis, the visitor leaves the site through a fragmented

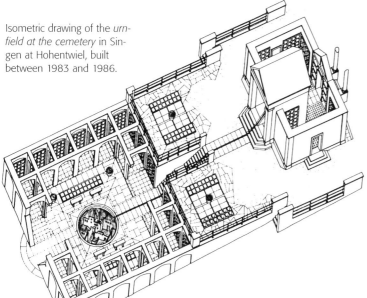

Isometric drawing of the *urnfield at the cemetery* in Singen at Hohentwiel, built between 1983 and 1986.

colonnaded portal. The entire complex of buildings blends in with the landscape of the terrace-like site and, at the same time, its monochrome white and grey clearly stands out against the surrounding cemetery landscape.

The effect of the *urnfield* in the middle of the cemetery is strange, almost like a piece of architectural stage design; its monochrome light grey is in sharp contrast to the dark green of the cemetery.

The spectacular staging of the complex evokes the impressive stage sets of Hans Dieter Schaal, revealing the architect's preference for classical quotations which are intended to root his work in Western cultural history. Nor can a certain tendency to Romantic emotionalism be denied in view of the symbolism of ruins and the archaic axiality. While all of this may provide the visitor to the cemetery with a wealth of possibilities for emotional identification and satisfy the general need for a clearly understandable architectural language, the question remains whether the neoclassical formal language and the elaborate symbolic expression do not tend to depend upon superficial images which deny the discreet simplicity of the genius loci.

The approach which Hans Dieter Schaal adopted for the 1993 project of the dilapidated, overgrown site of the *Villa Moser-Leibfried* in Stuttgart, which had been forgotten for decades, reveals his sensitivity to the special nature of the place. The villa, which was built in 1875 by the owner of a chocolate factory, was modelled on the buildings of the High Renaissance in Italy. The large garden was almost completely destroyed in the Second World War. Only parts of the foundations, a terrace and an artificial grotto remained intact. The ruin was to be opened to the public for the 1993

Hans Dieter Schaal

The adytum of the "temple remains", where a spring symbolising the beginning of life emerges from a marble vessel, lies at the highest point of the *urnfield at the cemetery* in Singen.

At the end of the water axis, which has its source in the spring, there is a circular pool containing a model of a ruined city, a metaphor for transitoriness and death.

The visitor enters the stone cinerarium containing the urn niches through a narrow, V-shaped opening in the wall.

An artificially fragmented columned doorway marks the rear entrance to the "urn tympanum".

View from the upper level over the courtyard with the urn walls and the "cloister". The cloister is broken up in the central axis of the site.

Hans Dieter Schaal

International Horticultural Exhibition in Stuttgart. Hans Dieter Schaal's basic idea was to leave the uncanny ensemble of villa and garden as it was, superimposing only a light wooden structure, which leads the visitor along an imaginary path through time. "Fundamentally, there are two ways of approaching the world and the landscape, actively or contemplatively," Schaal said to explain his purpose. "The path represents movement, reality is perceived in passing, the surface grazed in pictures. The place represents lingering, becoming absorbed, penetration, becoming involved with reality." A raised wooden footbridge does not lead to the main axis of the villa, but passes through the trees to the side of the complex, providing different insights into the history of the building and the garden. A barrel-shaped arbour which repeats the form and volume of the stone grotto, seems to form the entrance to the villa, but in fact only frames the view of the overgrown garden. A further meditative station along the path through the Romantic wilderness is the belvedere, an enclosed circular building with observation slits permitting only restricted views of the tops of the trees, instead of the expected panorama. The footbridge ends at the steps of a tower with an observation platform, which, however, is inaccessible and invites the visitor to let his imagination take over. Schaal's interventions disconcert the beholder and encourage him to get involved in mysterious structures of the mind. Unlike in the *urnfield* in Singen,

where the visitor is confronted with finished images, the decisive elements here are the place, the landscape and the garden, leaving space for the visitor's own imagi-nation. The conscious or unconscious dialogue with the unusual perspectives opens up new interpretations and ways of reading the environment without making any actual changes to the existing landscape. Schaal's *Villa Moser-Leibfried* project is undoubtedly one of the best examples of the successful transformation of an intellectual artistic experiment into the reality of the place.

Hans Dieter Schaal lives and works in the seclusion of the former vicarage of Attenweiler, a village near Ulm. The building, which is under a preservation order, is literally packed with books, sketches, plans, models and paintings from cellar to attic. The wealth of ideas contained in the inconceivable volume of material can only be guessed at. A small selection of the best models is housed in an outbuilding, where what was once a hayloft has been converted into an exhibition room. The artist, who otherwise normally shuns publicity, uses a visit to this small private exhibition to explain the philosophy of his work.

The barrel-shaped gateway is a reference to the former entrance to the *Villa Moser-Leibfried*, but ends at a wall overgrown with leaves.
International Horticultural Exhibition, Stuttgart, 1993.

Contrary to expectations, the belvedere, an enclosed circular building, only affords visitors a limited view through small openings.

The basic idea of the *Villa Moser-Leibfried* project the was to leave the core of the uncanny area of nature untouched and make visual exploration of the ruin possible from a footbridge.

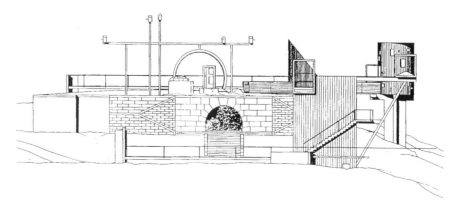

Hans Dieter Schaal

It is only at isolated points that the tower of steps and belvedere penetrate the trees of the *Villa Moser-Leibfried* setting. The precise, cautious intervention allows the visitor's mind to develop its own interpretation of the traces of the past.

The long footbridge leads to the tower of steps, from which a wooden beam projects, supporting an open cube. The supposed observation point reveals itself as an illusion.

How did you find your way to architecture and landscape architecture?

I had some fascinating experiences during the time when I was a student of architecture in Hanover: one was my involvement with the Herrenhäuser Gardens, on which we were making a film at the time. To my mind, these gardens are superb landscapes. The other key experience was walking in the mountain regions on the Aichelberg. I have often tried to draw the characteristic incision in the cone of a volcano. In one way, I anticipated today's situation: the motorway route now cuts through the landscape. I am a person who walks and travels through landscapes and towns, observes, analyses them in drawings and photographs, calls them into question and develops them intellectually. The design of landscape extensions and conversions, of new, different places follows on from this. So in this way landscape has been my concern from the very beginning.

What influence has studying history of art and architecture had on your work?

My study of the history of art, which I broke off in 1964 after only one year, has had a lasting influence on me. I think it's important to have detailed knowledge of the major works in architecture, urban planning and garden art in order to be in a position to do serious designs of one's own. Studying architecture was interesting, but it didn't really advance my thinking very much. I had to work out all the important aspects myself.

What were the particular influences on you at the time?

Land Art was definitely important for me. Particularly in the eighties a relatively large number of artists became involved in landscape, Werner Nöfer and Alan D'Arcangelo for example. However, I must add that, although I was aware of Land Art, I never related the work of the American artists to the environment here. The Land Art projects in America were realised in remote desert areas, which don't exist in Central Europe. Nor was I influenced by the work of any particular individual. Basically, my search for a link for my own work was unsuccessful. In architecture Alvar Aalto and Le Corbusier were important for me at that time. Apart from that, I was fascinated by literature, philosophy, theatre and cinema.

Hans Dieter Schaal

You just mentioned your liking for remote expanses of landscape. Is the Nordic, Scandinavian landscape your type of landscape?

Yes and no. The aspect of remoteness and solitude was once a very important one for me. The plateaus between Sweden and Norway provide a very powerful experience of solitude and remoteness. You really come face to face with the harshness of the Northern climate there. I would say that my Nordic time was the seventies. The garden aspect and everything which appears to be part of that is something I'm sure I would have despised at the time. This didn't come until I discovered the South. I was awarded a Rome scholarship in 1981 and

so I had the opportunity of spending a lengthy period in this fascinating city. It was at this time that I discovered the garden as an art theme. I couldn't see Italy's villa gardens often enough: Villa d'Este, Villa Medici, Villa Borghese, Villa Lante, Villa Torlonia and Villa Massimo. I experienced each of them as a poetic picture which had turned its back on the loud, bleeding, stinking wound which is 'Rome'.

Are you an introverted person, who likes to withdraw to the intimate seclusion of a paradisiacal garden?

Well, I'm both actually: extroverted and introverted. But I feel that the kind of people who are interested in gardens tend to be introverted and romantic.

What was your own experience of the work you did as part of the International Horticultural Exhibition in Stuttgart in 1993?

A number of artists were invited to take part in the exhibition. I put forward a relatively large

The Grand Garden of Herrenhausen in Hanover is a geometrical Baroque garden dating back over three hundred years. Hans Dieter Schaal sees this garden, considered to be one of the most beautiful Baroque gardens in Europe, as having had an important influence on his work.

number of projects, but was ultimately only able to realise two of them. Herman de Vries was sitting next to me at one of the discussions and he kept attacking me throughout the session. De Vries had developed a counter-proposal for the *Villa Leibfried*, which was actually not bad. He didn't want there to be any public access to the villa and so he intended to fence it off. That's okay, you can do it; only then nobody sees the Romantic interior.

Are you saying that you consider it important for people to have access to your work? Is the public reaction to your work important for you?

Of course it affects me when my works are wilfully destroyed. After all, everyone is looking for a fan-club. I've often had the experience of people coming up to me and saying, "I've never seen such a load of rubbish." At times like this I have to switch off, I think that's a natural reaction. Incidentally, I don't read any negative reviews. I'm only interested in who likes my work and who doesn't. When I design a stage

The *Stangenwald-Platz* is an artificial forest made of white concrete pillars in a regular order and covered with a steel trellis. International Horticultural Exhibition, Stuttgart, 1993.

Hans Dieter Schaal

set, it is perhaps seen by between 1000 and 5000 people and of these maybe 100 like it. That's something I have to accept.

Frank Werner writes that Hans Dieter Schaal is a "migrant". What do you see as being the advantages and dangers of such an approach in today's world?
Anyone who studies architecture soon realises that it is not a single discipline. Artists anyway don't see architecture and landscape architecture as being art in the strict sense. What interests me is the whole: the whole person with his body and soul, the whole world with natural sciences and art. Knowledge, clarity, the quest for understanding. So what I do can only be seen in such interdisciplinary terms. After I studied, I painted and drew a lot and was involved in a number of exhibitions. It was during this time that I got to know the art market and it was a place where I never felt quite comfortable. I always felt uneasy when I painted pictures in order to sell them. As I began to get more involved in architecture and landscape, the art market became less and less important for me. During my time in Rome I often heard remarks like: "Aha, he's betraying art!" This is the problem which every architect and every landscape architect faces: he is always in the dilemma of having to provide a service and wanting to give expression to his own creativity. When I was in Rome the first time in 1976, I lived next to Anselm Kiefer. He covered up his windows after just one week so that I couldn't see what he was working on. It was then that I decided to turn my back on this scene and focus my attention on the surrounding gardens, something which these creative people always found totally unacceptable. I still have no idea why the theme of the garden always meets with such rejection.

There is the artist's view: "When art is applied to gardens it's not art any more."
The first time I read that garden art was one of the visual arts and was even called the mother of the arts was in *Verlust der Mitte* by Hans Sedlmayr. Actually, all that I'm doing is fighting to have garden art recognized as art again. I consider garden design to be an art, and I hate it when landscape architecture practices confine themselves to providing greenery for streets. Every work of art is an expression of a poetic vision of a more beautiful world, of a higher order. If we abandon this utopian vision, we are no more than a cog in the ultimate cogwheel. Those who persist in this utopian vision – vociferously or quietly, openly or covertly – can create works of art in any medium.

Isn't garden art historically even more or less equated with the loss of artistic autonomy? After all, it was always the ruling classes which commissioned the great garden artists of the past in order to increase their own standing. Isn't this something which still influences the thinking of garden artists today?

Yes, but Land Artists also sold what they did to collectors and galleries. I don't see any difference. Nor do I really think that it's important. What counts for me is the view of Beuys – someone whose work I actually don't particularly like – that it is necessary to widen the concept of art. Anyway, there is no such thing as artistic autonomy. Everybody is bound by the constraints of his age and the society he lives in. What matters today is to invent new images which mediate between the outside world and the inner world and which have the same power as Hollywood's images. It's a matter of transcending the banality and nihilism of the cities, squares and parks. In my opinion, understanding of art was much more developed at the time of the Renaissance than it is today.

In your book *New Landscape Architecture* you say that you feel it's important to win back the landscape as a place of artistic design. Does this mean your primary concern is creating a link between art and all areas of life, or is it the landscape itself which is a particularly important?
What matters to me is the dialectics between inside and outside. I primarily understand outside to be landscape. Architects design buildings as a rule, but they often pay no attention to the space which surrounds the walls. I don't think the appearance of these buildings is so important.
The crucial question for me is: "what is at the centre of our conception of the world?" Sedlmayr touched on this topic. Now that the gods are, in a manner of speaking, dead, I think the best thing would be to make nature the central issue again. By this, I don't mean in the way that an ecological party focuses on nature, but in the pantheistic sense. In this sense each tree can be regarded as a valuable being. What happens when we treat this being with contempt is something we're all too familiar with now. So I would probably describe myself as a pantheist who has his main focus on nature and incorporates architecture into this context.

Returning to the issue of art and landscape once more: are there, in your view, contemporary examples of successful collaboration between the two disciplines?
To be honest, I don't know any such examples in Germany. This is not always our fault, but is, I feel, often due to the fact that people who commission projects are completely lacking in any understanding of such ideas. I see interesting approaches in the Parc Citroën in Paris, which is self contained, and in the Parc de la Villette, which reinstates the theme of architecture in the garden.

How would you describe the relationship between your work and the tradition of garden art?
I see Karl Friedrich Schinkel as being one of the master builders who sought a close relationship between urban planning and

landscape. I'm sure he worked with two components which should come together again today: Romanticism and Rationalism in the form of Classicism. Schinkel experienced difficulties in reconciling these contradictory movements, but he was capable of recreating a link, of uniting the North and the South. For me the interesting period of garden art ends around 1850. Ermenonville, designed by the Marquis de Girardin on the basis of the ideas of Rousseau, and Wörlitz, which was designed by Franz von Anhalt-Dessau, are, along with the Italian gardens, some of the most beautiful places I know.

Romanticism of ruins, old and new: decaying factories of the present and ruins from the past.

Transforming a place into a poetic topos is very important for my work. I feel that sites like Stonehenge play a special role: its reference to the endlessness of time and infinite space undoubtedly gives it a key significance for me. I see similarities between this and, for example, the cemeteries of Erik Gunnar Asplund; these are capable of conveying the feeling of remoteness and emptiness. Strangely enough, I also have an affinity to places with negative connotations. These include, on the one hand, refuse dumps, cemeteries and the like. I am also frequently drawn to places where something of significance has happened. It's rather like in a play: an event changes what was a neutral place into a special place.

Archetypal elements are important in many of your projects. What meaning do these elements have for you?
Archetypal forms are not only typical and important in art, they also play a similar role in garden art. They are what is universally understood, what is – as in a dream – accessible to everybody. For me such archetypal motifs only have meaning when they are part of a living context, are part of civilisation. When, for example, any architect talks about Versailles, he is thinking of the indissoluble link between building and landscape, making them part of a whole. Today, things are increasingly just placed in the landscape as isolated items. After all, it takes a number of words linked in a meaningful way to form a sentence.

Do you believe that landscape architecture is capable of regaining the same significance – as a kind of synthesis of arts – that it once had in classical garden art? Is this even conceivable in view of the conditions which exist in society today?
Yes it is. To my mind, it's the only salvation. Of course, there's no longer a palace in the middle of the park, except when there was one there anyway. My fundamental questions are directed towards the centre and are in search of content. I believe that nature must be at the centre of things, or of man, or – bearing in mind the circle – of the cosmic relationship between man and nature. The forms themselves will never change. I know that today most architects reject the notion of axis. The axis is attacked on the ridiculous grounds that it is no longer appropriate to our time, that it's even fascist. Today, an axis is referred to as a tangent or something similar. Man is forced to come to live with the dilemma that he is symmetrical and asymmetrical at the same time: he has two eyes and two ears, but only one heart and it's not in the middle. What is important for the beholder is that there is a composition, and this happens quite naturally when there's an axis. We know immediately if there's an axis and the components fit together. It's easy to see that the parts belong together when there's an axis or a symmetrical picture. It's much more difficult to convey decay.

Postmodernism has played a significant part in shaping the attitudes towards historical influences in both architecture and landscape architecture.
I can well understand the point of discussing Postmodernism in terms of historical interest. However, I have little time for the banal architectural manifestations of this interest.

Do you have problems with making use of classical references?
No, I like making quotations. I don't have any problems with classical references; on the contrary, the deeper the roots go back in history

Hans Dieter Schaal

and the more surreal the references are, the better I like it. The entire historico-cultural span is important to me. Small-minded works such as those of Leon Krier are an anathema to me. Then I would prefer Cape Canaveral.

Your work is often linked with the theory of Deconstructivism and, in this context, reference is made to your stage sets. What do you see as the reasons for this interpretation?

The first time that I did away with the traditional structures of architectonic design was in 1983 in the context of the production of *Les Troyens* at the Städtische Oper in Frankfurt. The artistic director wasn't happy with the traditional design of the set. What he said to me at the time was: "Everything is always so beautifully oblique in your books". He was referring to my isometric representations. He was of the opinion that I should build this way: built views. This is something which I still concern myself with today. I work a lot with photos in order to discover the laws governing the way we see. I experiment with photographs, turn them upside down, copy them and try to find new, unimagined, interest-

Architectural stage design for *Lulu* by Alban Berg at the Royal Opera House in Brussels, 1988.

ing perspectives. "Building the way you see" has definitely become an important principle for me. In addition, the stage sets have always been a reflection of psychoanalytical conditions, angst became an important theme here.

Do you see stage design as being preliminary practice for landscape design projects?

Landscape in the room and the room in landscape are still favourite subjects for me. This approach sometimes produces very unusual space, if, for example, the wall of the house is interpreted as a rock face and the floor as a hill. Quite a few singers who appeared on stage cursed me after their first performance because movement in such abnormal space is very unfamiliar. Such projects take you into areas which have Expressionist features. All that Expressionism is about is revealing inner experience. This is the other movement to which I feel drawn: the Expressionism of artists such as Oskar Kokoschka or Ruth Berghaus.

Of course, the essential question is the extent to which this can be applied to landscape. I do sometimes dream of my stage designs being realised in nature. I see my white structures

scattered over white expanses of sand and deserts like mirages. As theatres are black, unlit buildings, nature has no place in them, appearing, at best, in the form of painted scenery. Here in Europe there are virtually no possibilities of creating theatre architecture in the landscape. America is more progressive in this respect: take the gardens which have been staged in Las Vegas and in Epcot, Florida.

As landscape architects we are constantly involved in spreading images and influencing the way our environment is read. By doing so, we shape the way nature looks, either consciously or unconsciously.

This is precisely the point where landscape architects are unable to provide answers. You need to be an artist to do this, or both. Of course every built design interprets and shapes our relationship to nature and landscape. This is where we have a great deal of responsibility. As, however, the banality of everyday life always succeeds in prevailing, aesthetic gardens, parks and also squares can only be windows which have been opened to afford a view of the inner world of the self and nature.

Romanticism was mentioned earlier. It almost seems as if the images you have described are of a Romantic nature. In your book you call for a new Romanticism. Can you describe its essential qualities?

This is a very important question. A lonely junction where a single light flashes at night is in some way a picture associated with this new Romanticism. This is something which everyone has to seek in his own landscape. I don't see it as being possible any longer to just say: ugh, a filling station, a sewage plant and so on. These are all necessary evils which are part and parcel of urban life. They can all have their intrinsic poetry.

Doesn't this amount to aestheticising ugliness?

An artist's work constantly involves altering aesthetic standards. For example, I'm thinking of Andy Warhol and Pop Art. Andy Warhol came from advertising and he made the "Campbell Soup" can into his Mona Lisa. I don't know whether this is cynical or not. But it's something which I consider to be very important because when things are made visible and reinterpreted this is a means of overcoming certain problems. If I mention filling stations in connection with Romanticism, this is a way of saying that I am also very interested in cinema. Think of American films where the lone filling station often is an extremely important topos.

My liking of the moon and ruins is naturally Romantic. I have been a fan of ruins since my childhood. Ruins are – in the same way that water is – thresholds to a special inner world. This is where I see transcendence beginning. For me ruins embody futility, time, transience and the fact that nature always triumphs.

"Gardens in space? Gardens
on other planets, on meteors?
Gardens on the Moon?"
Hans Dieter Schaal. Collage

Petrified garden in desert-like
landscape. Collage

Hans Dieter Schaal

Biography and Selected Works

Hans Dieter Schaal was born in Ulm on the Danube in 1943.
He lives and works in Attenweiler near Biberach on Riß.

1963/1964	Studied history of art, philosophy and German language and literature at Tübingen and Munich
1965–1970	Student of architecture at the Technische Universität Hannover, graduating from the Technische Hochschule Stuttgart
1981	Villa Massimo award, Rome
1982	Sponsorship prize for architecture awarded by the Akademie der Künste in Berlin

Except where noted, locations are in Germany

Realised projects:

1983–1986	*Urnfield* at Singen cemetery, Hohentwiel
1986	Main entrance for the Regional Horticultural Exhibition in Freiburg/Breisgau
1989	Planning for the 1995 Federal Horticultural Exhibition in Berlin
1993	Project for the *Moser-Leibfried Villa* and *Stangenwald*, International Horticultural Exhibition in Stuttgart
Since 1994	planning for the new public park in Biberach on Riß (building work to start in 1996)
1995	Planning for the St.-Johann cemetery and the area around the Limes-Museum, Aalen

Exhibition Design/Architecture:

1987	*Berlin-Berlin*, exhibition in the context of the 750th anniversary of Berlin
1991	*Otto Dix*, Kunstgebäude Stuttgart
1993	*Walther Rathenau*, Zeughaus Berlin
	Pompeji, Kunstgebäude Stuttgart and Hamburg stock exchange
1994	*1200 Jahre Stadt Frankfurt*, Bockenheimer Depot, Frankfurt/Main
1995	*Kino, movie, cinéma*, Martin-Gropius-Bau, Berlin

Stage sets, including:

1983	*Les Troyens* by Berlioz, at the opera-house in Frankfurt/Main
1985	*Wozzeck*, by Alban Berg, Grand Opéra in Paris, France
1986	*Orpheus*, ballet by Werner Henze, Staatsoper Wien, Austria
	Elektra by Richard Strauss, Dresdner Staatsoper
1987	*Moses und Aaron*, Staatsoper in East Berlin
	1988 *Lulu* by Alban Berg at the opera house in Brussels, Belgium
	Tristan und Isolde, Hamburger Staatsoper
	Fierrabras by Franz Schubert, Staatsoper Wien, Austria

1989	*Eintagswesen* by Lars Norén in Gent, Belgium

Numerous competitions, including:

1978	Competition, Federal Horticultural Exhibition, Berlin, 1985 (1st special prize)
1985	Görlitzer Park in West-Berlin (2nd prize)
1987	Gateway to the city of Mannheim (5th prize)
1989	Conversion of former Hamburger Bahnhof station building in Berlin to a modern art museum
1994	Lustgarten international competition, Spreeinsel, Berlin
1995	New theatre building and garden in Potsdam

Numerous one-man exhibitions in Germany and abroad

Selected Bibliography

Schaal, H. D. *Anregungen für eine neue Landschaftsgestaltung*. Kiel, 1977

Schaal, H. D. *Zum Beispiel Ulm neu*. Ulm, 1978

Schaal, H. D. *Paths and Passages*. Stuttgart, 1978, revised editions 1980, 1984 and Berlin, 1993

Schaal, H. D. *Architektonische Situationen*. Stuttgart/Attenweiler, 1980, Berlin, 1986

Schaal, H. D. *Mond*. Attenweiler, 1981

Schaal, H. D. *Denkgebäude*. Wiesbaden, 1983

Schaal, H. D. *Architectures 1970–1990*. Stuttgart, 1990

Schaal, H. D. *New Landscape Architecture*. Berlin, 1994

Schaal, H. D. *Interior Spaces*. Berlin, 1995.

Acknowledgements

Kindly provided by the artist:
Peter Horn: 189, 194, 195, 196, 197, 199
Joap Piper: 202
Hans Dieter Schaal: 193 top l./m./bottom, 198
as well as:
Udo Weilacher: 191, 192, 193 top r.

Martha Schwartz, green areas
and parking facilities for *The
Citadel*, the former premises
of a tyre manufacturer. City of
Commerce, California,
1990–1991.

Pop, Baroque and Minimalism –
Martha Schwartz and Peter Walker

The American landscape architects
Martha Schwartz and Peter Walker have
fuelled the discussion on the relationship
between landscape architecture and
visual art in a way which has been
unparalleled in recent years. Both the
quick-witted "enfant terrible of garden
art" and the creative "old hand", husband
and former teacher of Martha Schwartz,
are firmly convinced that landscape
design is an independent art form and is
in urgent need of revival. They have an
outstanding knowledge of modern art
and their collection of modern works is
impressive. Although the designs of
Martha Schwartz and Peter Walker
differ from each other significantly, they
may fundamentally be described as a
distinctive, sometimes eclectic amalgam
of the formal principles of historical garden art and allusions to contemporary
art movements such as Pop Art, Minimal
Art and Land Art.
In addition to classical garden art, Peter
Walker is particularly interested in the
Minimal Art of artists such as Carl Andre,
Robert Smithson and Donald Judd. He
feels that Minimalist reduction transforms
the garden from functional scenery into

a meaningful, perhaps even mystical object, capable of withstanding the test of time. Thus, the Ryoan-ji Japanese Zen garden in Kyoto is for him a good example of an abstract garden in which different levels of meaning are superimposed upon each other. *Tanner Fountain*, created on the campus of the University of Cambridge, Massachusetts in 1984, is one of Peter Walker's projects which particularly reveals the influence of Minimal Art. 159 erratics placed in a perfect circle at regular intervals, shimmering through fine mist in summer and shrouded in clouds of steam in winter, are clearly reminiscent of *Stone Field Sculpture*, a work by Carl Andre in Hartford, Connecticut. In 1977 Andre placed 39 erratics, witnesses to the forces of nature dating back to an earlier ice-age, in an urban context.

Peter Walker has been a successful landscape architect in the United States since the late fifties. Major projects, including ones in Japan and Korea, have earned him international recognition. However, it was only recently that the Berkeley-based firm Peter Walker, William Johnson & Partners realised its first projects in Europe. One of the world's most modern airport hotels, designed by the Chicago architect Helmut Jahn, was completed at Munich airport in June 1994. Peter Walker designed not only the large, glass atrium of the two-wing *Hotel Kempinski* but also the imposing outside areas. His purpose was to create a green, pleasant, recognisable place of arrival, a place which travellers and visitors can experience at different speeds, from different angles and at any time of the day or night. The formal design of the complex is based on superimposed grids and axes, each establishing a relationship either to the buildings, to the history of what was once an agricultural site or to the infrastructure of the airport. The large formal garden, the visual focus of the hotel, is additionally shaped by its own grid; its low, clipped box hedges, oak trees, immaculate lawns and paths of different coloured gravels reflect Peter Walker's admiration of both the great formal gardens of the eighteenth and nineteenth centuries and the garden art of Modernism. In contrast, the design of the atrium, which is traversed diagonally by a free-standing, six-metre high, segmented glass wall, is reminiscent of Pop

Whereas a fine mist provides coolness in summer, a cloud of hot steam hangs over the *Tanner Fountain* in winter.

Art. The glass welcoming wall links the interior of the foyer with the surrounding outside space, a link which is emphasized by a light pipe let into the floor. The artificiality of the ambiance in the atrium is underpinned by endless rows of artificial red geraniums placed in the glass wall, by palm-trees in the hotel bar and cubic steel trellises which, overgrown with climbing plants, are reminiscent of topiaries. Critics of Peter Walker's designs see his expressive use of colours, forms and images as superficial showiness, advancing the demise of meaning in the garden and the landscape. For Peter Walker, they are an attempt to work freely with historical and contemporary models in order to create places of meaning which have not capitulated to functional, economic and ecological requirements.

In contrast to her husband, Martha Schwartz works much more in the field of art and, by her own admission, sees her work as being directly related to the American Land Art and Pop Art of the sixties. She became acquainted with Land Art during her time as an art student and was a keen observer of the way it developed. "The awareness of the land itself as a powerful medium for expression was first explored by these artists," says Martha Schwartz. "The emotional power of the landscape was ignored by landscape architects and architects alike. For information and inspiration in the 'new' medium, the artists were the only source."[1]

Whereas Land Artists were mainly active in areas well away from cities, the young landscape architect has deliberately sought the challenges of cities and is trying to return the Land Art ideas of interaction and intervention to the urban complexity.

[1] Schwarzt, M. In Stichting Conferentie Artivisual Landscapes, editor. *Artivisual Landscapes*. The Hague, 1992. p. 40

The *Tanner Fountain* by Peter Walker, realised on the campus of Harvard University in Cambridge, Massachusetts in 1984, provides an experience of the changing seasons in nature.

Martha Schwartz
Peter Walker

The *Kempinski Hotel* at Munich
airport, 1993/94, by the Chicago architects Murphy/Jahn,
is surrounded by the imposing
gardens designed by Peter
Walker, William Johnson and
Partners. The formal layout
consists of intersecting layers
of different lines and grids.

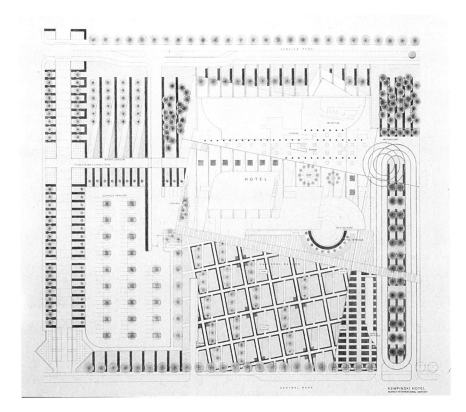

Oak trees, hedges of box and
yew, rectilinear lawns and
gravel areas in different colours
give the imposing garden in
front of the *Kempinski Hotel*
its Baroque character.

The orthogonal design of the
Kempinski atrium is continued
in the outside space. Pyramid-
shaped steel trellises will gradually be covered by climbing
plants, eventually resembling
topiaries.

The view from the lounge on
the top floor of the *Kempinski
Hotel* reveals the particular
features of the landscape
design.

**Martha Schwartz
Peter Walker**

The glass wall cuts through the glass envelope of the *Kempinski* atrium.

The six-metre-high segments of the "welcoming wall" contain countless artificial red geraniums in plastic flower-pots.

The view from the lounge on the top floor of the *Kempinski Hotel* reveals the particular features of the landscape design.

Martha Schwartz
Peter Walker

She sees America's cities as being competition-orientated, fast-moving places, frequently vulgar and narrow-minded, as places which are controlled by people with money but all too often devoid of any taste, any sense of urban obligations or any sense of responsibility towards the future. It is against this background that society's schizophrenic understanding of nature becomes particularly clear. One minute nature is seen through a cloud of romantic notions, only to be the victim of one-sided economic considerations the next. Martha Schwartz rejects this kind of two-facedness and refuses to create idealised landscapes modelled on classical English gardens, arguing that these would, anyway, not stand up to the test of environmental compatibility. She understands the artificial and the natural as being inseparable parts of a whole. In the seventies, influential thinkers in the United States such as Professor Ian McHarg were still propagating the notion that landscape is an ecological system and that ecologically meaningful planning would by itself lead to aesthetic quality.[2] Martha Schwartz interprets such one-sided sacrifice to heightened ecological awareness as a helpless attempt at self-justification.

[2] cf. McHharg, Ian. *Design with Nature*. New York, 1969

The projects realised by Martha Schwartz are often of a temporary nature and, in some cases, experimental. However, they have one thing in common: a choice of materials

In Fukuoka, Japan, Martha Schwartz cooperated on a housing project in 1990–1991 with Mark Mack, architect, and created a cupola of ceramic tiles to mark the entrance to the B-4 housing complex.

which, also in terms of colourfulness, knows no limits. She uses coloured pebbles, gaudily coloured tiles, plastic flowers and, occasionally, even perishable bakery products in her projects. *Bagel Garden*, one of her earliest temporary projects, which she realised in front of her own house in Boston in 1979, met with outrage on the part of other members of the profession and sparked off a controversial public debate. Using purple aquarium gravel and eight dozen, weatherproof bagels, she transformed the 55-square-metre front garden of the Georgian terrace house, a square enclosed by wrought-iron garden fence and low, clipped box-hedges, into a humorous and also serious artistic arrangement which she named *petite parterre embroidery*. She used the tradition of the formal French garden as a link between the nearby Japanese maple in its royal purple and the familiar bagels arranged in a strictly geometric layout. The resulting aesthetic garden was also to be understood as an ironic comment on the petit-bourgeois ideal of a front-garden.

"Ideas must be challenged in order to prove their viability in a culture," concludes Martha Schwartz and points out the necessity for invention.[3] She creates very individual spaces of experience and openly challenges the beholder to rethink his own established standards of values. On the occasion of a lecture she gave at the Rhode Island School of Design, she maintained "that we, as landscape architects, were limited

[3] Schwartz, M. In Stichting Conferentie Artivisual Landscapes, editor. 1992: p. 40

Using only a few elements,
Martha Schwartz transformed
the small front garden of her
Boston terrace house into a
humorous artistic installation.
Bagel Garden, 1979.

213

Martha Schwartz
Peter Walker

The ingredients in the *Bagel Garden*: purple aquarium gravel, eight dozen impregnated bagels and the courage to face the outraged comments of neighbours and colleagues.

in our sights as to what landscape architecture could be, and that our own lack of imagination and courage had deadened the profession."[4] In her fight against the narrowness of her profession, she creates courageous projects using all the means at her disposal: plastic vegetation, as in the *Roof Garden of the Whitehead Institute* in Cambridge, Massachusetts, or the golden garden frogs in her sensational *Rio Shopping Center* project in Atlanta, Georgia. She counters the accusations of her critics by arguing that one cannot ignore phenomena of outside space just because they are ugly and hostile. Difficult commissions such as these offer the landscape architect the freedom she needs for unconventional experiments, which she sometimes even accords a liberating and educational side-effect. However, this "stimulus for the heart, mind and soul"[5] is in danger of reaching saturation point quickly by the all too one-sided use of provocative techniques.

It is only recently that Martha Schwartz Incorporated in Cambridge, Massachusetts has been given large-scale public commissions in the United States. Her redesign of *Jacob Javits Plaza* in the heart of New York City is one such commission and is currently being realised. This neglected public plaza with an area of 3,760 square metres consists of an angle bounded by two large office buildings and lies on top of an under-

[4] Schwartz, M., quoted by Boles, Daralice. "P/A Profile. Peter Walker and Martha Schwartz." In *Progressive Architecture*, 7/89: p. 56

[5] Schwartz, M. In Stichting Conferentie Artivisual Landscapes, editor. 1992: p. 40

Rio Shopping Center in Atlanta, Georgia, 1987–1988. An award-winning project of Martha Schwartz.

ground garage and various services areas. It is a typical plaza in Manhattan, mainly frequented by people who work in the nearby offices during lunch hour. In order to give the plaza an image both witty and reflecting its particular character, Martha Schwartz has selected design elements which are typical of parks in New York – benches, street lamps, paving-stones, fences and so on – and, by using these familiar forms in an unfamiliar way, creates a kind of inner-city parterre. The design is deliberately modelled on the broderie-parterre of the French Baroque garden, but, instead of sweeping, clipped hedges, the long, sweeping New York park benches snake across the entire plaza. Circular hills of lawn, spread out like large green cushions, are bordered by typical metal hoop-fences. The plaza is lit by traditional street lamps, the posts of which have been considerably lengthened. However, in contrast to her bold experiments in private outside space, this project reflects the constraints which functional, financial and planning criteria in the public context have placed on her creativity. But she makes use of all means available to her, including a good dash of humour, to create inspiring public spaces without, at the same, everytime and everywhere deprecating the alleged inhospitableness and hostility of the city. For the sake of giving expression to her own joie de vivre and making it possible for people to experience the outside space, Martha Schwartz is refreshingly indifferent to the

Martha Schwartz
Peter Walker

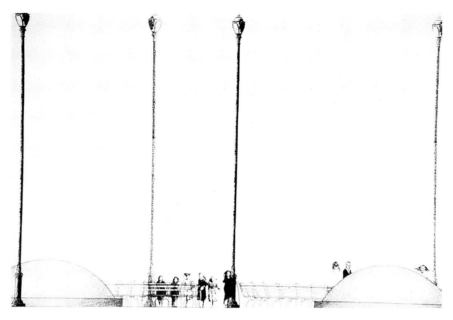

Jacob Javits Plaza in New York, 1995

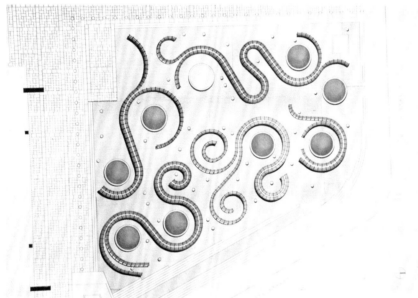

Martha Schwartz's design for the *Jacob Javits Plaza* is modelled on the formal parterre of classical French gardens.

Endless lines of benches wind their way across *Jacob Javits Plaza* between the strictly formal cushions of lawn.

**Martha Schwartz
Peter Walker**

political correctness of her profession, social correctness and even ecological correctness.

Martha Schwartz is invited to lecture in Europe and to speak at symposiums and workshops as she is seen as a landscape architect able to give direction to a profession which is seeking a new identity. Particularly her experimental projects have often given rise to controversial discussions on the claim of landscape architecture to be an art form. On the one hand, there is admiration for American freshness and willingness to experiment, on the other hand, there is widespread belief that this kind of contemporary garden art can only be realised in the United States, where people are used to the gaudiness of "Disney design". Whereas this dedicated landscape architect has not yet had the opportunity to demonstrate her ability in Europe by realising a project in the European context, the major projects in which Peter Walker has been involved include, in addition to the Munich airport project, the Europa Haus project in Frankfurt and the design of the Sony Center at Potsdamer Platz in Berlin. Neither of them feel that they are able to act as freely in the European arena as in the "land of unlimited opportunities".

Peter, can you remember your first visit to Europe?

About thirty years ago, just after I'd finished school, I did a three-week tour of Europe and visited the capitals and the great gardens, I travelled through Spain, France and Italy. Just like any design student I was particularly interested in looking at gardens and architecture. I tried to visit all the places that I'd heard of in school during those three weeks. And I realised that I didn't know anything, that I knew nothing of the language or the history of the countries that I was visiting. I could follow a road map, but that was about all I knew of the places I was visiting. Everything was so overwhelming, so complicated and so deeply rooted in different cultures.

Germany, which I got to know quite well, was in the process of reconstruction. Some people wanted to build something new and others wanted to rebuild the old things. Some cities wanted to re-establish the past and others, such as Frankfurt and Rotterdam, wanted to build for the future. I went to some of the first garden festivals, which, at that time, were more about rebuilding cities than exhibiting gardens. My second or third trip to Europe focused on new towns in Scandinavia, Germany and England. This was very exciting because we were building suburbs in the United States, but not new towns. Unlike American suburbs, European new towns were sponsored by the city centres, which extended their transportation lines out to create a successful connection between city centres and suburbs. I spent a lot of time looking at this aspect of European growth. This was my first impression of Europe and was the aspect I found the most interesting, in fact more so than the gardens. This interest in new towns and reconstruction was not a particular American interest, but there were eleven new towns in America and I worked on five of them.

Martha, how did you first experience Europe?

I've been coming to Europe since I was sixteen years old. I'm from the East coast, and so I'd been coming to Europe for ten years before my first trip to California. I couldn't figure out any reason to visit California. It was also ten years after I started coming to Europe that I first heard anything about landscape architecture. So I came over as a teenager with my parents and we visited a few gardens. I can remember Versailles well, but at the time I found it incredibly boring. We went to look at churches and museums of art and all the things that tourists visit. We returned to Europe every year for many different reasons. One year I came with a group of college students from Pennsylvania in order to compete in a European mini-golf competition. Probably my most powerful recollection was seeing all these people who didn't speak English and who didn't do things the same way that an American would have done them. Despite all these differences, everything seemed

to work quite nicely. It was a real awakening that there were other worlds, other people and other cultures. I began to view the world with more respect. It made me realise that the United States is not the centre of the universe and that I am not the centre of the universe.

Did you experience this differently when you came back as a professional?

I only started coming back as a professional a couple of years ago. It's only recently that I've been participating in competitions with European designers and have been asked to lecture here. It's very ironic that most of my professional involvement in Europe has been in Germany. When I was travelling, I never wanted to visit Germany. It wasn't until I turned forty that I decided to go and see what Germany was like. Actually, this was the country where there was the greatest interest in the kind of work I do. Today, I have a much more focused interest in the landscape and the way people live over here. I also have a much better idea of the differences between the way of life in Europe and the way people live in the United States. People in Europe see the land in a different way. The pressure on the land in the course of history has been so great, something which Americans find hard to understand. Nonetheless, these circumstances have still led to outstanding landscape artefacts, which are clear evidence that landscape can be a cultural art form. I often ask myself: "What works here?" "Why does it work here?" This gives me some idea of the direction we should be going and of things that we'll probably never achieve. I'm very interested in the designed landscape, particularly in the great classical gardens of the past. We don't have these kinds of gardens in the United States. It's important for me to come over here and get in touch with this spirit again.

My roots may well be here because I was trained as an artist and I'm interested in the making of things, of artefacts and what people leave behind. I'm interested in sculpture, in movies, paintings and landscapes which, so to speak, represent culture. As far as the landscape tradition is concerned, I feel much closer to Europe than to the West coast of the United States. When I take a look at Versailles today, I am reinforcing my own interests. Versailles communicates to me as an artist.

P.W. The first time we came to Europe together was with a group of students. Martha had just graduated. We came over with some of her classmates and some students from Michigan and made an intensive and systematic study of the French gardens. Shortly afterwards, we bought a house in Italy and for a period of six to seven years we used it as a base to visit many cultural sites in Europe. Ever since we've been deeply interested in European culture. Our basic driving force was the notion that here not only architecture, painting and sculpture but also landscape architecture were clearly part of

Peter Walker

Martha Schwartz

historical culture. Studying gardens became the rootstock of our whole interest in the formal aspects of landscape architecture. We each made our own use of these impressions, but these were the roots which we grafted onto and which have influenced us, if not directed us since then.

M.S. On the one hand, I admire the way that Europeans live, their knowledge of art is much more a part of their general education and that's reflected in what they eat, the way they plan their towns, their attitude to the environment, the way they create open spaces and so forth. The feeling for aesthetics and the way it affects all areas of life is far more integrated. In contrast, the United States is wild and woolly and, in many cases, downright ugly. But then of course my dilemma is that in terms of what I do artistically I'm pretty unsuited for life in Europe. I couldn't work here because of the numbers of

have the same problems as their colleagues in the United States and they see less clearly the connection which Martha and I depend on, namely the long-term view that landscape is part of culture and not part of bureaucracy. Ultimately, landscape architecture is, along with art and painting and sculpture, judged in terms of its contribution to culture. None of the landscape architects who I have so far met in Europe sees this as a central issue. I think they want to win recognition for their discipline, but most of them see themselves as being helpless and underprivileged peripheral figures, particularly when they see themselves in the context of historical garden art.

Martha Schwartz's "Blue Crab Park" for *Baltimore Inner Harbour* is planned as a two-hectare earth sculpture in the form of a crab, the symbol of the city of Baltimore.

rules. I tend to be anarchic in the way I approach things, and there are far more opportunities in places which are not so regulated. In other words, I benefit from the lack of regulations and, at the same time, I suffer because of this lack as it means that I lead a fairly insecure existence.

P.W. I've had an easier time as far as this is concerned as my practice is now corporate and Europe is now less governmental and more corporate. I don't find the difference as great as Martha does as she works more in the artistic realm and is often dependent on sponsors or patronage. One of the dilemmas that I experience working here is that landscape practice in Europe parallels trends in the sixties and seventies in the United States. Most landscape architects in Europe work for either very small or medium-sized companies and are very much caught up in bureaucratic rules and regulations; in consequence, they're very frustrated. They

M.S. There are simply too many rules here and they would drive me crazy, but I feel that there are reasons for the rules which exist here. The land has been used so much more intensively and for so much longer than in the United States, yet, despite this, it's much more beautiful. This can partly be explained by the fact that the landscape was not designed from the point of view of the car, whereas development of landscape in the United States began with the automobile. The medieval structure of compact European towns surrounded by agricultural areas is a beautiful model. When you're in a town it's very urban, but as soon as you get out of it you're in the country. But the decisive question

Competition project for *Baltimore Inner Harbour* in Baltimore, Maryland, 1994, photograph of model. The design aims to strengthen the link between the adjacent quarters and the harbour, and to lessen the linear impression of the harbour promenade by a series of different spaces: "Crab Walk", "Picnic Park", "Natural History Spiral", "Science Playground", are attractions for local residents and tourists.

is what is to happen when these structures disappear. Here the Europeans are no better off than the Americans. It looks damn ugly on the periphery and that's the problem.

Generally, I think there's less need to be inventive in Europe. People in Europe tend to have more respect for the history of the landscape. In the United States there are many reasons why we have to be inventive. We still have pieces of land which have barely been touched, and we need people who are able to imagine how things should be done the very first time. When I began working as a landscape architecture, one choice I made was at first only to work with cowboys. They're my clients. These wild people who just go off and try something. Architect cowboys, developer cowboys and so on. All these boys wanted to do something which would set them apart from the others, probably so that they would be able to market their projects better. But now that we've been through a recession, there aren't very many cowboys left. Now the administrators are in control, and I'm starting to work on public projects. I don't know if these are going to turn out the way I want them to.

P.W. The idea that all of America is controlled by cowboys is, of course, wrong. Most of America is in fact very conservative, but, because the country is vast, things can still develop in niches. There's no room for niches in Europe. Everything is overlaid with five different regulations.

Peter, you have been working in different parts of the world for a number of years and, recently, you've been doing more things in Korea and Japan.
My moving around the world really started in Japan, and wherever I go I learn something new. Japan is a most bewildering place and I can't imagine anywhere less like America. We started doing projects there and tried to find out how the system worked and how you get things built in Japan. We had really invaluable assistance from the Japanese architects because they were not frightened by what we were doing. Because they knew of us, they were asking for what we did, and that was a great advantage. Instead of having to prove ourselves in Japan, what we had to do there was to figure out how to do what we did even better. It's always easier if somebody already likes your work. If you don't know whether people like your work, it's a lot harder. When the Japanese began publishing our work and these publications appeared in Europe, things started to get going in Europe. In fact it was through the Japanese publications that we became known in Europe. People in Europe began to read about us in magazines, but they didn't commission us to realise a project, they invited us to take part in a competition. I soon realised that even if you don't win a competition, it's good promotion provided you get short-listed. Scarcely any attention is paid to competitions which are held

in America. Competitions have been a powerful way of making the kind of work we do known in Europe.

What concept of landscape and landscape design do you base your projects on? Is there a "recipe" for good gardens in Japan or Korea?
I think it's the same recipe which anybody who does something artistic has to have. It's a mixture of practicality, vision and content – something that people can recognise in it. Martha has taught me a lot about using other media of communication. My notion of landscape design was that a landscape architect would design a garden, and then people would visit it and either like it or not like it. And that would be the way that reputations grew. Today, I realise that very few people ever actually visit these gar-

The design of the outside area of the *Center for Advanced Technology in the Harima Science Garden City* in Japan, 1993, reveals Peter Walker's admiration of Minimal Art and the art of Japanese Zen gardens.

dens. Instead, they have access to them through various kinds of media.

George Hargreaves, a friend of ours, once said to us, "Whenever I do anything which is geometric, it can be conveyed well in photographs and I get a lot of attention; but whenever I do work of another kind, this receives very little attention." I think that this is one of the qualities of modern landscape architecture. We are becoming more and more attuned to the media of our age and we can't help being influenced by them, because we see how we can get a reaction. This doesn't mean you're only designing to get media attention. In the past it was the aristocracy who talked about gardens like Le Nôtre's and it was through this word of mouth propaganda that garden art spread throughout Europe. Frederick Law Olmsted travelled all over the United States in order to prepare the small

Martha Schwartz
Peter Walker

publications which he intended to write about gardens. People heard about the gardens through the publications and then went to see the actual garden. The only difference today is that the method of propagation is slightly different.

Jailhouse Garden by Martha Schwartz for the King County prison in Seattle, Washington, 1982–1987.

Martha, what personal reasons do you have for the work you do in landscape architecture?

My reasons are very personal. It's not my intention to show "this is the way it should be". The objectives which Pete and I have is to create landscapes which can be seen and objectified. In order to create a landscape which can be seen you often have to make it completely different from its surroundings. In order to initiate a dialogue on landscape, the landscape first has to be visible and sometimes this calls for a very radical approach. And a lot of what we do we

do for personal interest. For example, Pete sometimes realises geometric projects because they photograph well and sometimes just because he likes this formal language.

P.W. But the dialogue is also important to us. Although I think that an artist primarily does creative work for his own satisfaction, he also wants to enter into a dialogue with the world rather than live in splendid isolation. Twenty-five years ago we were interested in the common man and the way he used things. That was very functionalistic in its orientation. In the course of time, Martha and I have increasingly gone over to engaging people not only physically but also intellectually. We wanted to create something which could be discussed. Something which we and our colleagues as well as our clients and their friends could discuss. It's an attempt to reintegrate people into culture. Novels are written to express ideas and give people the possibility of discussing these ideas. Why shouldn't a garden be designed for exactly the same purpose?

M.S. I think saying that we design gardens or even new art so that people can discuss them sounds like an apology, as we actually design gardens for our own satisfaction. We make apologies because our profession tends to be very moralistic. Landscape architects always try to do "what is right", to be socially correct, politically correct, ecologically correct. Everybody expects us to play by the rules. It's very dangerous to stand up and say: "I'm doing this garden because I think it's going to be very beautiful." Or, "I'm working on a project of this kind because I find it interesting." What I'm interested in is recreating a value for this kind of thinking because I believe that spaces that are not designed from a very personal point of view tend to be uninteresting and unimportant spaces. All the things which distinguish a culture are things which are produced by individuals with their own points of view, their own feelings and aims. Such things can then be assimilated into a culture and become part of it. I feel that landscape architects should be allowed to say: "Look, I just really love circles, I want the whole world to be a big circle."

Landscape architects usually work in public space which is part of our earth and so it belongs to everybody. Doesn't this prevent us from claiming a bit of land as our own to do whatever we want on?
M.S. That's right, but if we don't do it, who is to do it?

P.W. I don't think it's a question of egocentricity on the one hand and selflessness on the other. Ultimately, the artist always gives his paintings away. So, in a certain way, he is extremely altruistic, maybe not in terms of his intentions, but in the end effect.

The *Jailhouse Garden* is a pleasant place for prisoners and visitors as well as a political statement. Whereas the building would prefer to avoid public attention, Martha Schwartz forces passers-by to stop and look.

M.S. It's a question of the role of the public garden and its function. Working in public space undoubtedly means making allowances. This is also one of the greatest challenges. It is said that architecture is the greatest art form because it not only has to function but also has to satisfy aesthetic needs. Landscape architecture is also an art form! The fact that landscape designs function doesn't get you off the hook. They also have to function at a higher level. There's a higher level that nobody talks about, a metaphysical level at which human beings exist.

Your designs appear in magazines and journals which are published internationally. Everybody is familiar with the same ideas and pictures. Do you think that you will create an international style in time?
M.S. I don't think that this will lead to an international style in landscape architecture. Actually, I think it would be pretty scary to see the same

Artificial landscape at a site hostile to vegetation: plastic hedges, plastic flowers, dyed gravel and plenty of green paint in Martha Schwartz's *Splice Garden* on the roof of the Whitehead Institute for Biomedical Research in Cambridge, Massachusetts, 1986.

style repeated over and over again. What might happen is that landscape architects could find their own personal voices, and this would lead to a great proliferation of different forms of expression. That would be part of a movement and less of a style. That would be good to see.

P.W. I don't think that style is ultimately important. In my view, style is something that you look at afterwards. It's a device used by historians to categorise things. I think it's ridiculous to belief that a designer decides from the outset that he's going to do something in an international style.

M.S. I see a whole series of gardens around the world which could be classified as contemporary gardens. I don't want to call them postmodern as I'm not sure that modernism has ever existed in garden design. Probably there will be a wide diversity in the future. It's the same in art: the Minimalists are quite different from the Abstract Expressionists and, in turn, they are dif-

ferent from the Conceptual Artists. And yet they're all part of the Modern art movement. So if you start seeing gardens like Pete's all around the world that would be the "Pete Walker school".

P.W. It would probably have to be called the "Carl Andre style". If you really want to understand a development, you have to go back to its origins.

Artists such as Carl Andre had a certain understanding of their environment and the society they lived in and reacted to the society of the sixties in their own way. Martha, you were just talking about your own very personal reasons for designing gardens and using colours and forms you like without having to justify yourself all the time. Is having fun your philosophy?
M.S. I didn't say "having fun". What I said is I want to do things which have some personal meaning. In one sense I'm very interested in the truth. I seek an explanation for what I see as being true. I want to find out how we see the landscape or how we would like to see the landscape and how we tackle this issue. What matters to me here is having as much clarity as possible.
When I'm working on projects, I always find myself up against the same problem. I'm always told "We all love the landscape. It's the most important part of the project." But reality is usually a bit different: there's no money, there's no backing, nobody cares about the garden, and I'm supposed to play along with this game. If they don't have money for the landscape, I can provide them with an image, only it will be made of plastic because that's what they can afford. If they want a real landscape, perhaps they should allocate money, space, time and all the other things and be prepared to make a commitment. For this reason, people see me as radical; they're afraid and only commission me to do small, low-budget projects. I am sometimes offered art projects which, although they don't bring in a lot of money, give me more freedom and more possibilities.

Of course your "honesty in plastic" produces a lot of rejection and aggression. People say: "Martha Schwartz realises landscapes which are typical of our consumer society. All she is doing is reinforcing what we're all fighting against."
M.S. Exposing it. I'm trying to expose it. People say: "You know what, she hates plants." I don't hate plants at all. If I work with artificial plants, it's because I have no other choice. There's no basis for a landscape, because all the parties involved have decided that landscape is completely unimportant. Then I say: "Okay, we'll just paint it green, that's all we can do with the budget we've got." Maybe this will make people think about the landscape.
The other thing is that not everybody will be in

a position to have a piece of landscape of their own. There are many people who can't afford to have a garden. What do they do? Do we just forget about them? After all, most of America's landscape consists of roof tops and other ugly things. Do we say that this is not landscape and it can't be green and therefore I'm going to ignore them? So I would like to think about the image of a landscape and implant it in a place where real landscape is not possible. Although this whole situation makes me very angry, I like to feel that there is something hopeful and positive about it.

Many people ask themselves what constitutes honesty in landscape architecture. Is camouflage honest? Is substitute nature honest?

P.W. You're putting philosophical questions to a profession that has no philosophy. In the seventeenth and eighteenth centuries people had a very clear vision, and even in the nineteenth century people in the United States had a very clear vision of what our profession was supposed to do and of the value of its creative work. Today, this clear vision has been lost. We need to find a contemporary way of defining our profession.

There are two ways a profession can be defined: a Le Nôtre or an Olmsted can emerge and define it by their example. Then everyone knows what the profession does. Or it can reflect philosophically on what its purpose is in the way that Karl Marx did. There may well be other models, but these are the two historical models that spring to mind. People no longer know what it is we are supposed to be doing, and I suspect that we don't either.

The fact that landscape architecture is different from architecture, painting and sculpture has resulted in landscape architects no longer knowing what their role is. Environmentalism has broadened the field and created confusion. We're landscape architects and not scientists. We're not environmentalists in the sense that we can go out and count the trees and derive some knowledge from our statistical findings. We don't do that, who the hell wants to do that. That's what foresters do. So what is it that we do?

Minimalism and other movements were developed in painting, sculpture, drama, music and other formats, but have yet to be developed in our format. Minimalism in music is entirely different from Minimalism in painting and Minimalism in sculpture is completely different from either. What we now have to do is develop our own format. That's what we're trying to do. But it's first important to be clear what the landscape is. If people say that plastic isn't landscape, I want to know why. It's landscape to me, it's outdoors, it serves a particular purpose, it's to scale, it's even green. It tries to do everything which a landscape is supposed to do.

By creating the *Bagel Garden* Martha made a joke, and I think it's a very profound joke, about a bagel being a very good piece of landscape material. Her joke explains what a landscape material is, what is needed to design a landscape and where the material is going to be put and, to some extent, to what purpose the material in question is going to be put. Our age doesn't have a transcendent genius who answers all these questions for us. So we will have to try to do this ourselves.

M.S. I'm sure we'll succeed!

P.W. I really don't think we are anywhere near to finding answers. When people run around not knowing what profession they really belong to, not knowing the nature of their art, not understanding what the means of the twentieth century are, the resulting set-up is very confusing. People are going round in circles. Martha doesn't have a lot of weapons, in other words she doesn't have a lot of money. Clients aren't banging at her door all the time, but at least she's faced in the right direction and she's not running around in circles.

M.S. Very often the people who succeed in understanding what it's all about are driven by an internal flywheel. There's something like a little mouse in there which keeps turning the wheel and just keeps on going and nobody knows why. It's not anything you can give to anybody or teach anybody. If you can give this little mouse a philosophy, if you can give it a direction and a reason which then makes it part of a superordinate idea, that should get you somewhere. But you need the flywheel which is driven by "I just love to do plastic landscapes", or "I just love to make people angry", or "I just love circles and squares!" The flywheel is very important, it's fundamental to getting things done. You have to have real personal reasons for fighting and not giving up.

From what you've both said, I have the impression that you are both going in the same direction and that your work has many parallels. Are there differences in the way you think and your approach to your work?

M.S. I think we often like to dwell on all the differences, but actually these differences aren't very great. I intrinsically know what Pete is after. I have always been interested in geometrical relationships and mystical qualities that are inherent in geometry. I could show you great piles of drawings and etchings. If you looked at these and compared them with my landscapes, they'd be very similar. The formal language that Pete uses is interesting to me and I like it. I've always been interested in making gardens into art, making them objective so that they can be seen. There are very few people who are genuinely interested in this. In one sense, we need reinforcement from each other because it's difficult to develop things that actually

223

Martha Schwartz
Peter Walker

An enclosed garden forms the entrance to the *Dickinson Residence* in Santa Fé, New Mexico, 1990–1991, Martha Schwartz. Four wells and six olive trees create an introverted ambiance. Water channels made of coloured tiles, forming an orthogonal pattern, link the wells.

The large *Dickinson Residence* in traditional adobe style lies on a hillside and commands an impressive view of the surrounding countryside.

The four wells are illuminated at dusk.

225

Martha Schwartz
Peter Walker

nobody wants. Nobody wants large, expensive projects which serve no apparent purpose.

P.W. Looking at it this way, there are no rational reasons for opera.

M.S. There's no practical reason for painting or sculpture. You don't need them. Nobody needs one of Pete's garden and certainly nobody needs one of my gardens. So why are we doing what we do? I would say that we're doing it because we can. We have been lucky enough to be born into a situation where we can do this kind of work, instead of having to fight just to stay alive.

P.W. I hope that there are people who can benefit from this work and understand it. I'm interested in seeing what use people are able to make of the knowledge I have gained. For example, for me Minimalism has to do with light, weather and the seasons and how they can be read against an artefact. This artefact can be something very simple. Perhaps I can't take this idea any further, but, maybe, if I succeed in communicating it, somebody else will be able to. It took me years to get just this little bit of information clear in my mind. I try to encourage people to think analytically, to be self-critical and to be aware of their own processes so that they can pass on what they have learned and others can build upon this.

M.S. Coming back to your question about what we do for each other. When I first met Pete and came out to California, he was the head of a firm which had 130 employees. I had done just one year of landscape architecture at college and was about to drop out because it seemed like the most boring thing I could imagine. And this was right after art school.
Pete was the first person I met who saw that landscape architecture and art are actually related. He asked the class: "if you're not going to make art or something else which people will remember, why are you here?" And I thought: "God, that's great! Now I can take all my training and apply it to this new field which I find myself becoming really interested in." So I stayed with landscape architecture, and, at the same time, Pete was interested in finding a way to get out of landscape architecture and into art. He had been collecting art for a long time and he was aware of the discrepancy between the things he was collecting and the things he was doing. I knew all about the artists and what they were doing. Essentially, I would say that Pete helped me to become a landscape architect and I helped Pete to become an artist. I encouraged him to forget the other stuff and to try things out and experiment. I think that we have really helped each other to get where we are. Otherwise, I would definitely not have become a landscape architect.

P.W. We have a whole group of people who are sympathetic to what we do in one way or another: some clients, some architects, a few other landscape architects.

Which landscape architects would you make "club members"?
P.W. Le Nôtre, Olmsted, Jens Jensen, Thomas Church, Larry Halprin, Isamu Noguchi, Garret Eckbo. I see us as being part of what is still a very small group, which has its roots in history. I don't think that our work is particularly unique or brand-new. There have been people who have been a lot better than we are and people who have probably not been as good as we are. In terms of what we do, it's a small, but continuing group. All the truly great gardens have come out of this group. I see them as contemporary garden artists although they didn't all work in this century. I don't see any difference between, in particular, the later works of Le Nôtre and what I do.

Is this a longing to restore garden art to the position that it once had?
P.W. We have to define it in terms which were successful in any given era. For example, I don't think that Le Nôtre was operating in circumstances which are completely different from those of today. I think that there were a lot of problems at his time. He was able to find the equation to work in, and I think that it's up to us to find today's equation to work in.

M.S. I think that people have to be inventive. If people want to look for a system, it's going to be a long search. I think that people have to go out and start. It's a question of "think globally, act locally". They have to start in their own backyards. Start there and see where that takes you. It's not going to come from anybody but ourselves.

P.W. I have got to a point where people will look. I have experienced a number of instances where we have proposed something quite incredible. People looked at it and decided not to realise it. I've come this far, but I'm not the first person to have achieved this. But at least I've got to a point where I've been able to try something out and I hope that one day I'll actually be able to realise a part of it.

Biography and Selected Works

Martha Schwartz was born in Philadelphia, Pennsylvania in 1950.
She lives and works in Boston, Massachusetts.

1973	Bachelor of Fine Arts at the University of Michigan in Ann Arbor.
1974–1977	Student of landscape architecture at the University of Michigan in Ann Arbor and at the Harvard University Graduate School of Design.

Except where noted, locations are in the U.S.A.

Practice of Landscape Design and principal teaching activities:

1976–1982	Worked for Sasaki, Walker and Associates (SWA), Boston, Massachusetts
1982–1984	Martha Schwartz Incorporated, Boston, Massachusetts
1984–1990	Peter Walker/Martha Schwartz, Landscape Architects, New York and San Francisco
1990–1992	Martha Schwartz, Ken Smith, David Meyer Incorporated, San Francisco
Since 1991	Adjunct Professor at the Harvard University Graduate School of Design Guest lecturer at the Rhode Island School of Design and at the University of California in Berkeley Participation in many workshops and symposiums, numerous guest lectures Collaborated on numerous art commissions in the U.S.A.
Since 1992	Martha Schwartz, Incorporated, Cambridge, Massachusetts and San Francisco

Selected realised projects:

1979	*Bagel Garden* in Boston, Massachusetts
1986	*Splice Garden*, Whitehead Institute for Biomedical Research in Cambridge, Massachusetts
1986–1988	Center for Innovative Technology in Fairfax, Virginia with Arquitectonica International, architects
1982–1987	*Jailhouse Garden,* King County in Seattle, Washington
1987	International Swimming Hall of Fame in Fort Lauderdale, Florida with Arquitectonica International, architects
1987–1990	Rio Shopping Center in Atlanta, Georgia with Arquitectonica International, architects
1989–1990	Interior design of the Becton Dickinson Immunocytrometry Division in San José, California with Gensler Associates Inc., architects
1990–1991	The Citadel, City of Commerce, California with The Nadel Partnership, architects
1990–1991	Fukuoka International Housing, Site B-4 with Mark Mack, architect
	Garden for the Dickinson Residence in Santa Fé, New Mexico with Steven Jacobson, architect
Since 1992	Redesign of the Jacob Javits Plaza in New York City
1994	Baltimore Inner Harbour, West Shore and Rash Field Competition (1st prize) with Design Collective Inc., architects
1994–1995	Garden of the Davis Residence in El Paso, Texas Redesign of Hud Plaza in Washington, D.C. with architrave p.c., architects

Numerous international awards

Selected Bibliography

Schwartz, M. "Landscape and Common Culture Since Modernism." In *Architecture California*, vol. 14 (1992)

Schwartz, M. "Parc de la Citadelle." In *Pages Paysages*, no. 4 (1992)

Roche-Soulie, S./Roulet, S. *Piscine*. Paris, 1992

Schwartz, M. "Our Culture and the Art for Public Spaces." In *Stichting Conferentie Artivisual Landscapes*, edited by International IFLA Conference 1992. The Hague, 1992

Schwartz, M. "Landscape and Common Culture Since Modernism." In *Modern Landscape Architecture: a critical review*, edited by M. Trieb. Berkeley, 1993

Numerous articles in international journals of landscape architecture, particularly in *Landscape Architecture* and *Progressive Architecture* (USA).

Martha Schwartz
Peter Walker

Biography and Selected Works

Peter E. Walker was born in Pasadena, California in 1932.
He lives and works in San Francisco.

1955	Bachelor of Science in landscape architecture, University of California, Berkeley
1955–1956	Graduate studies in landscape architecture at the University of Illinois
1957	Master of Landscape Architecture at the Harvard University Graduate School of Design.

Practice of Landscape Architecture and principal teaching activities:

1957	Founding partner of Sasaki, Walker and Associates (SWA), Watertown, Massachusetts
1975	Establishment of SWA office in San Francisco
1983	Establishment of Peter Walker/Martha Schwartz, Landscape Architects, New York and San Francisco
Since 1992	Peter Walker, William Johnson and Partners, Berkeley
Since 1958	Lecturer at the Harvard University Graduate School of Design. Guest lecturer at numerous international universities

Selected realised projects:

1957–1960	Foothill College, Los Altos, California with E. J. Kump and Associates and Masten and Hurd Associates, architects
1972	Weyerhaeuser Company Corporate Headquarters in Tacoma, Washington with Skidmore, Owings & Merrill, architects
1983	Burnett Park, Fort Worth, Texas
1984	*Tanner Fountain,* Harvard University, Cambridge, Massachusetts IBM Clearlake, Clearlake, Texas Herman Miller Incorporated, Rockland, California
1984–1989	IBM Solana Westlake and Southlake, Dallas, Texas
1989	Redwood City Center, California
1990	Outside areas at the Olympic Village in Barcelona
1991	IBM Japan Makuhari Building in Makuhari, Chiba Prefecture, Japan with Taniguchi and Associates and Nihon Sekkei Inc., architects
1991–1993	Ayala Triangle in the Makati district, Manila with Skidmore, Owings & Merrill, architects
1992–1993	Longacres Park in Renton, Washington with Skidmore, Owings & Merrill, architects Principal Mutual Life Insurance Company, Des Moines, Iowa with Jahn/Murphy Associates
1993	Design of the Europa-Haus, Frankfurt on Main with Jahn/Murphy, architects Center for Advanced Science and Technology in Harima Science Garden City, Hyogo Prefecture, Japan with Arata Isozaki, architect
1994	Outside areas and interior design of Kempinski Hotel, Munich airport, Germany with Jahn/Murphy Associates

Numerous international awards and successes in competitions including:

1988	Marina Linear Park, San Diego, California
1992	Federal Triangle, Washington, D.C. Clark County Administration Complex, Nevada
1993	Industrial and Commercial Bank of China, Peking T. F. Green Airport, Rhode Island Sony Center, Berlin, Germany

Selected Bibliography

Process Architecture no. 85. *Peter Walker: Landscape as Art.* Tokyo, 1989

Dillon, D. "Peter Walker. Solana, un grande parco nel Texas." In *Domus* 746 (1993): pp. 70–77

Process Architecture no. 118. *Peter Walker, William Johnson and Partners.* Tokyo, 1994

Walker, P./Simo, M. *Invisible Gardens. The Search for Modernism in the American Landscape.* Massachusetts, 1994

Yamagiwa Corporation, editor. *The Way of Collaboration. Peter Walker, William Johnson and Partners.* Tokyo, 1994 (catalogue)

Numerous articles in international journals of landscape architecture.

Acknowledgements

Kindly provided by Martha Schwartz and Peter Walker:
Art on File: 221
Pamela Palmer: 219
Rion Rizzo: 214 m.
Office Martha Schwartz Inc.: 212, 217 r., 218, 220, 224, 225
Office Peter Walker, William Johnson and Partners: 208 bottom, 210, 211 r., 217 l.
Jay Venezia: 205
Alan Ward: 206, 207, 213, 214 top, 222
as well as:
Udo Weilacher: 208 top, 209, 211 l.

Hyperrealistic Shock Therapy – Adriaan Geuze

Charcoal-coloured tiles with the imprints of fossilised birch branches for the parking deck of the *V.S.B. Bank* in Utrecht, 1995.

In order to understand the work of Adriaan Geuze, it is necessary to be aware of the nature and history of Dutch landscape. It is the product of the century-old fight of man against the elemental force of the sea. The aim was to obtain cultivable, inhabitable land by building dykes. The consequence has not only been a high degree of urbanisation but also a functional, largely linear structuring of the low-lying land. The rational and technological approach to nature and environment has also influenced Dutch landscape architecture. Whereas the landscape design of the sixties and seventies adopted a largely defensive strategy towards unrestrained urban growth, a new generation of landscape architects is using offensive approaches in order to give landscape design a more defined profile and to intervene actively in ongoing problems of the urban and natural landscapes. Adriaan Geuze, the founding partner of West 8, a Rotterdam planning office, is a member of the avant-garde of European landscape architecture. Geuze's designs originate in the typical relationship of the Dutch to their landscape. They are, at the same time, characterised by their powerful simplicity and whole-hearted endorsement of the unvarnished aesthetics of popular culture. Many see the projects of West 8 as being an exemplary symbiosis of art, ecology and landscape architecture. Others describe the radical designs as blatant provocation. It is virtually impossible to describe the typical characteristics of Geuze's work; the Dutchman, who was born in 1960, is, as he himself admits, still very much in the process of development, the end of which cannot be foreseen.

One of the first projects of West 8, landscaping the large sand dumps at the eight-kilometre-long storm-barrier *Oosterschelde Weir*, is one of the young Rotterdam planner's most exciting projects and demonstrates his goal of combining design factors with economic and ecological aspects in a meaningful way. When the huge dam became operational in 1986, the embanked areas which had served as islands to work from were left behind. The Rotterdam office was commissioned by the Rijkswaterstaat, the Dutch Ministry of Transport and Water Management, to landscape these areas. A first section of the work covering an area of 2.5 hectares at the northern end of the weir was realised in 1991/1992: the "largest living Zen garden",[1] a garden composed of the black shells of the common mussel and the white shells of the cockle – waste from the nearby mussel farms. The rectilinear stripes of the surface, which has been levelled to a plateau, are a clear indication of the artificial nature of the

The *Oosterschelde Weir* became operational in 1986. The computer-controlled storm barriers seal off the North Sea along an eight-kilometre stretch when storm tides threaten.

[1] Geuze, A. In Koenigs, T., editor. *Stadt-Parks*. Frankfurt am Main, 1993: p. 39

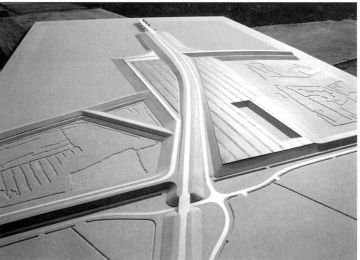

The northern end of the *Oosterschelde Weir*, model by West 8.

intervention; it is in sharp contrast to the soft line of the coast and unequivocally rejects the imitation of nature which was originally called for.

Geuze plans with the everyday user in mind. In consequence, the scale and layout of the site establish a relationship to the car driver as, rushing past, he suddenly experiences the view across the expanse of the sea and the striking play of colours of the plateau. Geuze's main concern is increasing people's sensitivity to their everyday environment, something which he does not seek to achieve by using the Romantic images of the nineteenth century, but by employing and exaggerating the potential of the everyday, sometimes even of the vulgar.

It is surprising that the rebellious landscape architect includes ecological qualities in his projects which otherwise seem to be so radically orientated to aesthetics and functionality. His preliminary studies for numerous projects include detailed investigation of the ecological conditions existing at the site. The mussel beds at the *Oosterschelde Weir* are suitable breeding grounds for a number of species of sea-birds. In other words, ecological planning does not automatically entail imitating what is natural, rather, as Geuze puts it, nature is to a certain extent successful in developing evolutionary strategies to adapt to the areas inhabited by man.

Geuze's work is, however, not only based on a changed understanding of nature. He also feels that the behaviour of man, his requirements of the environment, his style of life and his image of himself have changed so radically that the old models of urban green space, in particular the municipal park of the nineteenth century, no longer serve their purpose. The individual at the end of the 20th century is self-confident, mobile, makes intelligent use of new media and technologies and takes possession of all kinds of space in a resourceful way. "Contemporary life is permanent flight," concludes Geuze and "the new city generates (…) its own escape routes."[2] Presence in public life, opportunities for expression of the individual and of the prevailing zeitgeist are deemed to be important parameters for the development and invention of new space. The project for the *Schouwburgplein*, Rotterdam's 15,000 square metre theatre square in the heart of the lively port city, demonstrates what Geuze understands by hyperrealistic shock therapy: the things are shown in a bluntly realistic way, as a scenario of emptiness. As an underground garage is located below the square, the site is treated like a roof: covered, like an artificial surface, with steel plate and perforated sheet-metal, interspersed with ventilation shafts and entrances and dotted with greenery in mobile containers. Metal grids allow a Milky Way of light to emerge at night, and bizarre, monumental light masts provide a disquieting ambience, a mixture of the subterranean and the supernatural, which the visitor is to conquer and interpret consciously. At the same time, some of the square's elements react to natural influences, corrode or erode in the course of time or change their character

[2] Geuze, A. In Uitgeverij Thoth, editor. *Modern Park Design*. Amsterdam, 1993: p. 47

Black shells of the common mussel and white shells of the cockle, waste products of the mussel industry, were used by West 8 to create an impressive art landscape.

as a direct consequence of weather conditions: the spray of the fountains, for example, varies in height depending on the surrounding temperature. The square is intended to be in a permanent state of flux, reflecting the discontinuity and changing nature of a world to which the individual continually has to adjust.

Adriaan Geuze

What formed your close relationship to the Dutch landscape?

You could say that my roots are truly Dutch. My father worked as a diesel engineer as a young man and my grandfather was a dyke engineer. He told me a lot about building dykes and hydraulic engineering and this inspired me from a very early age. I obtained a traditional degree in landscape architecture at the end of a course of studies which was the equivalent to similar courses in Germany, Denmark or France, but was typically Dutch: Dutch landscape architecture is based on the question of how to win land from nothing, from water. So this means that landscape architecture is not a luxury here, but an essential feature of our existence.

My studies were an absolute disaster as the idea of landscape was somehow inside me and I had problems with the scientific approach. During my studies I devoted a lot of time to the study of architecture as this was something I was greatly interested in. I was so fascinated by the work of the Russian constructivists that I read everything about it that I could get my

A converted building in the dock area of Rotterdam serves the young team of West 8 as an office.

hands on and even went to Moscow. I worked in Amsterdam to earn money to pay for my studies and graduated after about two years. I made a spontaneous decision to move to Rotterdam and to set up an office here in the dock area. I wanted all the things you can see out there in the docks to inspire my work as a landscape architect. I believe that West 8 has made an important contribution to Dutch landscape architecture as we have given landscape a contemporary definition. We love popular culture, we love the dock culture, the technical effects, we love the aesthetics of non-design. This kind of perception, our different way of looking at things has led to many new ideas in the way landscape is approached. Unlike many of our Dutch colleagues, we are not hampered by reservations regarding form and fashion. Many of them model their designs on the principles used in the gardens and parks of Paris or the squares of Barcelona. Instead, we are very keen to formulate a new, unusual hyperreality. This is to be understood as a kind of style and certainly as a central theme of our work.

Are there examples of current European landscape architecture you think particularly highly of?

I am very enthusiastic about Danish landscape architecture. The Danes succeed in creating very simple landscapes of beautiful texture using only very few elements. They also know a lot about the use of plants. Many of Sven-Ingvar Andersson's works are good examples of this. The overall approach holds a lot of promise for the future. There are also some examples of French landscape architecture which I very much like, for instance the work of Yves Brunier, who died in 1991 and who I see as having been one of the best young French landscape architects. I also like some of the projects which have been realised in Barcelona on account of their successful integration of architecture and art.

Are there any links between your work and traditional garden art?

Yes, of course. I feel very strong links with the early period of modern Dutch landscape architecture. No independent landscape architecture existed in Holland until around 1950. It was only then that the first Dutch landscape architects began using the ideas of Leberecht Migge, only with a delay of thirty years. I found the representatives of the generation of the fifties and sixties very inspiring. But then I lose the thread of the development in Holland. I have no roots in the seventies or eighties.

Many of your contemporaries are still influenced by the Italian Renaissance, the French Baroque Garden and the English Landscape garden. Is this all just history as far as you are concerned?

No, but I happen to be a Dutch hyperrealist and also, to a certain degree, a functionalist. At the same time, I love Pop Art because it is about mass society. After all, I work in the Randstad, where around six million people live in a very small area. There is not a single square metre of land here which has not been worked at least ten times. The entire landscape is man-made, and I love it. I don't feel the need to keep having ecological experiences of nature.

Looking at your projects, they are not something which people would readily associate with ecology.

I have studied ecology, I know our landscape and nature as it exists in north-western Europe. I am familiar with its flora and fauna and ecological cycles. I can read a soil or vegetation map and know the botanical names of plants. And I also enjoy French fries and ketchup and drive a car. The two different aspects are not mutually exclusive.

In order to better understand the way your work has developed, I would be interested in knowing more about the origins of West 8.

After I had finished my studies, I immediately set up a practice in Rotterdam and started

Adriaan Geuze

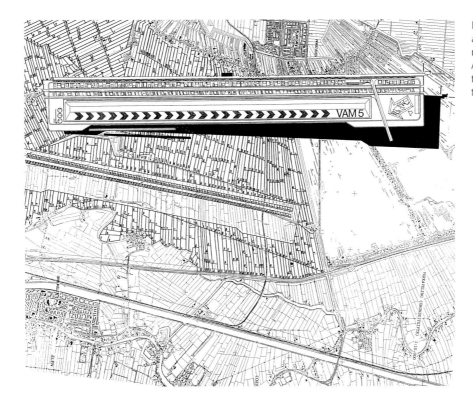

Plan of *VAM 5*, a project for a large refuse disposal plant near Breukelen-Vinkeveen. Adriaan Geuze was awarded the 1990 Prix de Rome for this project.

VAM 5, photograph of model. West 8 planned a refuse island, 5 kilometres long and 640 metres wide, as part of a recreation area.

Adriaan Geuze

looking for suitable premises in the dock area. I spent the last of my money on a telephone and asked two people if they would like to work with me. The day after we got the telephone, we set ourselves up in the Hotel New York, which had once been the head office of the Dutch-American shipping line. The building was rather dilapidated and so the rent wasn't very high. At some point the telephone rang, and we had a research job in Rotterdam. I don't quite know how this happened. Three years later I won the national prize for landscape architecture and urban planning, the 1990 *Prix de Rome*, and we became well-known overnight. I won a few prizes, and we were also lucky. We were literally working day and night.

All we produced in the first five years was paper. It was not until 1992 that we had the

How does collaboration with artists work at your office?

I well understand how to design strategies on a large scale, how to analyse the context. The artist understands when I talk about the different colours of types of mussel and is aware of the meaning of this form of expression. If we had commissioned a Land Artist to design an object for the *Oosterschelde Weir*, it would probably have turned out to be something ridiculous, a sculpture or the like. Now the design has developed more as a bundle of layers superimposed upon each other. The landscape architect devises a plan and offers others the possibility of formulating their own elements within this structure. Each element takes on real meaning as it's a part of the whole. This interaction is, to my mind, one of the principal reasons for the success of our work.

The 1995 plan of *Schiphol airport*, the "green airport", clearly shows the strategy of the "green guerrillas": planting a total of 130,000 birches, 26 hectares of clover, 1,925,000 bulbs on all available open spaces.

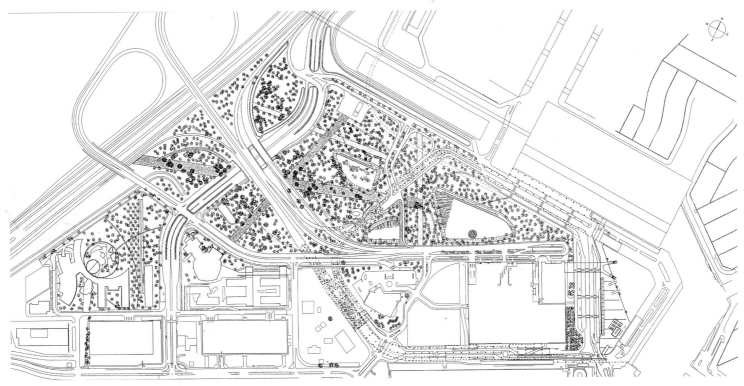

first opportunity to actually build something. The *Oosterschelde Weir* project, one of the first we realised, was something of an exception. Of course, my teaching posts at various schools played an important role: schools of architecture, urban planning, interior design, industrial design, in Amsterdam, Rotterdam, Germany, Belgium, Barcelona, Paris. I got to know a lot of people in a short space of time and was invited to collaborate on various projects. We worked with young people a lot, crazy people, and sometimes it's no longer possible to control the energy involved. This is reflected in our designs: there's always something special, we always reach a certain point in our projects. Today three architects, two industrial designers and a botanist work at our office.

How would you describe the way you see yourself as a contemporary landscape architect?

I'm still young, am still developing my ideas and so I can't give you a definitive answer to this question. But, nevertheless, I already feel responsibility in my work for a kind of reconciliation. I would like to make contemporary landscape accessible again to the people who live in it. I don't want to continue to create new illusions which strengthen the misconception that our landscape is ruined, that our society is bad, that we destroy the landscape, that we change the entire earth, that we will soon have to die, that we must protect ourselves and our landscape. This pessimism is not my way. I find it ridiculous to have this attitude in Holland, and I'm proud of the wonderful landscape which

Temporary garden in the courtyard of a building at *Schiphol airport*: white birches, dark-grey gravel, light-grey concrete slabs and red clay shards.

The production of honey in the birch-wood of *Schiphol airport* as a collage and …

… in reality

A chess-board pattern of red and white tulips between the runways at *Schiphol airport*.

Adriaan Geuze

people have created. I'm quite serious about this: if we continue to make simple and powerful interventions in the landscape – something which has a tradition of six hundred years in Holland – not for the sake of enjoyment and design but for the sake of having it work, we will undoubtedly be in a position to continue development of this landscape in the future.

Is the manipulative attitude to nature typical of the Netherlands? What does the concept of nature mean to you?

That's a difficult question. I'm a landscape architect body and soul and I love nature very much. Sometimes people think that we're making fun of nature. That's not true, we have a great deal of respect for nature and we are very familiar with it. We fully understand the ecological foundations of landscape. We know what biotopes are contained in a planning area, how the interaction of vegetation and soil works and what influences the local microclimate has. At the same time, I firmly believe in evolution, that nature will survive. I think that, to a certain extent, our knowledge qualifies us to design nature. Landscape architecture always means changing nature, and this is something most landscape architects don't want to admit. Even laissez-faire is a way of shaping nature. The interventions of a landscape architect always change nature, even if he adopts a scientific approach. If we are conscious of this, we can adopt another, much freer approach to design.

A number of anthors have linked your work with Land Art. On the other hand, you mentioned your own particular liking of Pop Art. How would you define your position?

The Pop Art of the sixties inspired me because the artists used absolutely horrible, banal, everyday materials for their work. In doing so, they clearly demonstrated their love of their own age. Of course they made fun of the times they lived in, but this didn't stop them from loving them, just as we love airports and magnificent motorways. These are part of our society, we deal with them every day, and so we should take them seriously as being a form of expression of the way we deal with nature. We were, for example, commissioned to provide greenery for the site of *Schiphol airport*, which had been enlarged to three to four times its original size. At present the site extends over an area of more than 2,000 hectares. We explained that we would be able to provide the airport with greenery at relatively low cost, but that we first wanted to remove all the vegetation from the nineteenth century. So we dug up roses and shrubs and began planting trees; but first we carried out a preparatory ecological study in collaboration with the state forestry institute to establish what types of vegetation were best suited to the site. The conclusions reached by the study showed that a particular kind of birch, the betula pubescens, was well-suited. Over a period of six years we planted hundreds of thousands of these trees in a way

which did not follow any fixed planting plan. We planted a tree wherever there was room: on the central reservation of roads, in front of traffic signs, along cable routes, even in front of the terminals and the hangars. We operated like a sort of green guerrilla, and we met with opposition wherever trees were alleged to be in the way. We planted clover under the trees as organic fertiliser so that the trees would grow better. As you probably know, clover binds nitrogen. The trees grew better, and we created a microclimate which attracted lots of insects and birds. Then we commissioned a bee-keeper to install beehives. Now these tiny "helicopters" are buzzing around all over the place and help to spread the clover. We have, so to speak, begun a tiny ecological cycle, and our strategy has improved the situation considerably. Everyone is happy. The area becomes greener with each passing year. This is landscape architecture for me: reflecting on the problem and then developing a good strategy to improve the landscape. Landscape of this kind cannot be

Zen nature on the shores of the North Sea. *Oosterschelde* project by West 8.

created in a single year, but should be left to grow for a period of perhaps twenty years. To my mind, the *Oosterschelde* project is a further example of an approach which combines ecology and design in a new way. After the extensive construction work to the *Oosterschelde dam* was completed, what was left over from this work was strewn over the entire area. The building site was never properly cleared because there was no money left to pay for this. Huge docks and kilometres of dykes which had only served a purpose during construction work were left behind. In between all the garbage there was a vast quantity of sand, which was in three or four dumps. The original plan to build a motorway here was never implemented. So we were given the job of clearing up in order to get rid of the mess and, in the process, we were also to landscape the area. The suggestion was made that we should create artificial dunes on the wrong side of the dam, on the inside. This would have been ludicrous. Anyway it would have been boring to drive along the dam

A nature reserve on the *Oosterschelde*, designed by West 8 as a striped carpet woven of black and white mussels. Tuesday, 28 July 1992, 9.11 p.m.

Adriaan Geuze

without ever seeing the sea. We Dutch spent six billion guilders on building this idiotic dam and used a lot of steel and concrete to block our view of the sea. The landscape is ruined. The *Oosterschelde* may be a nature reserve today, but it's not possible to see either the water, the seals or the birds there. We thought that the idea of building an artificial landscape of dunes was ridiculous as it would have made the situation worse than it was anyway. Instead, we decided to build plateaus. If you travel along the road today, you can enjoy an impressive view of the sea.

In addition, we made the plateaus into a kind of Land Art project. We decided to improve the surface of the plateaus by covering them with a layer of mussel shells. So what was created was artificial landscape architecture in nature and using nature. The funny part of it is – and it's something we really like – that the mussel project which we proposed uses waste products. The mussel farms in Yerseke produce large quantities of mussel shells which they also have to dispose of. So all we needed to say was, "dispose of them in our direction!"

We collaborated with ecologists on this project; they wanted a breeding site for an endangered sea-bird species. When we proposed the pattern of mussel shells that we had in mind, they were particularly taken with the white cockle shells as these birds prefer white surfaces as breeding grounds. It was recognised that our planning would create good conditions for colonisation by birds. Gulls prefer flat resting places close to the sea. When the tide comes in, they leave the sandbanks for flat areas. This behaviour fitted in well with our proposal.

The nature of the *Oosterschelde* is artificial nature which came into being when the dam was built. We control nature. We wanted to give visual expression to this relationship and, in this way, put people in greater contact with their own nature again. Realising the project by using mussels of two different colours arranged in alternating stripes enabled us to link the work with the tradition of the Dutch fine arts, in which the linear landscape has always played a significant part. All landscape in south-western Holland is linear. The decision was taken in the thirteenth century to create a linear pattern of cows, frogs, cows, frogs, cows, frogs and so on. This is linear nature and was even then something akin to Zen nature. So this is actually not something which is so unusual for the Dutch. At the same time we designed the striped pattern in order to provide the car driver with a visually striking experience. The pattern changes with speed and starts to become Land Art.

The project is ecological, consists of waste products, provides an experience of movement, and is humorous. The combination of these aspects creates a kind of tension, but this is something that only very few people understand. Holiday-makers understand it, but the average Dutchman is incapable of understanding the nature which surrounds him. He asks what it's all supposed to mean. When you look at the Dutch landscape with all its ditches and the linear pattern of reed vegetation, frogs and fish you don't ask this question. Of course, I'm not a preacher and I can't enlighten society. All we can do is bring new things into society in order to bring about a little bit of change. If there's a purpose in my work, it's to promote optimism with regard to the landscape, to put people back in contact with their own environment.

In Flevoland there are still a few of the old Land Art projects such as Robert Morris' Observatory. Do you see such projects as meaningful ways of finding access to the Dutch landscape?

No, definitely not. I hate this sort of stuff. The landscape is far more powerful than the Observatory. If you drive through the Flevopolder in summer, eighty per cent of the landscape is bright yellow on account of the huge fields of flowering rape. This landscape derives its scale from the high-voltage power lines and the dyke on the horizon, which is of such an unbelievably rich green that it takes your breath away. I don't think you can convey any greater experience than this.

It is sometimes claimed that you intend your designs to be provocative. Is this the case?

No, it's not true. Of course, it's conceivable that the planning of, for example, *Schouwburgplein* is perceived as a provocation as we use contemporary everyday material which people find around them all the time – on motorways, at work and so on. When we use this material in the unusual context of an inner-city square, we are trying to give it a new value.

Is working with landscape different from working in the city?

No, it's the same. At the most, time makes it different. If you work in the landscape, you organise a process to a certain extent. If you're working on a project like the *Schouwburgplein* in Rotterdam, you behave more like an architect and tend to neglect the time aspect. All the same, I will be interested to see what the square looks like in twenty years. Will the material mature? Will the square react like a chess-board and be made more mature and more beautiful by use? Sensitivity to time is one of the most important qualities of a landscape architect. I believe that the natural environment and the public urban space are areas which will always be settled by man. I am interested in this process of settlement, in the creation of space in which individuals can express themselves, discover new interpretations, make inventions. My design of space can be understood as an invitation to individuals or as a means to provoke them into taking action.

You have made an intensive study of the people's attitudes towards public space. What conclusions have your observations led you to?

I spent ten years studying the dock areas of Rotterdam, in particular the Maasvlakte area.

Plan of the *V.S.B. Bank* in Utrecht. West 8 designed the open spaces, which cover an area of 25,000 square metres in spring 1995. The sober design is characterised by a limited number of sensitive design elements. The base of the bank building serves as a car park and is covered bearing charcoal-coloured tiles with the imprints of fossilised birch branches. Much of the rest of the site is planted with slender birches, broken by a long strip of plants in red stone chipping.

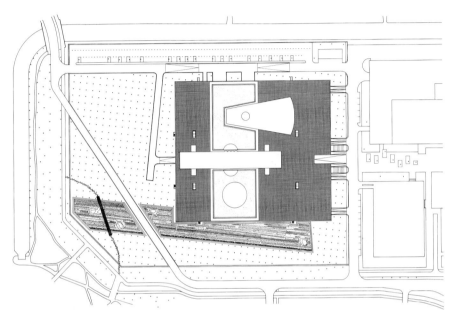

Large rough blocks of stone, placed at irregular intervals along a linear hedge relief of long, clipped box hedges, give the garden of the *V.S.B. Bank* in Utrecht a meditative character. The garden was completed by West 8 in May 1995.

Adriaan Geuze

Maasvlakte is a major landfill project on the coast, an absurd landscape, with huge terminals for the steel industry, container terminals, the largest oil storage facilities in the world, a dump for toxic sludge from the docks, dumps for chemical waste, huge new wind energy plants and so on. All the things which have no place in the Dutch landscape, all problematic installations are banished to Maasvlakte. This mixture of docks and strange, bizarre phenomena produces an extraordinarily wild, windswept landscape. The peculiar thing is that people make use of this absurd landscape. A couple of hundred thousand people are out there in the summer, in between the power stations, gantry cranes und gigantic supertankers. There are people moto-crossing, doing dog-sledging training and so on. A hang-gliding school has recently opened and there's an airfield for ultralight flying. It's the site of the first Dutch nudist beach and there's an entire surfing community out there. It's absolutely amazing.

Maasvlakte is a kind of new town which people don't actually talk about, but aren't ashamed of either. Freedom of function, freedom of scale, freedom of architecture, freedom of urban building structures; freedom is the crucial feature of this area. All the things which are impossible elsewhere happen there. It's a kind of future landscape, and after twenty years the result is quite astonishing. It's really beautiful. You see, Goethe travelled to the classical landscapes of Italy in the eighteenth century. He wrote novels about them and experienced very exciting things. The contemporary individual is a kind of reincarnation of Goethe; he's free and makes his own conquest of the world. At Goethe's time it was only intellectuals who were in a position to discover the world, today this is something anyone can do. People today are mobile, have money, education and the ability to make decisions. In its day, the public park served to make nature accessible to people, but in our times the individual knows himself where he can best enjoy nature. He goes to the mountains in winter, to the Riviera in summer and what does he do at the weekend? – he goes out to Maastvlakte.

You have written an article on contemporary landscape architecture in which you proclaim the end of park planning. In what way do you envisage the public inner-city space of the future?
In the article you just mentioned I spoke about the absurdity of new parks in suburbs, and what I wrote is often misunderstood. Each new suburb in Holland comes into being by marking out a certain area and covering it with layers of sand; these layers have to be several metres thick because the subsoil would otherwise be unable to support the buildings and roads. So, first the existing landscape is destroyed and then green areas and parks are created. That's absolutely ridiculous as people cannot use these areas today; instead they go to the beach to surf, travel to the Alps to climb and to the sea to go sailing. Today every family has a car; or at least one member of every family has a car. So, I don't think we should waste our energy on building new parks in suburbs and new towns; after all, nearly every existing town already has one or several examples of the wonderful parks of the nineteenth century, for example Buttes Chaumont in Paris, Central Park in New York or the marvellous public parks in Germany. The quality of these impressive nineteenth-century parks is something we can never hope to achieve today. We don't have the possibilities of creating such parks. And seeing that they already exist, there is, in my opinion, no need to build any new ones. That's my story.

On the other hand, some experts plead for the creation of inner-city parks to help prevent the increasing destruction of holiday landscapes all over the world due to the growth in tourism. It's an established fact that tourism which is motivated by the search for romantic places destroys the very thing it is seeking: unspoilt nature.
That's a pessimistic view. Of course, I think that improvements are necessary in Switzerland and Austria. We need to increase our knowledge of local conditions, in other words we should channel our energies into creating viable winter sports areas which don't have a destructive effect on nature. This is possible, and the Swiss have already shown how it can be done.

Do you think we need to develop a new language in the landscape?
Yes, definitely.

What might it be like?
I think we should begin by using materials which come from our landscape. People used to be surrounded by stone and vegetation. Today we are surrounded by metal, asphalt, crash-barriers, bicycle routes and concrete. So we should use them. Woodland in Holland mainly consists of poplars, plantations with a grid-like arrangement of trees. Typical of Holland are also the pitch-black basalt dykes on granite-like ground which is almost white; the water makes the granite green and the result is this black-green-white pattern. Take a look at it, it's art and it's beautiful!

These are the same materials that you incorporated in your planning of *Schouwburgplein*. And water also plays a decisive role in this project.
There are three pools on the square, paddling pools for children in the summer, which exist because the mayor wanted to provide an activity for children in association with the cinema complex it was planned to build there. For us it was important to create an environment on *Schouwburgplein* which changes with the weather conditions, the temperature, time of day, incidence of sunlight, the seasons. That's why we made an intensive study of all conceivable ways of continually changing this

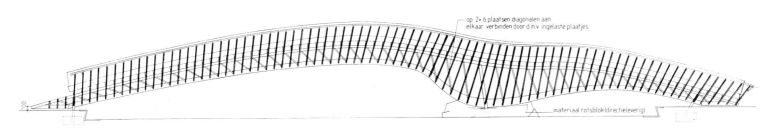

op 2× 6 plaatsen diagonalen aan
elkaar verbinden door d.m.v. ingelaste plaatjes

materiaal rotsblok (directieleverig)

A touch a East Asian garden art: a curved footbridge with a long wooden bench spans the linear garden of the *V.S.B. Bank*.

Adriaan Geuze

technomorphous square. We didn't use things like apple trees, roses and so on, but the objects which people are surrounded by. And it's still possible to perceive the seasons. At night the metal surfaces will reflect all the lights of the city. A kind of horizontal Milky Way will be created, it'll be incredible!

How will the environment change over time? Will it acquire more character or become more boring?

One of the materials we have used for the square is wood, because we are quite sure that thousands of names and messages will have been carved into it a few years from now. Also I should point out that our planning includes the eventuality of the square having to be built twice in thirty years! In other words, we have a budget which is sufficient to conserve and renew about five per cent every year. All the metal will be removed after ten years and

Jean-Jacques Rousseau and the philosophy that man is part of all-powerful nature, in other words the philosophy of Romanticism. At the beginning of the last century, Charles Darwin travelled to the Galápagos Islands, where he discovered an unbelievable diversity of species. He found out that nature, and I see man as being part of nature, was capable of adapting to the environment. Western Europeans and above all Americans are obsessed with adapting the environment to man. For decades they have been trying to create a world for children, a world for women, a world for the elderly. It was seriously believed that man was evil and had to be protected from his own wilful behaviour, his garbage, his pollution and so on. Of course, there's some truth in this and it goes without saying that I detest the way that resources are wasted and the environment polluted. But there's more to it than that. Take big cities like New York where the individual has

Endoscope photographs of the model of *Schouwburgplein* clearly demonstrate the effect of the four hydraulically movable masts as mobile outside elements.

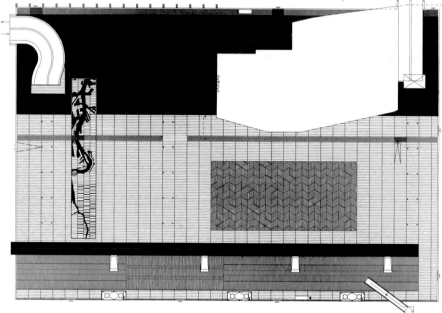

Redesign of *Schouwburgplein* in the centre of Rotterdam, 1993. The ground-plan of the planned complex of theatres, cinemas and music-theatres is on top right. Three media towers and a "ballet" of light masts border the square on the opposite side.

the underlying structure renewed. The entire square will have been rebuilt after a period of thirty years. Although the square is one of the most important in central Rotterdam and will probably be kept under proper surveillance, we're still concerned about the possibility of vandalism. We have already made arrangements to ensure that everything is kept clean and well maintained. Well, not quite everything. I like the idea of the names carved in wood and I like the idea that the steel plates will rust. The result will be an area of bright orange and a beaten path of gleaming metal. It will be wonderful.

You like to speak of post-Darwinism when characterising the relationship between man and the environment. How would you define post-Darwinism?

It's very simple. Landscape architects are in a way a reflection of our society, and we still have a very Romantic disposition. I'm not thinking of classical ballet and ballerinas in white, but of

adapted to changed environmental conditions over the decades. Man found the way back to the bicycle because cars either meant sitting in traffic jams or because these cars were stolen or damaged. We should stop adapting the environment to people. Rather, we should pay greater attention to the intelligence and humour of people who are capable of adapting to the environment. This is post-Darwinism. Post-Darwinism is basically very simple: if we create a kind of artificial jungle, there will be rats and pigeons and all sorts of animals which are sufficiently adaptable to survive. If we design a pattern in the landscape, as in the case of the *Oosterschelde* project, the white birds will prefer one part and the black birds another. This is something you can see out there. Nature isn't stupid, it's smart. It knows how to survive, this is something I am very optimistic about. This attitude can certainly be equated with the development of what may be seen as a Dutch style: hyperrealism.

Computer simulation for the redesign of *Schouwburgplein*. Three ventilation towers for the underground garage beneath the square are to tower above the square as 15-metre high, parallelepiped light objects. In front the series of movable light masts.

Adriaan Geuze

Biography and Selected Works

Adriaan Geuze was born in Dordrecht, the Netherlands, in 1960.
He lives and works in Rotterdam.
He studied at Wageningen Agricultural University and graduated in landscape architecture in 1987.
In 1987 he founded the West 8 planning office.
Adriaan Geuze was awarded the Maaskant prize for young architects in 1995.
He has held teaching posts at the Academy of Architecture in Amsterdam and in Rotterdam, at the Institute of Architecture in St. Lucas, Belgium and at the Institute of Architecture and Urban Planning in Barcelona.

Except where noted, locations are in the Netherlands

Selected designs and realised projects:

1990	Design for the VAM 5 refuse disposal project, Breukelen-Vinkeveen
1990	Design for Grote Visserij square, Rotterdam
1991	Oosterschelde project
1990–1992	Design for Schouwburgplein in Rotterdam; start of realisation in 1996
1992–1996	Green areas at Schiphol airport, Amsterdam
1993	Urban planning Borneo/Sporenburg, Amsterdam; start of realisation in 1995
1994	Design for Ede/Doesburg, Ede Design for Ij-burg, Amsterdam
1994/1995	Design of open spaces at University of Utrecht
1995	Inner Rotte, Rotterdam Aelbrechtskade, Rotterdam Design for Ij shore, Amsterdam Design for the garden of the Interpolis insurance company Garden for the Kröller-Müller Museum, Otterloo Garden for Zoetermeer prison

Numerous competitions including:

1990	Prix de Rome (1st prize)
1992	Lille municipal park, France
1993	Station square in Bergen op Zoom (1st prize)
1994	Chassee site, Breda Limited competition held by city of Amsterdam (1st prize) Monbijou Park, Berlin, Germany

Selected Bibliography

Geuze, A. "Accelerating Darwin." In *Nederlandse Landschapsarchitectuur. Tussen traditie en experiment.* Amsterdam, 1993

Geuze, A. "Parks für Städter." In Koenigs, T., editor. *Stadt-Parks. Urbane Natur in Frankfurt am Main.* Frankfurt am Main, 1993

Geuze, A. "Die 'Sensation' des Unprogrammierten. Manifest für die Maasvlakte." In *Archis,* 1993

Uitgeverij Thoth, editor. *Modern Park Design.* Amsterdam, 1993

Verein PlanBox, editor. *Oranje Landschap. Aktuelle niederländische Landschaftsarchitektur.* Wien, 1993 (catalogue)

Geuze, A. "Wastelands. Storm Surge Barrier." In *Architectural Design,* 1994

Adriaan Geuze. Landschapsarchitect. Amsterdam, 1995

Since 1989 numerous articles have been published on the work of Adriaan Geuze and West 8 in international journals including *De Architect* (Netherlands), *Groen* (Netherlands), *Topos* (Germany)

Acknowledgements

Kindly provided by the landscape architect:
Jannes Linders: 229, 239, 241
Hans Werlemann: 237, 242
Office West 8: 230, 231, 232, 233, 235, 243
as well as:
Udo Weilacher: 236

General Bibliography

Books

Abakanowicz, Magdalena/ Kowalski, Piotr/ Raynaud, Jean-Pierre/Sonfist, Alan/ Daval, Jean-Luc (Eds.): *Paris – La Défense. L´art contemporain et l´axe historique*. Genève, 1992.

Adorno, Theodor W.: *Ästhetische Theorie*. Frankfurt/M., 1970.
English edition: *Aesthetic Theory*. London, 1984.

Allemandi, Umberto & C. (Ed.): *Art in Arcadia. Collezione Gori – Fattoria die Celle*. Torino, 1994.
English edition: *Art in Arcadia. The Gori Collection, Celle. A Tuscan Patron of Contemporary Art at his Country House*. Torino, 1994.

Appleton, Jay: *The Experience of Landscape*. London, 1975.

Asensio Cerver, Francisco: *World of environmental design*. Landscape Art. (Span./Engl.) Barcelona, 1995.

Bahrdt, Hans Paul: *Umwelterfahrung*. München, 1974.

Baudson, Michael (Ed.): *Zeit – Die vierte Dimension in der Kunst*. Weinheim, 1985.

Beardsley, John: *Earthworks and Beyond. Contemporary Art in the Landscape*. New York/ London/Paris, 1984, 1989.

Belting, Hans: *Das Ende der Kunstgeschichte?* München, 1983.
English edition: *The end of the history of art?* Chicago, 1987.

Benjamin, Walter: *Das Kunstwerk im Zeitalter seiner technischen Reproduzierbarkeit*. Frankfurt/M., 1936/1963.

Bihalji-Merin, Oto: *Ende der Kunst im Zeitalter der Wissenschaft?* Stuttgart/Berlin/Köln/ Mainz, 1969.

Bogner, Dieter (Ed.): *Kunst und Ökologie. Materialien zu einer latenten Kunstdiskussion*. In: Kunstforum International Bd. 93, Febr./March 1988.

Bourdon, David: *Designing the Earth. The human impulse to shape nature*. New York, 1995.

Brand, Jan/De Muynck, Catelijne/Kleerebezem, Jouke:

Allocaties. Kunst voor een natuurlijke en kunstmatige omgeving. Zoetermeer, 1992. English edition: *Allocations. Art for a natural and artificial environment*. Zoetermeer, 1992.

Broer, Werner/Schulze-Weslarn, Annemarie (Eds.): *Gartenkunst und Landschaftspflege. Vom Paradiesgarten zur Land-Art*. Hannover, 1989.

Burckhardt, Lucius: *Die Kinder fressen ihre Revolution*. Köln, 1985.

Cauquelin, Anne: *L´invention du paysage*. Paris, 1989.

Claus, Jürgen: *Treffpunkt Kunst. Gegenwart und Zukunft des Schöpferischen*. Bonn, 1982.

Claus, Jürgen: *Kunst und Technologie. Aufbruch in neue Wirklichkeiten*. Bonn, 1984.

Claus, Jürgen: *Expansion der Kunst. Beiträge zu Theorie und Praxis öffentlicher Kunst*. Frankfurt/M./Berlin/Wien, 1982.

Colpitt, Frances: *Minimal Art. The Critical Perspective*. Seattle, 1990.

Coracle Press/Scottish Arts Council/Graeme Murray Gallery (Eds.): *The unpainted Landscape*. London/Edinburgh, 1987.

Dewey, John: *Art as Experience*. New York, 1934.

Eco, Umberto: *La struttura Assente: introduzione alla ricerca semiologica*. Milano, 1968.
English edition: *Theory of Semiotics*. Indiana, 1978.

Eco, Umberto: *Opera aperta*. Milano, 1962, 1967.
English edition: *The Open Work*. London, 1989.

Editions d'Art Albert Skira S.A./Sécrétariat général des villes nouvelles (Eds.): *L´Art et la ville: Urbanisme et Art Contemporain. Art and The City: Town-planning and Contemporary Art*. Genève, 1990.

Falazik, Ruth/Romain, Lothar/ Kunstverein Springhornhof Neuenkirchen: *Kunst-Landschaft. Neuenkirchener Symposien 1974–1987*. Neuenkirchen, 1987.

Fieldhouse, Ken/Harvey, Sheila (Eds.): *Landscape Design: An International Survey*. Woodstock, N.Y., 1992.

Förderverein Kulturlandschaft Niederlausitz e. V. (Ed.): *Kunstszene Tagebau. Dokumentation eines ungewöhnlichen Kunstereignisses*. Heidelberg, 1992.

Förderverein Kulturlandschaft Niederlausitz e.V. (Ed.): *Europa-Biennale Niederlausitz. Kunst und Landschaftsgestaltung – Art in Nature – Intermediale Aktionen. II. Biennale Pritzen 1993*. Cottbus, 1994.

Fujie, Atasushi: *Le land art americain et les notions de pittoresque et de sublime*. Paris, 1993.

Goldwater, Robert: *Primitivism in Modern Art*. New York, 1938. Cambridge/Mass./London, 1986.

Gombrich, Ernst H.: *Art and Illusion. A study in the psychology of pictorial representation*. New York, 1961.

Grant, Bill/Harris, Paul (Eds.): *The Grizedale Experience. Sculpture, Arts & Theatre in a Lakeland Forest*. Edinburgh, 1991.

Gröning, Gert/Herlyn, Ulfert (Eds.): *Landschaftswahrnehmung und Landschaftserfahrung*. München, 1990.

Groh, Ruth/Groh, Dieter: *Weltbild und Naturaneignung. Zur Kulturgeschichte der Natur*. Frankfurt/M., 1991.

Guccione, B.: *Paesaggio Parchi Giardini*. Firenze, 1990.

Hartmann, Wolfgang/Pokorny, Werner: *Das Bildhauersymposion*. Stuttgart, 1988.

Häusser, R./Honisch, D.: *Kunst, Landschaft, Architektur*. Bad Neuenahr-Ahrweiler, 1983.

Havlice, Patricia Pate: *Earth Scale Art. A Bibliography, Directory of Artists and Index of Reproductions*. New York/ London, 1984.

Herd, Stanley James: *Crop Art*. New York, 1994.

Art and Design (Ed.): *Art and The Natural Environment*. London, 1994.

Holt, Nancy (Ed.): *The Writings of Robert Smithson*. New York, 1979.

Hughes, Robert: *The Schock of the New*. London, 1980.

IGBK, Internationale Gesellschaft der Bildenden Künste, Sektion Bundesrepublik Deutschland (Ed.): *Erde Zeichen Erde*. Bonn, 1993.

Jappe, Georg (Ed.): *Ressource Kunst. Die Elemente neu gesehen*. Köln, 1989.

Jellicoe, Geoffrey/Jellicoe, Susan: *The Landscape of Man. Shaping the Environment from Prehistory to the Present Day*. London, 1975.

Johnson, Jory: *Modern Landscape Architecture. Redefining the Garden*. New York, 1991.

Jung, Carl Gustav: *Man and his Symbols*. New York, 1964.

Kellein, Thomas: *Sputnik-Schock und Mondlandung. Künstlerische Großprojekte von Yves Klein zu Christo*. Stuttgart, 1989.

Kemal, Salim/Gaskell, Ivan (Eds.): *Landscape, Natural Beauty and the Arts*. Cambridge, 1993.

Krauss, Rosalind E.: *Passages in Modern Sculpture*. New York, 1977.

Krauss, Rosalind E.: *The Originality of the Avant-Garde and Other Modernist Myths*. Cambridge/Mass., 1985.

Lancaster, Michael: *The New European Landscape*. Oxford, 1994.

Leblanc, Linda/Coulon, Jacques: *Architecture Thématique: Paysages*. Paris, 1993.

Lévi-Strauss, Claude: *La pensée sauvage*. Paris, 1962. English edition: *The Savage Mind*. Chicago, 1966.

Lippard, Lucy R.: *Overlay. Contemporary Art and the Art of Prehistory*. New York, 1983.

Lörzing, Han: *Een Kunstreis door Flevoland*. Rotterdam, 1991.

Lyall, Sutherland: *Designing the New Landscape*. London, 1991.

Magistrat der Stadt Kassel, Kulturamt (Ed.): *Aversion/Akzeptanz. Öffentliche Kunst und öffentliche Meinung*. Kassel, 1992.

Mai, Ekkehard/Schmirber, Gisela: *Denkmal – Zeichen –*

Monument. Skulptur und öffentlicher Raum heute. Bonn, 1989.

Mahabadi, Mehdi: *Kunst in der Freiraumplanung. Zeitgenössische Plastik/Skulptur*. Berlin, 1990.

Martin, Rupert: *The Sculpted Forest. Sculptures in the Forest of Dean*. Bristol, 1990.

Matilsky, Barbara C.: *Fragile Ecologies. Contemporary Artists' Interpretations and Solutions*. New York, 1992.

Metken, Günter: *Spurensicherung. Kunst als Anthropologie und Selbsterfahrung. Fiktive Wissenschaften in der heutigen Kunst*. Köln, 1977.

Miyagi, Shunsaku/Yokohari, Makoto: *Contemporary Landscape Architecture. An international Perspective*. Tokyo, 1990.

Moore, Charles W./Mitchell, William J./Turnbull, William Jr.: *The poetics of gardens*. Cambridge/Mass., 1988.

Mosser, Monique/Teyssot, Georges: *L´architettura dei giardini d´Occidente. Dal Rinascimento al Novecento*. Milano, 1990
English edition: *The history of garden design: The Western tradition from the Renaissance to the present day*. London, 1990.

Moure, Gloria: *Configuracions Urbanes*. Barcelona, 1994.

Norberg-Schulz, Christian: *Genius loci – paesaggio, ambiente, architettura*. Milano, 1979.
English edition: *Genius loci: Towards a phenomenology of architecture*. London, 1980.

Ohff, Heinz: *Kunst ist Utopie*. Berlin, 1972.

Ohff, Heinz: *Anti-Kunst*. Köln, 1973

Otto, Walter F.: *Die Gestalt und das Sein*. Darmstadt, 1955.

Otto, Walter F.: *Gesetz, Urbild und Mythos*. Stuttgart, 1951.

Paflik, Hannelore (Ed.): *Das Phänomen Zeit in Kunst und Wissenschaft*. Weinheim, 1987.

Panofsky, Erwin: *Meaning in the Visual Arts*. New York, 1957.

Panofsky, Erwin: *Perspective as Symbolic Form*. Cambridge/Mass., 1991.

Petrikat, Wolfgang: *Land Art, Landschaftsverpackung, Landschaftsanalyse*. Kassel, 1988.

Plagemann, Volker: *Kunst im öffentlichen Raum. Anstöße der 80er Jahre*. Köln, 1990.

Poinsot, Jean-Marc: *L'Atelier sans mur*. Villeurbanne, 1991.

Ritter, Joachim: *Landschaft, Zur Funktion des Ästhetischen in der modernen Gesellschaft*. Münster, 1978.

Rubin, William (Ed.): *Primitivism in 20th Century Art: Affinity of the Tribal and the Modern*. New York, 1984

Sandler, Irving: *American Art of the 1960s*. New York, 1988.

Sedlmayr, Hans: *Verlust der Mitte*. Berlin, 1956.

Seel, Martin: *Eine Ästhetik der Natur*. Frankfurt/M., 1991.

Senator für Bau- und Wohnungswesen Berlin (Ed.): *Kunst im Park. Bundesgartenschau Berlin 1985*. Berlin, 1985.

Smuda, Manfred (Ed.): *Landschaft*. Frankfurt/M., 1986.

Sonfist, Alan: *Art in the Land. A Critical Anthology of Environmental Art*. New Nork, 1983.

Städtisches Museum Leverkusen (Ed.): *Landschaft – Gegenpol der Fluchtraum*. Leverkusen, 1974.

Stichting Conferentie Artivisual Landscapes (Ed.): *Artivisual Landscapes. International IFLA Conference 1992. Focussing on the interface between Landscape Architecture and the Visual Arts*. Amsterdam, 1992.

Szeemann, Harald: *Der Hang zum Gesamtkunstwerk*. Aarau, 1983.

The Museum of Modern Art, New York (Ed.): *Denatured Visions. Landscape and Culture in the Twentieth Century*. New York, 1991.

Thomas, Karin: *Bis heute. Stilgeschichte der Kunst im 20. Jahrhundert*. Köln, 1994.

Tiberghien, Gilles A.: *Land Art*. Paris, 1993, 1995 (French and English editions)

Toyka, Rolf (Ed.): *Bitterfeld: Braunkohle-Brachen. Probleme – Chancen – Visionen*. München, 1993.

Uitgeverij Ploegsma (Ed.): *Verbeelding in Flevoland. Image-making in the new polder Flevoland*. Amsterdam, 1988.

Wedewer, Rolf/Romain, Lothar: *Kunst als Flucht. Zur Kritik künstlerischer Ideologien*. Jahrbuch 1971, Opladen, 1971.

Werkner, Patrick: *Land Art USA. Von den Ursprüngen zu den Großraumprojekten in der Wüste*. München, 1992.

Zagari, Franco: *L'Architettura del giardino contemporaneo*. Milano, 1988.

Zimmermann, Jürgen: *Das Naturbild des Menschen*. München, 1982.

Exhibition Catalogues

Andrew Dickson White Museum of Art, Cornell University: *Earth Art (February 11–March 16, 1969)*. Ithaca/ USA, 1969.

Arte Sella (Ed.): *Arte Sella. International Art Meeting. Sella di Borgo Valsugana. Documentazione 1994*. Milano, 1995.

Atelier 340 (Ed.): *Nils-Udo – Bob Verschueren. Avec arbres et feuilles. Mit Bäumen und Blättern. Met bomen en bladeren. With trees and leaves*. Bruxelles, 1992.

Beardsley, *John*/Hirshhorn Museum and Sculpture Garden (Eds.): *Probing the Earth. Contemporary Land Projects*. Washington D.C., 1977.

CAPC Bordeaux (Ed.): *Sculpture/Nature*. Bordeaux, 1978.

Centre d'art contemporain, Genève (Ed.): *Centre d'art contemporain de Genève 1984–1989*. Genève, 1989.

Crafts Council/Arts Council (Eds.): *The Furnished Landscape. Applied Art in Public Spaces*. London, 1992.

Deste Foundation for Contemporary Art Athen (Ed.): *Artificial Nature*. Athens, 1990.

Fernsehgalerie Gerry Schum (Ed.): *Fernsehgalerie Gerry Schum. Land Art*. Hannover, 1970.

Frauen Museum (Ed.): *Umwelt – Naturkunst*. Bonn, 1985.

Galerie Falazik (Ed.): *Material aus der Landschaft. Kunst in die Landschaft*. Neuenkirchen, 1977.

Galerie m/Ernst Gerhard Güse (Eds.): *Richard Serra*. Stuttgart, 1987.

Galleria Civica d'arte moderna (Ed.): *Conceptual Art, Arte Povera, Land Art*. Torino, 1970.

Kölner Kunstverein (Ed.): *Landschaft in der Erfahrung*. Köln, 1989.

Kulturstiftung Stormarn (1989): *Projekt: Schürberg. Die Natur sprechen lassen*. Hamburg, 1989.

Kunsthalle Bielefeld (Ed.): *Concept Art, Minimal Art, Arte Povera, Land Art*. Sammlung Marzona. Bielefeld, 1990.

Kunsthaus Zürich (Ed.): *Mythos und Ritual in der Kunst der siebziger Jahre*. Zürich, 1981.

Kunstverein Gelsenkirchen (Ed.): *Dokumentation Kunstmeile Gelsenkirchen*. Gelsenkirchen, 1992.

Kunstverein Hasselbach (Ed.): *Skulptur im Tal*. Hasselbach, 1989.

Lindau/Etablissement Public pour l'Aménagement de la région de La Défense/Ministère de la Culture et de la Francophonie, Délégation aux arts plastiques (Fiacre) (Eds.): *Différentes Natures. Visions de l'art contemporain*. Paris, 1993

Museé d'art contemporain de Montréal (Ed.): *Elementa Naturae*. Montréal, 1987.

Museé du Québec (Ed.): *Territoires d'artistes. Paysages verticaux*. Québec, 1989.

Museo de Arte Moderna, Rio de Janeiro/Goethe Institut (Eds.): *Arte Amazonas. Ein künstlerischer Beitrag zur Konferenz der Vereinten Nationen über Umwelt und Entwicklung Rio 92*. Brasilia, 1992.

Museum Fridericianum (Ed.): *Schlaf der Vernunft*. Kassel, 1983.

Museum Ludwig, Köln (Ed.): *Europa/Amerika. Die Geschichte einer künstlerischen Faszination seit 1940*. Köln, 1986.

Museum of Contemporary Art, Chicago: *Charles Simonds*. Chicago, 1982.

Neue Sammlung, München. Staatliches Museum für angewandte Kunst (Ed.): *Kalenderbauten. Frühe Astronomische Großgeräte aus Indien, Mexico und Peru*. München, 1976.

Neuer Berliner Kunstverein e.V. (Ed.): *Dimensionen des Plastischen – Bildhauertechniken (21.03–20.04.81)*. Staatliche Kunsthalle Berlin, 1981

Rüth, Uwe/Galerie Heimeshoff, Essen (Eds.): *Material und Raum*. Essen, 1991.

Seattle Art Museum/King County Arts Commission (Eds.): *Earthworks: Land Reclamation as Sculpture. A Project of the King County Arts Commission*. Seattle, 1979.

Storm King Art Center (Ed.): *Enclosures and Encounters Architectural Aspects of Recent Sculpture*. Mountainville/New York, 1992.

Verlag Werner Druck AG, Basel (Ed.): *Skulptur im 20. Jahrhundert, Merian Park*. Basel, 1984.

Ville de Niort/Ministére de la Culture (Eds.): *Sites choisis*. Niort, 1991.

Westfälisches Landesmuseum für Kunst und Kulturgeschichte in der Stadt Münster (Ed.): *Skulptur Projekte in Münster 1987*. Münster, 1987.

Wiener Festwochen (Ed.): *Von der Natur in der Kunst. Eine Ausstellung der Wiener Festwochen. 3. Mai bis 15. Juli 1990*. Wien, 1990.

Württembergischer Kunstverein: *Vergangenheit – Gegenwart – Zukunft. Zeitgenössische Kunst und Architektur*. Stuttgart, 1982.

Württembergischer Kunstverein (Ed.): *Natur – Skulptur. Nature – Sculpture*. Stuttgart, 1981.

Index

Acknowledgements

This book would not have been possible without the help of the artists, landscape architects and architects it portrays. For this reason, I would like to express my special thanks to them for their openness, hospitality and help. A number of the staff and partners in their individual offices and studios put a lot of work into ensuring smooth communications and supplying texts and photographs. I am particularly grateful to Inge Breughem and Elien Bil in Rotterdam, to Carine Cohn in Paris, Amy Hau of the Noguchi Foundation in New York, Erika Kienast-Lüder and Günther Vogt in Zurich, Anneliese Latz in Ampertshausen and Ingrid Voth-Amslinger in Munich for their valuable assistance. Claus Reisinger and Ferdinand Werner of the Wernersche Verlagsgesellschaft in Worms on Rhine also made an invaluable contribution to getting the project off the ground.

The outstanding photographic material was generously made available to me by a large number of artists and photographers. My special thanks go to the artists Alfio Bonanno, Andy Goldsworthy, Michael Heizer, Richard Long, Nikolaus Lang, Nils-Udo and Alan Sonfist, the photographers Thomas Kläber in Cottbus, Christa Panick in Vollmar and Maria Otte in Melle as well as the art expert and gallery-owner Ruth Falazik in Neuenkirchen.

I would like to express my particular thanks to all the staff at the Institute of Landscape and Garden at the University of Karlsruhe for the many ways they supported this project. Special mention should be made of the valuable assistance provided by Michael Schramm in London in the form of intensive research of source material in British libraries.

I will always remain indebted to Tim Day, assistant professor at the Department of Landscape Architecture at the California State Polytechnic University in Pomona, Los Angeles for his generous and kind help. Sadly, Tim Day died in a fatal accident in January 1996.

For encouraging me to realise the project and providing invaluable editorial assistance I would like to express my particular thanks to Andreas Müller in Berlin. The book owes its finishing touches to his committed and critical approach. The same enthusiasm, flexibility and wealth of ideas were contributed by the graphic designer Bernd Fischer in Berlin. The outstanding design of the book is the result of his work.

It only remains to be said that such an elaborate and at times very demanding project would scarcely have been possible without the unreserved support, infinite patience and assistance of Rita Weilacher. She deserves my very special thanks.